The Oral Ethos of the Early Church

Biblical Performance Criticism Series

Orality, Memory, Translation, Rhetoric, Discourse

David Rhoads, Series Editor

The ancient societies of the Bible were overwhelmingly oral. People originally experienced the traditions now in the Bible as oral performances. Focusing on the ancient performance of biblical traditions enables us to shift academic work on the Bible from the mentality of a modern print culture to that of an oral/scribal culture. Conceived broadly, biblical performance criticism embraces many methods as means to reframe the biblical materials in the context of traditional oral cultures, construct scenarios of ancient performances, learn from contemporary performances of these materials, and reinterpret biblical writings accordingly. The result is a foundational paradigm shift that reconfigures traditional disciplines and employs fresh biblical methodologies such as theater studies, speech-act theory, and performance studies. The emerging research of many scholars in this field of study, the development of working groups in scholarly societies, and the appearance of conferences on orality and literacy make it timely to inaugurate this series. For further information on biblical performance criticism, go to www.biblicalperformancecriticism.org/.

Books in the Series

Holly Hearon and Philip Ruge-Jones, editors
The Bible in Ancient and Modern Media

James A. Maxey
From Orality to Orality

Antoinette Clark Wire
The Case for Mark Composed in Performance

Robert D. Miller II, SFO
Oral Tradition in Ancient Israel

Pieter J. J. Botha
Orality and Literacy in Early Christianity

James A. Maxey and Ernest R. Wendland, editors
Translating Scripture for Sound and Performance

J. A. (Bobby) Loubser
Oral and Manuscript Culture in the Bible

Joanna Dewey
The Oral Ethos of the Early Church

Richard A. Horsley
Text and Tradition in Performance and Writing

The Oral Ethos of the Early Church

Speaking, Writing, and the Gospel of Mark

JOANNA DEWEY

CASCADE *Books* • Eugene, Oregon

THE ORAL ETHOS OF THE EARLY CHURCH
Speaking, Writing, and the Gospel of Mark

Performance Biblical Criticism Series 8

Cascade Books
An Imprint of Wipf and Stock Publishers
199 W. 8th Ave., Suite 3
Eugene, OR 97401

www.wipfandstock.com

ISBN 13: 978-1-60608-852-4

Cataloguing-in-Publication data:

Dewey, Joanna, 1936–

The oral ethos of the early church : speaking, writing, and the gospel of Mark / Joanna Dewey.

Biblical Performance Criticism Series 8

xviii + 204 p. ; 23 cm. Includes bibliographical references.

ISBN 13: 978-1-60608-852-4

1. Bible. Mark—Criticism, interpretation, etc. 2. Bible. John—Criticism, interpretation, etc. 3. Performance—Religious aspects—Christianity. 4. Oral traditions. I. Title. II. Series.

BS2585.52 D48 2013

Manufactured in the USA

To David Rhoads
Editing Companion for three decades
Coauthor
and above all Friend

Contents

Acknowledgments

The author and the publisher gratefully acknowledge the permission to publish the following articles and essays in revised form.

"Textuality in an Oral Culture: A Survey of the Pauline Traditions." *Semeia* 65 (1994) 37–65.

"The Gospel of John in Its Oral-Written Media World." In *Jesus in Johannine Tradition*, edited by Robert T. Fortna and Tom Thatcher, 239–52. Louisville: Westminster John Knox, 2001.

"The Literary Structure of the Controversy Stories in Mark 2:1—3:6." *Journal of Biblical Literature* 92 (1973) 394–401.

"Mark as Interwoven Tapestry: Forecasts and Echoes for a Listening Audience." *Catholic Biblical Quarterly* 53 (1991) 221–36.

"Oral Methods of Structuring Narrative in Mark." *Interpretation* 53 (1989) 32–44.

"The Gospel of Mark as Oral/Aural Event: Implications for Interpretation." In *The New Literary Criticism and the New Testament*, edited by Elizabeth Struthers Malbon and Edgar V. McKnight, 145–63. Journal for the Study of the New Testament Supplement Series 109. Sheffield: Sheffield Academic Press, 1994.

"The Gospel of Mark as Oral Hermeneutic." In *Jesus, the Voice, and the Text: Beyond "The Oral and the Written Gospel*," edited by Tom Thatcher, 71–87. Waco, TX: Baylor University Press, 2008.

"From Storytelling to Written Text: The Loss of Early Christian Women's Voices." *Biblical Theology Bulletin* 26 (1996) 71–78.

"Women on the Way: A Reconstruction of Late First-Century Women's Storytelling." In *The Bible in Ancient and Modern Media*, edited by Holly E. Hearon and Philip Ruge-Jones, 36–48. Biblical Performance Criticism 1. Eugene, OR: Cascade Books, 2009.

"The Survival of Mark's Gospel: A Good Story?" *Journal of Biblical Literature* 123 (2004) 495–507.

Introduction

A MAJOR FOCUS OF New Testament research in my academic career has been on the oral/aural media world of the first century, especially as that media world has interacted with two other research interests, the Gospel of Mark and feminism. In my years as a graduate student in the 1970s, I became fascinated by the Gospel of Mark, especially with the way in which it was put together. The scholarly work at the time was primarily concerned with the redaction history of the text, which focused only on connections in the seams or transitions between episodes; yet I became intrigued with the text itself as a whole. Reading *Die Zusammensetzung des Markusevangeliums* by Johannes Sundwall, I became aware that there were not only connections between adjacent passages but also interconnections across multiple passages. The gospel was not just "pearls on a string" but rather an interwoven tapestry. As a result of my interest in the literary dynamics of Mark's story, I became active in the Markan Seminar at the Society of Biblical Literature and then the Literary Aspects of the Gospels Group. I read widely in literary criticism, continued work on the extensive interconnections in Mark, and became coauthor with David Rhoads of the second edition (and eventually the third edition) of *Mark as Story*.

Also during my graduate years I became involved in and committed to feminist criticism of the New Testament. In 1975, Letty Russell gathered Elisabeth Schüssler Fiorenza, Sharon Ringe, and me in her living room in New York to write and publish *The Liberating Word: A Guide to Non-Sexist Interpretation of the Bible* under the auspices of the National Council of Churches. Although the book seems somewhat naïve now, at the time it was one of the very first on feminist approaches, and it was badly needed. By the early 1980s, two things in regard to feminism had become clear: first, the extent to which biblical scholars had ignored the positive material about women that is found in the New Testament; and second, the fact that the New Testament material represented men's views of women and not women's views of themselves.

Then in the early '80s, I discovered the oral/aural media world of antiquity. Werner Kelber's *The Oral and the Written Gospel* was published in 1983, and at the same time the Bible in Ancient and Modern Media Group at the SBL began. Particularly formative for me was an extended conversation I had with Tom Boomershine over lunch at an annual SBL meeting. Tom had published articles on the orality of the New Testament period and was spearheading The Bible in Ancient and Modern Media Group. He convinced me that the first century was an oral and aural media world and that the communication medium mattered. I became aware that we had been studying the New Testament writings as if they were printed texts read silently by individuals. We had been reading Mark as a print document for what information it could give us about Mark's theology or community or the historical Jesus. By contrast, hearing a performance of the gospel in a group was an experience aimed at persuading listeners to be or to remain faithful disciples of Jesus. The oral/aural media world was concerned with persuasion, not knowledge. Also, I quickly realized that all the verbal repetitions and interconnections I had seen in the Gospel of Mark made more sense if the gospel was heard. And I could see why scholars, trained as we are to read print, had remained so oblivious to these interconnections. Furthermore, consideration of the media world offered a way to approach the study of women's voices, which are significantly underrepresented in the New Testament texts and often minimized or distorted.

I was embarked on new research. I read what was available about literacy in antiquity. I read widely about oral literature in antiquity and modern times. I read about women and orality. I was active in the Bible in Ancient and Modern Media Group, cochairing it from 1989 to 1996. Since this time period to the present, I have been actively studying and writing articles about oral dimensions of the New Testament and the early Christian world. I am delighted now to bring these articles together in the Biblical Performance Criticism Series. What follows is a brief introduction to each of the articles, which have been arranged in three parts.

Part 1 gives the broader view of "The Oral-Written Media World" of the New Testament, a world still not familiar to many New Testament scholars today. The first article, "Textuality in an Oral Culture: A Survey of the Pauline Traditions" explains what is known about ancient literacy—literacy rates, who was literate, uses of literacy, and interactions of orality and literacy. It makes use of the development of Pauline traditions (authentic letters, pseudonymous letters, Acts, and the *Acts of Paul and Thecla*) to delineate a complex and nonlinear spectrum of oral and literate emphases and interactions.

The second article in Part 1, "The Gospel of John in its Oral-Written Media World," also deals with the overall first-century media world. In this essay, however, the emphasis is on the key characteristics of orality and the ongoing interactions between oral and written communication. The focus here is on the Gospel of John, identifying seven areas where recognition of the oral/aural media world may assist in the interpretation of John's gospel.

Part 2 is called "Oral Patterning in Mark and the Implications for the Interpretation of Mark." This part comprises five articles on Mark's oral style and the implications oral performance has for understanding Mark's gospel. These articles are presented in the order in which they were written. The first article is on "The Literary Structure of the Controversy Stories in Mark 2:1—3:6." It was published in 1973 at the onset of the narrative analysis of the Gospels. Although I wrote the article in terms of literary patterning, the analysis can better be reconceived as oral features of narrative—aural forecasts and echoes, structural patterns of repetition, and elegant detail developed over many oral and written iterations. This article, along with my dissertation, *Markan Public Debate*, which built upon the article, laid the groundwork for my subsequent research on oral style in Mark.

The next three articles explore Mark's oral style and its significance for interpreting Mark. "Mark as Interwoven Tapestry: Forecasts and Echoes for a Listening Audience" explores the Markan verbal threads at all the places in the text where scholars have previously posited major breaks in Mark's narrative; it suggests that hearers would not sense major breaks but would instead experience continuity. In "Oral Methods of Structuring Narrative in Mark," I use the descriptions of oral composition posited by Eric Havelock and Walter Ong to demonstrate how oral composition techniques pervade the overall narrative of Mark's gospel. Both of these articles offer implications of Mark's oral style for a fresh understanding Mark's story and its rhetorical impact. The third article on Mark's oral style, "The Gospel of Mark as an Oral/Aural Event: Implications for Interpretation," explores the oral nature of Mark in greater depth, unpacking the implications of its agonistic tone and the participatory nature of oral performance.

The final article in Part 2 was written for a volume honoring Werner Kelber's work. My article contests Kelber's three arguments for considering Mark to be a written counterform to oral hermeneutics: namely, that Mark rejects the oral authorities (disciples, family, and prophets/christs), that Mark silences the oral teachings of the sayings material, and that Mark's emphasis is on death rather than life. I argue that it is not necessary to posit a shift from orality to writing in order to explain these three features of Mark. Rather, they can all be readily and sometimes more cogently explained from a point of view that retains the fundamentally oral nature of Mark's Gospel.

Part 3 comprises four articles that address some of the "Wider Implications of the Oral/Aural Media World" for our understanding of early Christianity and the gradual shift to manuscript authority. The first two articles concern the fate of women as the church moved from oral to written authority beginning in the mid-second century. This shift in the fate of women was due to a very limited population of educated, literate men responsible for our written texts—men who tended to ignore or subordinate women. The first of the two articles on women, "From Storytelling to Written Text: The Loss of Early Christian Women's Voices," provides evidence that as the written-manuscript tradition developed, it tended to minimize or exclude the presence of women. The second article, "Women on the Way: A Reconstruction of Late First-Century Women's Storytelling," is my attempt to retell Mark's gospel from the perspective of a Gentile woman storyteller in the late first century; the telling is short enough for performing to classes and church groups. My version moves the women followers of Jesus from the periphery of the story world to the center. Fifteen verses before the end of the Gospel of Mark, the audience is told that women have accompanied Jesus in Galilee from the beginning and have gone up to Jerusalem with him. So I retell the story in such a way as to include them as disciples from the beginning. Versions similar to mine may well have been told and been in circulation in the early Christian movement. In these two pieces, I am attempting to reintegrate women into our imaginative picture of early Christianity, countering the tendency for the later manuscript medium significantly to diminish and often to expunge early Christian women from our memories. The distortion of our historical understanding of early Christianity due to the loss of women's voices in the developing manuscript tradition has had and continues to have a deleterious impact on the lives of women.

The last two articles in Part 3 raise historical questions about the text of Gospel of Mark. They also make use of new directions in contemporary textual criticism, particularly in the work of Eldon J. Epp and D. C. Parker. In "The Survival of Mark's Gospel: A Good Story?" I argue that the gospel survived to become part of the New Testament because it was a good story, widely known and told orally throughout early Christian communities. Given the incorporation of so much of Mark's story into the Gospels of Matthew and Luke, and given the realities of the ancient media world, it is reasonable to expect that the Gospel of Mark would no longer have been copied. By all rights, Mark should have disappeared, gone the way of Q. Yet its continued and geographically widespread existence in oral performance offers an explanation for why it survived to become part of the canon.

The last article in Part 3, "Our Text of Mark: How Similar to First Century Versions?"(published for the first time here), raises questions about how close our earliest extant texts of Mark from the fourth and fifth centuries are to the original composition or to first-century performances of Mark. We know that manuscripts of the New Testament changed the most in their first one hundred to one hundred fifty years of transmission, changes we cannot track because we do not have any extant manuscripts from this period. Therefore, our contemporary reconstructed Greek texts of Mark most likely represent fourth-century versions, versions that may be quite different from what Mark actually composed around 70 CE. If our media picture of a succession of oral performances and written versions, and then even more oral performances and written versions, does indeed represent what happened, then we need to assume that multiple changes occurred over time in the early manuscript tradition before we have any records. This observation certainly makes any reconstruction of the first century Markan community problematic and raises broader issues for our reconstruction of early Christianity.

Finally, I offer three notes for readers of this collection of articles. First, I use the name Mark to refer to the author/composer of the Gospel of Mark. This is partially a matter of convenience. The Gospel of Mark, however, is a very tightly interwoven narrative; this suggests that one person has put his stamp on the narrative.[1] I imagine that there was a particularly gifted oral

---

1. If the person had been a woman, I suspect she would have included the women followers earlier than fifteen verses before the end of the gospel.

storyteller, probably named Mark, who reworked the oral narrative tradition around 70 CE, and that it first got put in writing at about that time. The story was refined in both oral performance and written versions over time. I cannot of course demonstrate this, but it seems to me most probable.

The second note concerns the idea that the Gospel of Mark was composed orally. In antiquity, people familiar with storytelling traditions were certainly capable of composing lengthy stories in the course of oral performance. Or they could compose in an oral style in the act of writing, especially since a story would have been composed in writing with the expectation that it would be performed orally. Although we can discern an oral style in a written text, we cannot be sure whether the Gospel of Mark was originally composed orally or in writing with the goal of being performed orally. In the earlier articles, I discuss Mark's oral style without arguing that the gospel was orally composed. As I learned more about the ancient media world and investigated social-memory theory, I became more convinced that the Gospel of Mark was not only composed in an oral style; it was composed orally and only afterward written down. And this is the position I present in the later chapters.

Finally, there is some repetition throughout the chapters. In order for each essay to stand on its own, it was necessary to preserve the repetition. It also seemed appropriate to restate arguments and repeat significant quotations in light of the fact that biblical scholars and students are still unfamiliar with much of this material. It takes time to grasp the full implications of this new oral/aural approach, because it is a significant paradigm shift in biblical studies. It has been a paradigm shift for me, and I assume it may be for others as well. My hope is that this volume will assist us in making that shift by bringing new life and fresh insights into our study of the New Testament.

I am grateful to David Rhoads for his constant encouragement to get this collection together over the years and for his practical help in making it happen. I wish to thank Matthew Frost and Chingboi Guite, graduate students at the Lutheran School of Theology at Chicago, for their assistance in getting the essays into the proper format for publication. I am grateful to the Lutheran School of Theology at Chicago for providing financial support for the graduate students.

Abbreviations

ABD	*The Anchor Bible Dictionary.* 6 vols. Edited by David Noel Freedman. New York: Doubleday, 1992
BETL	Bibliotheca Ephemeridum theologicarum Lovaniensium
BTB	*Biblical Theology Bulletin*
CBA	Catholic Biblical Association
CBQ	*Catholic Biblical Quarterly*
CRBR	*Critical Review of Books in Religion*
GRBS	*Greek, Roman, and Byzantine Studies*
HTR	*Harvard Theological Studies*
HvTSt	*Hervormde Teologiese Studies*
Int	*Interpretation*
JBL	*Journal of Biblical Literature*
JR	*Journal of Religion*
JSNT	*Journal for the Study of the New Testament*
JTS	*Journal of Theological Studies*
LB	*Linguistica Biblica*
LCL	Loeb Classical Library
NICNT	New International Commentary on the New Testament
NA[25]	Nestle-Aland Greek New Testament, 25th ed.
NAB	New American Bible
NEB	New English Bible
Neot	*Neotestamentica*
NovT	*Novum Testamentum.*
NovTSup	Supplements to Novum Testamentum
NRSV	New Revised Standard Version
NTS	*New Testament Studies*
PMLA	*Publications of the Modern Language Association*

Abbreviations

PRSt	*Perspectives in Religious Studies*
RSR	*Recherches de science religieuise*
RSV	Revised Standard Version
SBL	Society of Biblical Literature
SBLDS	Society of Biblical Literature Dissertation Series
SBLSP	Society of Biblical Literature Seminar Papers
SemeiaSt	Semeia Studies
SJT	*Scottish Journal of Theology*
STRev	*Sewanee Theological Review*
SNTSMS	Society of New Testament Studies Monograph Sseries
SV	Scholars Version
TDNT	*Theological Dictionary of the New Testament.* 10 vols. Edited by Gerhard Kittel and Gerhard Friedrich. Translated by Geoffrey W. Bromiley. Grand Rapids: Eerdmans, 1964–76
UBS³	United Bible Societies Greek New Testament, 3rd ed.
UBS⁴	United Bible Societies Greek New Testament, 4th ed.
USQR	*Union Seminary Quarterly Review*
VD	*Verbum Domini*
ZTK	*Zeitschrift für Theologie und Kirche*

PART 1

The Oral-Written Media World

1

Textuality in an Oral Culture

A Survey of the Pauline Traditions

Introduction

In studying the development of early Christianity scholars have generally assumed that the first-century media world functioned much as our modern print media world does, giving priority to logical linear thinking and to written texts. Since the early days of form criticism, we have acknowledged that there was an oral stage prior to the written gospels. We have, however, assumed that the progression from oral performance to written text was a continuous linear development, with writing rapidly becoming the primary medium for Christians, and with written texts supplanting oral tradition as soon as they were composed. We have tended to equate Christianity with written documents, whether with extant texts or our own hypothetical reconstructions. We have yet fully to grasp the implications the ancient oral/aural media world has for understanding the formation of early Christianity.

It is true that scholars have become more aware of ancient orality since the publication of Werner Kelber's *The Oral and the Written Gospel: The Hermeneutics of Speaking and Writing in the Synoptic Tradition, Mark, Paul, and Q* in 1983, and since the formation of the Bible in Ancient and Modern Media Group of the Society of Biblical Literature by Thomas Boomershine in the same year.[1] As a result, it is no longer unusual to find biblical scholars who have read the work of Walter Ong and who stress that early Christians

---

1. Kelber, *Oral and Written Gospel*; Silberman, *Orality*.

heard rather than read the gospels. Nonetheless, we are still a long way from understanding the high degree of orality in ancient Mediterranean cultures and the ways orality and literacy interacted, working together and working against each other. We have only begun to investigate how literates and nonliterates shared the same culture and, at the same time, participated in quite different cultural worlds. We do not yet have an overview of how orality and literacy affected the development of the early churches and the formation of the New Testament canon. We have yet to consider fully how Christianity itself participated in orality and literacy. We are just beginning to develop a sense of the first-century media world and how Christianity fits within it.

Stated provocatively, my guiding hypothesis is that Christianity began as an oral phenomenon in a predominantly oral culture within which the dominant elite were literate and made extensive use of writing to maintain hegemony and control. Only gradually did Christianity come to depend upon the written word. The growing number of Christian texts and of literate Christians[2] in the second and following centuries helped facilitate the shift to manuscript-based authority and to the hegemony and control of Christian churches by a small, educated male elite.[3] Our tendency to equate Christianity with written texts, and to see these texts as typical of all of early Christianity, leads us to construct a distorted and one-sided view of the nature and spirit of the early churches. This chapter represents an exploratory step toward investigating the hypothesis by studying the roles of literacy, textuality, and orality in the Pauline traditions.

In order to do so, we need some grasp of the extent and uses of literacy in antiquity. Therefore, Part I looks at literacy and, to a lesser extent, at oral-communication media in the first-century Mediterranean world. Part II is an investigation of the role of literacy and orality in the extant texts related to Paul: the undisputed letters, the deuteropauline letters, the canonical Acts of the Apostles, and the apocryphal *Acts of Paul*. I have chosen to focus on the Pauline materials for two reasons: first, we have sufficient materials to make such a study possible; and second, the Christian churches based in urban Mediterranean cities were likely the most literate of the early Christian groups. These two factors, of course, are not unrelated. In Part III, I

---

2. In sheer numbers, not necessarily in the percentage of Christians who were literate.

3. There were of course other sociological forces at work contributing to this change. The importance of the media shift to textuality, however, has not yet been sufficiently recognized.

shall suggest some implications that recognition of the relative unimportance of textuality among early Christians has for our reconstruction of early Christian history.

Part I: Literacy and Orality in the Ancient Mediterranean

The first-century media world was a manuscript culture with high residual orality.[4] But to define it that way is to define it from the perspective of the elite, those few who could read and write, and who ruled the empire. Most people living during the first century were not literate: occasionally for specific, very limited purposes they made use of writing, but that writing was done by someone else. Furthermore, writing and reading were not silent, individual activities. They were closely allied to the oral world, to speech. Pieter Botha writes, "Greco-Roman literacy—the little that existed—remained a kind of imitation talking."[5]

It is still not unusual to read scholarly estimates of widespread literacy in ancient cities. Recently, however, we have become aware that these estimates are gross overestimates. Scholars investigating cross-cultural agrarian and advanced agrarian societies estimate that only between 2 and 4 percent of ancient Mediterranean people were literate.[6] It is generally agreed that literacy rates were much lower among women than among men, and much lower in rural than in urban areas. William V. Harris's massive 1989 work, *Ancient Literacy*, attempts to summarize all the ancient evidence on literacy, and the following discussion draws heavily on his work.[7] He gives somewhat higher estimates than the social scientists do, suggesting perhaps as much as 15 percent for males in Italian cities,[8] and similar or lower levels for males in the eastern Mediterranean. What constituted literacy is also not clear. Reading and writing were distinct skills in antiquity; literacy could mean anything from the simple ability to write one's own name to fluency in both reading and writing. Harris tends to use a minimal definition of literacy. But whatever definition one chooses, it seems safe to

4. Ong, *Orality and Literacy*, 158.

5. Botha, "Greco-Roman Literacy," 206.

6. Malina and Rohrbaugh, *Social-Science Commentary*, 3; Rohrbaugh, "Social Location," 115; Bar-Ilan, "Illiteracy," 56.

7. For reviews of his work, see Humphrey, *Literacy in the Roman World*; and Keenan, "Ancient Literacy." While many have argued about specifics of Harris's description, as Humphrey (5) notes, few question his basic thesis of low literacy rates.

8. Harris, *Ancient Literacy*, 267.

conclude that literacy was not widespread in antiquity. For the purposes of this chapter, nonliterates were those who neither read nor wrote. And in the first century, most people were nonliterate.

That literacy rates were low should not surprise us. A very small, educated elite, plus a few literate slaves and freedpeople, could handle the writing needed to maintain an empire and to conduct long-distance trade, about the only activities in antiquity that absolutely depended on writing. Most people had little or no use for reading and writing skills. In the following sections, I shall describe, first, typical uses of literacy; second, who was literate; and third, means of literate and oral communication.

Uses of Literacy

Among the ruling elite, the top 2 to 5 percent of the population,[9] literacy was used for the arts. There was considerable production and consumption of literature. All literary works seem to have been written for this small group. Even the Greek romance was not the first-century equivalent of the mass-market paperback: rather than appealing to a wider audience, it was the light reading of the very limited reading public "possessing a real degree of education."[10] "Literature was a symbol of social status (and conversely, a point of access to the upper class, a way of making contact with the elite), and remained the preserve of the aristocracy."[11] This literature, however, was usually experienced aurally.[12] Readings and performances were common at the gatherings of the elite. "Texts were produced to be read out loud in a communal setting."[13]

The primary practical use of writing in antiquity was for ruling the empire.[14] The administrative letter was the essential tool for regulating the empire's business. "In the context of the Roman imperial administration,

---

9. Percentages as always are elusive. The governing classes rarely exceed 2 percent of the population in an agrarian society (Lenski, *Power and Privilege*, 219; Duling and Perrin, *New Testament*, 56; Rohrbaugh, "Social Location," 117). Since some of the higher status merchants and retainers may have participated in the elite culture, a somewhat higher percentage is perhaps an appropriate guess.

10. Harris, *Ancient Literacy*, 227–28.

11. Botha, "Greco-Roman Literacy," 206.

12. Yaghjian, "Ancient Reading."

13. Cartlidge, "Combien d'unités," 406 n.37; cf. Knox, "Silent Reading"; and Slusser, "Reading Silently."

14. Botha, "Greco-Roman Literacy," 208.

correspondence was the most important instrument with which the affairs of the vast and often distant provinces could be regulated and adjudicated."[15] Writing was a practical necessity for the empire. In addition to administrative correspondence, the government used writing for inscriptions of laws posted in public places. These inscriptions were not the normal way for officials to communicate with the public: this was done orally by means of public criers. Thus, the public inscriptions may have been more to convey the prestige and power of the law than to communicate the content to the populace. The inscriptions were symbols of the power and authority of Rome.[16] Perhaps precisely because it could be read by so few, writing carried a sense of authority and stature. "Virtually every culture that has mastered the art of writing, or even only come into direct contact with scribal or chirographic culture, has assigned immense importance and prestige to the written word."[17] The empire both used writing and also made use of the status of writing as a means to rule.

Long-distance trade, which was by definition largely luxury items, also required writing. In addition, personal letters to kin living at a distance were common. Nonliterates, and frequently also literates, would employ scribes for writing letters. Writing, whether for government, business, or personal matters, was primarily a tool that enabled communication at a distance, when oral communication was not possible.

Little use of reading and writing was necessary to get along in everyday life, either personally or economically, and it could be done by professional scribes. By the first century, among the wealthy, wills and marriage and divorce agreements were frequently written.[18] It was easy to have such documents drawn up by scribes even if one was not literate. In the economic sphere, there is extensive documentary evidence of contracts and apprenticeship agreements made on behalf of nonliterates. Most business transactions, however, would not require writing at all. Trading was usually face-to-face and oral. Tradespeople and artisans did not need writing to conduct their small businesses; only contracts for large sums of money were normally put in writing. One could live and conduct business without

---

15. Koester, "Writings and the Spirit," 355.

16. Botha, "Greco-Roman Literacy," 197.

17. Graham, *Beyond the Written Word*, 12.

18. Written wills and formal marriage and divorce agreements presuppose at least minimal property and thus were probably not needed by many in the population. Legal marriage (with written documentation) was the exception rather than the rule.

being literate. This would be true even for an elite man with extensive estates. For him it would be a social shame more than a practical inconvenience not to be literate, for his slaves or freedpeople could do the work for him.[19]

One final area for consideration is religion. Religions made some use of the written word for prophecies and inscriptions. The use of writing gave the content special power or solemnity: "The written word itself exercised religious power: it was sometimes believed (or simply felt) to have some special and profound quality that caused or allowed people to bring about extraordinary results. One need only remember the Sibylline Books . . . There are also the magical papyri and Jewish attitudes to writing the name of God."[20] This public use may be akin to the public posting of civil laws. Nonetheless, participation in religious ceremonies or looking after a household altar did not require literacy. Religious propaganda addressed to the general public was oral. Letter writing was not a typical means of religious propaganda, although writing to communicate at a distance was occasionally used for religious purposes. Jews and Epicureans seem to have used letters to connect geographically separated groups;[21] Paul certainly wrote to his churches to communicate at a distance.[22] Textuality was perhaps more central to Judaism since the Jews had created written texts—Scripture—as an integral part of their religion, and some among them engaged in oral interpretation of these written texts—developing the Oral Torah. To be a good Jew, however, did not require the ability to read the sacred texts.

In addition to the very limited need for writing for the large majority of the population, two other factors militated against the spread of literacy. First, writing materials were inconvenient and expensive.[23] The writing materials used for practical purposes were small potsherds or wax-covered tablets. The tablets, gathered in codices of ten, could hold about fifty words on a side. These were inexpensive and easy to reuse, but inconvenient, bulky, and useless for texts of any great length. Papyrus and parchment, used extensively by the elite, would have been prohibitively expensive for most people. In Egypt, about 45 CE, when skilled laborers earned six

---

19. Harris, *Ancient Literacy*, 248–51.

20. Botha, "Greco-Roman Literacy," 209.

21. Harris, *Ancient Literacy*, 220.

22. In "Writings and the Spirit," Koester suggests that Christians used the letter as the empire used the administrative letter—to create unity.

23. Harris, *Ancient Literacy*, 193–96.

obols a day, and unskilled three a day, a single sheet of papyrus sold for two obols;[24] prices were likely higher outside Egypt. Writing materials for texts of any length, such as most of Paul's letters or a gospel, were beyond the means of most of the population.

Second, given the limited use of literacy, there was virtually no public support for mass education. Schooling seems to have declined in the Eastern Mediterranean with the advent of Roman power.[25] Insofar as the Roman empire needed literate clerks, it trained slaves rather than the free population. Schooling, while relatively cheap compared to the price of papyrus, had to be paid for by the family, and there was little economic advantage to be gained by teaching one's sons or daughters to read or write. Schooling in elementary letters was uncommon even in the cities.[26] Unlike the situation in early modern Europe, there were neither economic nor religious forces fostering literacy.

Who Was Literate?

From a grasp of the uses of literacy in antiquity, it is relatively easy to describe who was literate. Literacy was nearly universal among the politically and socially elite men of the empire.[27] Harris writes, "Within the elites of the established Greco-Roman world a degree of written culture was a social necessity, and an illiterate male would have been regarded as bizarre."[28] However, even within this stratum of society, a person would not need to do much if any reading or writing. In addition to the elite themselves, a variety of functionaries of the elite—the males of the retainer class—were likely to have a fairly high literacy rate.[29] In the army, legionaries could sometimes read, and literacy did provide some chance for advancement. Not surprisingly, literacy correlated with military rank. In addition, there were literate slaves and freedmen who carried out much of the clerical work

---

24. Harris, *Ancient Literacy*, 194.

25. Ibid., 281.

26. Ibid., 235–46; Botha, "Greco-Roman Literacy," 202–4.

27. Harris, *Ancient Literacy*, 248–52.

28. Ibid., 248.

29. The size of the retainer class is difficult to ascertain from historical records. Lenski estimates it to be about five times the size of the governing class (*Power and Privilege*, 245).

of the empire, but they would constitute only a very small proportion of all slaves and freedpersons.

Outside of the social-political elite and their retainers, literacy was quite restricted.[30] Merchants in international trade might well be literate—or employ literates. Practitioners of a few crafts tended to be literate. In classical Greece, doctors,[31] engineers, surveyors, and rhapsodes were generally literate.[32] Some, such as doctors, were also often slaves, at least by the time of the empire.[33] There is little evidence that the number of crafts requiring literacy increased in Hellenistic or Roman times. In addition to those in specific occupations, wealthy businesspeople were also often literate. However, we know of historical and fictional wealthy businessmen who were not literate themselves.[34] Ownership of a prosperous business increased the likelihood that a person was literate but did not require it. The newly wealthy in particular often lacked education.[35]

Two groups require special consideration: women and Jews. At every social level, women's literacy rate was lower than men's. The difference would be least among the elite. Within this group, women may have been nearly as literate as men,[36] or considerably less literate.[37] Literacy skills would have been useful to these women as managers of large households. There were ancient women authors of considerable literary artistry, particularly in the genres of lyric and elegiac poetry.[38] Outside the elite, women's literacy was rare, but it did occur, generally associated with wealth or with a particular occupation.[39] There is considerable evidence of families in which the men were literate and the women not, and little evidence of the opposite.[40]

---

30. Harris, *Ancient Literacy*, 253–81.

31. Midwives, however, were sometimes exhorted to be literate, suggesting that many of them were not (ibid., 203).

32. Ibid., 82.

33. Meeks, *First Urban Christians*, 57.

34. Harris, *Ancient Literacy*, 197–98.

35. Ibid., 251.

36. Harris, *Ancient Literacy*, 252.

37. Veyne, "Roman Empire," 20.

38. Snyder, *Woman and the Lyre*; see also Kraemer, "Women's Authorship"; and Lefkowitz, "Ancient Women."

39. See Pomeroy, "*Technikai kai Mousikai*"; and Pomeroy, "Women in Roman Egypt"; 309–16; Cole, "Greek Women."

40. Harris, *Ancient Literacy*, 279.

The question must be raised as to whether the Jews were more literate than other nationalities in the Roman empire, since the importance of Scripture in their religion may have functioned to encourage literacy. Little evidence is available. On the basis of cross-cultural analysis and rabbinic references, Meir Bar-Ilan suggests a literacy rate of less than 3 percent in the lands of Israel—about the same as others estimate for the empire as a whole.[41] Harris also suggests that widespread Jewish literacy was very unlikely.[42] Literacy rates among Jews most likely correlated with their social status. Many of the chief priests, elders, and Pharisees were probably literate—and literate in more than one language. The chief priests and elders were the wealthy landowners, part of the governing elite who generally were literate. The Pharisees were retainers—bureaucrats for whom scribal skills were useful.[43] The Pharisees' literacy could be and was used for religious purposes in reading and interpretating Scripture. However, the Pharisaic emphasis upon the writings probably had not yet resulted in any increase in literacy beyond the retainer class.

In summary, literacy in Greco-Roman antiquity was quite limited both in the percentage of the population and in the ways literacy was used. It is virtually impossible for modern academics to realize how unimportant writing and reading were for the conduct of daily life. Although nonliterates would be familiar with the existence of written documents and might make use of writing through an intermediary a few times in their lives, they could nevertheless live nonliterate lives without shame or inconvenience. And likewise, even those who were most literate would have made very little use of reading or writing for either business or pleasure. On the other hand, writing was essential for the creation and maintenance of the Roman empire. It affected everyone's lives through written laws, administrative correspondence, and debt records. In a world in which most were nonliterate, writing was both an instrument of power and a symbol of power. So although few could read or write, reading and writing were fundamental in structuring relations in the ancient world. A partial analogy can perhaps be made to nuclear weapons. Few of us know how to make them; even fewer control their use. Yet a nation's possession or lack of nuclear weapons is

41. Bar-Ilan, "Illiteracy," 56. See also Malina and Rohrbaugh, *Social-Science Commentary*, 3; cf. Townsend, "Ancient Education," 154–57.

42. Harris, *Ancient Literacy*, 281; Catherine Hezser's extensive study of Jewish literacy in ancient Palestine confirms Bar-Ilan's and Harris's conclusions.

43. Saldarini, *Pharisees, Scribes, and Sadducees*; Horsley, *Spiral of Violence*, 73–75.

important in determining its status and power, and all of us are affected by our knowledge of the power of such weapons.

Means of Literate and Oral Communication

By the standards of modern industrialized society with its print and electronic communication systems, mass communication in the ancient world was extremely limited and usually oral. Literacy was essential to the formation and communication of the dominant culture. Among elite males, the formal rhetorical education with its attendant literacy, created a shared and relatively homogeneous culture and value system.[44] "And the homogeneity of the ruling elite has had the major consequence of permitting the expansion of empires."[45] This homogeneity facilitated control and hegemony by the governing elite.[46]

Yet even the elite were dependent upon word of mouth for most communication.[47] For them—as well as for less literate groups—literacy was used to enhance and facilitate orality. David Cartlidge writes, "The evidence from late antiquity is that oral operations (presentation and hearing) and literary operations (reading and writing) were (1) inescapably interlocked, and (2) they were communal activities. Chirographs were created for and by the community and in the service of orality."[48] This was true not only of literature. Letters were not read silently by individuals; they would be read aloud. Letters to groups would be performed orally. "One must reckon with the letter as having been prepared for a careful performance, and [with the fact] that eventually the letter was delivered like a proper speech."[49] Textuality, when it existed, existed as an aid to oral presentation.

As noted earlier, official communication to the population at large was by means of public criers (*kērukes, praecones*). They were numerous and attached to government officials at all levels.[50] But probably even more influential in diffusing knowledge among the nonliterates were the

---

44. Sjoberg, *Preindustrial City*, 119, 290.

45. Ibid., 290.

46. Botha, "Greco-Roman Literacy," 208.

47. Sjoberg, *Preindustrial City*, 286.

48. Cartlidge, "Combien d'unités," 407.

49. Botha, "Letter Writing," 24.

50. Harris, *Ancient Literacy*, 208.

street entertainers, storytellers, actors, and musicians.[51] When we think of oral performers in antiquity, we tend to think first of the rhapsodes who performed Homer and other ancient literature both at gatherings of the wealthy and in public theater performance. But the rhapsodes were literate and provided entertainment primarily for the elite. The street performers were normally nonliterates entertaining the nonliterate. Only a little information is available, because such people were scorned by the class that composed the written texts.[52] Those who earned their living by storytelling were among the many itinerant street artists of antiquity; they eked out a living telling stories in the company of musicians, dancing girls, astrologers, cynic street preachers, sword swallowers, and the rest. A second group consisted of official religious storytellers, associated with temples and synagogues, who told of the miracles accomplished by the particular god or goddess of the place. The temple storytellers would both amuse their listeners and teach them. This group had greater status than the street performers, who were usually outcasts; their social status was similar to that of the temple priests.[53]

In addition, there were many storytellers who did not make their living from performing, but who would be known in their village, town, or region as good tellers of tales. They would entertain and teach in the work places, in the evening after formal meals, to their neighbors in the evening, or while traveling. Storytelling was also particularly associated with women and children. There are numerous references to nursemaids, servants, or slaves in the houses of the elite, who told stories to frighten the children in their charge into obedience, or to lull them to sleep.[54]

It is through the stories of these popular storytellers that nonliterates would become familiar with the dominant tradition. "A prominent part of the repertoires of the story-tellers are [*sic*] selections from the society's most revered literature: the religious writings, the sagas of traditional heroes, and the great poets."[55] It is probably through such storytellers that most Jews gained their familiarity with Scripture. Storytellers were important not only in diffusing the dominant tradition but also in "distorting it."[56] Sjoberg

---

51. Sjoberg, *Preindustrial City*, 287.

52. Ibid., 287–9; Scobie, "Storytellers."

53. Scobie, "Storytellers," 241.

54. Ibid., 244–51.

55. Sjoberg, *Preindustrial City*, 287.

56. Ibid., 136–7, 289.

suggests that distortion is due partly to lack of literacy, that is, reliance on memory, and partly to "their efforts to dramatize a story to gain more listeners and thereby increase their earnings."[57] I would argue that distortion (i.e., change) is also due to the shift in social location of both the storyteller and the audience. The storytellers would reinforce values of the dominant culture embedded in the stories, but they would also alter the stories to reflect popular values and popular resentments against the elite that they shared with their audiences.[58] In addition, there would generally be local stories known to particular subgroups but not to the elite.[59] It was probably with good reason that the elite distrusted entertainers as "potential purveyors of ideas that threaten the authority structure."[60] Even the women's stories to children were suspect. Plato wrote in book 2 of the *Republic*: "We must begin, then, it seems, by a censorship over our storymakers, and what they do well we must pass and what not, reject. And the stories on the accepted list we will induce nurses and mothers to tell to the children and so shape their souls by these stories far rather than their bodies by their hands. But most of the stories they now tell we must reject."[61]

Contact between literates and nonliterates was probably rather limited. While governing elites and nonliterates would have little if any direct contact in ancient society, some of the retainer class and successful merchants probably would interact with urban nonliterates.[62] Within a city, outside of the elite area, people tended to live in ethnic and occupational groupings, often organized into guilds. Within these groupings, there might be some literates who interacted often with nonliterates. Certainly in many families in which there was any literacy, the man had some degree of literacy and the woman had none. Nonliterates would honor reading and writing as symbols of culture and status; they would also fear them as instruments of social, political, and economic oppression. It is in this milieu, largely nonliterate, mostly dependent on criers and storytellers for knowledge and communication, but with some connection to literates, that urban Christianity took shape.[63]

---

57. Ibid., 289.

58. Ong, *Orality and Literacy*; Scott, *Domination*.

59. Vansina, *Oral Tradition*, 154.

60. Sjoberg, *Preindustrial City*, 136.

61. Plato, *Republic*, 2.377b–c.

62. Sjoberg,, *Preindustrial City*, 108–44; Rohrbaugh, "Pre-Industrial City."

63. Rural Christianity would have had even less connection with literates (Oakman,

Part II: Literacy and Orality in the Pauline Tradition

It is difficult to determine the extent and functions of literacy in Greco-Roman antiquity. Given our lack of knowledge about the precise makeup of early Christian communities, it is even more difficult to estimate the degree of literacy among Christians. Furthermore, how much literacy and of what sort becomes an important question. It would require a high degree of reading literacy to read aloud a Pauline letter if one were not already thoroughly familiar with its contents. It would require only minimal literacy to present the letter orally to a congregation, if one had heard it and been prepared to deliver it to a group. Even the degree of literacy needed to compose and dictate letters such as Paul's is open to question. Nonetheless, it is possible to approach the issue with greater precision than heretofore and thus gain a better picture of the importance of literacy in the Pauline churches. I shall look first at the authentic letters of Paul for what we can learn about who was literate and how literacy was used in the early churches. Then I shall look at the deutero- and related Pauline material for what we can tell about both the development of a literate tradition and the continuing importance of orality.

Literacy and Textuality in Paul's Letters

Who Was Literate

Probably the best and most extensive discussion of social location in early urban Christianity remains Wayne Meeks's study of the Pauline communities.[64] Meeks's analysis supports the general consensus that the early churches contained a cross-section of the social scale, excluding at the top, the ruling elite, and at the bottom, the most destitute.[65] The exclusion of the top, however, means the exclusion of the only group for whom fluent literacy was the norm. To state this in another way, there may have been no Christians in the mid-first century who had received the education of the governing elites. Thus, for those early Christians who were to some degree literate, writing would have been a particular achievement, not something taken for granted as part of their social milieu.

"Countryside"; Rohrbaugh, "Social Location").

64. Meeks, *First Urban Christians*.

65. Ibid., 51–53, 73.

According to Meeks, the typical member of a Pauline church was a free artisan or small trader,[66] the person who worked for a living and could contribute to the Jerusalem collection only bit by bit.[67] Harris's evidence suggests that people in this group were generally not literate, for, as we have seen, there would be no need for literacy for the conduct of business or craft. If this group indeed made up the large majority of Paul's churches, then the literacy rate among early urban Christians was low, probably even in comparison to what was customary in ancient cities. The Pauline congregations included both slaves and slave owners. Those slaves who were clerks may have been literate; thus it is possible that a higher proportion of the slaves than of the free artisans and tradespeople were literate. However, most would not be literate, as slaves generally were not literate.

The writing of letters to and from the churches suggests, though it does not require, that some people in the communities were literate. Scribes could be employed to take dictation or to read letters aloud. Meeks discusses in detail the social location of all those named in Paul's letters about whom we can determine anything. Those who were prominent enough for the names to be mentioned were usually high-ranking in some aspect of status—although not part of the ruling elite. It is members of this group who were most likely to have some skills of reading or writing. Looking at Meeks's data, it is possible to make some observations about the literacy of this group.

First of all, Paul himself was literate. Furnish describes him as "apparently trained in the subjects that constituted the lower and middle levels of Hellenistic education."[68] Paul may have been literate because of his social class—he spoke of his craft labor as if it were choice rather than economic necessity—and/or because of his training as a Pharisee. Given our own literate biases, however, we may overestimate the degree of Paul's literacy and his reliance on writing. Like other literates, he often dictated rather than wrote himself.[69] We cannot really determine the extent of Paul's education. His letters are certainly not written in a high style, but letters often were not composed in a high style. Scholars have increasingly recognized Paul's rhetorical skill and sophistication.[70] Yet rhetoric was pervasive in the ancient

66. Ibid., 63–72.

67. 1 Cor 16:1–2.

68. Furnish, "On Putting Paul in His Place," 11.

69. Rom 16:22; see also 1 Cor 16:21; Gal 6:11; and Phlm 19.

70. For references on Paul and rhetoric, see Furnish, "On Putting Paul in His Place,"

world, permeating the nonliterate oral culture as well as the literate culture. It is fully possible that Paul may have been more of a street or popular rhetorician than someone the elite would have recognized as a polished rhetorician. What we can say with certainty is that Paul (or Paul and his coauthors) had enough rhetorical skill to invent lengthy letters.

Even Paul's literacy, however, has been called into question. Most recently, Botha has put forward this possibility.[71] He suggests that Paul's statement about writing in large letters in Gal 6:11 is actually a reference to his inability to write: "An interesting side issue is the very strong probability that Paul was *agrammatos*. Strictly speaking, Paul probably relied on scribes because he could not write Greek. A perusal of comments on Galatians 6:11 bears out that though the similarity to the illiteracy formula is well known, no-one wants to accept the implication of this similarity!"[72] Whether or not one wishes to pursue Botha's thought this far, he is certainly correct that literacy is much less necessary for the creation and reception of Paul's letters than we instinctively assume. Botha writes: "Paul's letter was not written by him as an individual, sitting at a desk and dropping a note to some friends. We must become aware of a much more complex event: some persons combined their efforts to deliberate and 'perform' a letter; there was someone involved in the creation and transportation of it, finally "recreating" for others a presentation/performance of the "message" intended for sharing."[73]

Some of the other traveling missionaries probably were also literate. The "superapostles" of 2 Corinthians apparently claimed great rhetorical skill, which implies education.[74] Apollos is described in Acts 18:24 as "an eloquent man, well versed in the scriptures," again implying education (if Luke can be trusted, given his bias for wealthy Christians). But traveling missionaries need not have been literate; Peter and John are described in Acts 4:13 as unlettered.[75] Literacy was not necessary for missionary work:

---

11 n. 21.

71. Botha, "Letter Writing," 22–23.

72. Ibid., 23.

73. Ibid., 22.

74. The debate about wisdom in 1 Corinthians 1–4 is cast in terms of speaking; it is unlikely that writing was involved (so also Kelber, *Oral and Written Gospel*, 173–75). Indeed, how much the contest between Paul and the superapostles in 2 Corinthians involved rhetoric as understood by the literate elite is open to doubt.

75. *Agrammatoi*. In ancient usage, the term could mean nonliterate, or more generally, uneducated, in which case the person could have received the first stages of education,

preaching was oral, and new cults were normally propagated by word of mouth.[76] Insofar as the missionaries were itinerant charismatics, writing would have been no particular advantage and not a likely skill.

The people who carried Paul's letters to the Christian communities may well have possessed some literacy, for that would assist them in using the letter as the basis for their presentation to the congregation. If Phoebe not only carried Paul's letter to Rome but was also Paul's representative in performing the letter to Roman Christians, which is the natural inference, then she was probably literate. Of individuals named in Paul's letters,[77] the only ones of whose literacy we can be reasonably sure on the basis of their occupations are Luke as a physician,[78] and Erastus as a city official, a keeper of accounts, whether slave or free.[79] Lydia, engaged in an international luxury trade, would either be literate or the employer of literate slaves.[80] Judging from their occupation as tentmakers, Prisca and Aquila would not have been literate. If Acts 18:8 is correct that Crispus, whom Paul mentions in 1 Cor 1:14, was the ruler (patron?) of a synagogue, then he may well have been literate, in light of the synagogue's respect for written Scriptures.

The Christian churches clearly contained members wealthy enough to offer their houses for Paul and others to stay at and to use for gatherings of the community. To what extent this wealth implies literacy is not evident. Such wealthy patrons were not part of the governing class; however, the extent of their wealth suggests use of writing, whether by themselves, by slaves, or by freedpeople in their employ. On the one hand, their status inconsistency of possessing greater wealth than social standing could have functioned as an incentive to better themselves socially through education. (Yet, their choice to join a despised and shameful religion does not suggest social climbing.) On the other hand, it is precisely this group, wealthy merchants and businesspeople, whom the elite often scorned as not literate and not educated. All that we can say is that literacy is a possibility but not

---

learning the letters, but little further education (Harris, *Ancient Literacy*, 5).

76. Harris, *Ancient Literacy*, 220.

77. See Meeks, *First Urban Christians*, 57–62.

78. Phlm 24; cf. Col 4:14.

79. Rom 16:23.

80. She is mentioned only in Acts (16:14, 40). If Schottroff is correct that Lydia is lower class, in a profession despised because of its foul odor (*Let the Oppressed Go Free*, 65), then Lydia is not likely literate.

a necessity for them. Even if literacy was high among this group, the overall literacy of Pauline congregations would remain low.

Uses of Literacy in Paul's Churches

Literacy comes into play in Paul's churches in four respects: the production of letters, the reception of the letters, the possible use of Scripture in worship, and the use of Scripture in debate. The primary use of literacy was for letters traveling a long distance: Paul's letters, at least one letter from Corinthian Christians to Paul,[81] and letters of recommendation.[82] Here letters are a substitute for personal presence, not the preferred means of communication.[83] Paul, however, may upon occasion have deliberately chosen to write rather than to go himself, as the more effective means of influencing a community.[84] Furthermore, as noted above, oral preparation seems to be an integral part of the creation of the written texts. Here, literacy seems definitely in the service of oral communication. While texts were produced that later became very important within Christianity as texts, these texts began as aids to orality, and seemingly had little importance in themselves.

Literacy is also less crucial to the reception of the letters than we are likely to assume. In the first place, given the nature of manuscripts, one needed to be quite familiar with a text in order to read it aloud, a familiarity that was perhaps more likely to have been gained by hearing it orally than by prior reading. "At the most basic level, the oral text was the 'base text,' if only because reading a manuscript text virtually demanded prior knowledge of the text."[85] The text was likely orally dictated and orally performed. In the initial instance the letter is likely to have been read—or performed— by the person carrying it.[86] William Doty writes: "I wonder if the Pauline letters may not be seen as the essential part of the messages Paul had to convey, pressed into brief compass as a basis for elaboration by the carriers. The subsequent reading of the letters in the primitive Christian communities would then have been the occasions for full exposition and expansion

81. 1 Cor 5:9.
82. 2 Cor 3:1–2.
83. Funk, *Parables and Presence*, 81–102.
84. Mitchell, "New Testament Envoys."
85. Graham, *Beyond the Written Word*, 36.
86. On the letters as performance, see Ward, "Pauline Voice."

of the sketch of material in the letters."[87] Performance of the letter to a congregation probably involved a complex of literate and oral activities—and need not have involved literacy at all.

Later repeated use of Paul's letters in the communities to which they were originally sent and the exchange of his letters among Christian communities would require literacy. The fact that the letters were written documents gave them a permanence that oral discourse never has, and thus constituted a first step towards a developing literate tradition, a tradition that eventuated in the Christian canon. Although Paul's letters themselves were in the service of orality, they provided, if you will, both the raw material for and the impetus towards a communication system based on written texts.

Among Jews, Scripture (i.e., the writings) had already come to play a central role.[88] Yet Scripture seems not to have played a role in worship in Paul's communities. Reading and interpretation of Scripture are not mentioned either in lists of gifts for church leaders or in instructions for orderly conduct of worship. When Paul lists gifts for church leadership in Romans and 1 Corinthians, there is no reference to the Scripture at all.[89] Both lists do refer to teaching and/or teachers, but there is no indication that teaching consists of Scripture or of readings of any sort. The Christian gospel proclaimed orally, or some aspect thereof, is the more likely content. The list of activities in worship likewise refers to someone having a teaching (*didachēn echei*),[90] but it seems to refer to someone standing up and speaking spontaneously during worship, not to reading the writings.

In his discussion of order in worship, Paul wants to limit the number prophesying and speaking in tongues, and to have only one person speak at a time.[91] He shows no concern, however, for order or silence while Scripture was being read. Interpretation refers not to interpretation of readings but of spoken prophecy or tongues. Thus, there is no evidence that Scripture readings were important in the worship of Paul's communities, and it seems unlikely that they occurred at all. There is also no indication in Paul's letters

---

87. Doty, *Letters*, 45–46.

88. See Boomershine, "Jesus of Nazareth." That written texts were integral to the religion of the Jewish elite (both the ruling and retainer classes) seems indisputable. To what extent popular Jewish practice drew on written texts is an area in need of investigation.

89. Rom 12:6–8; 1 Cor 12:27–31.

90. 1 Cor 14:26.

91. 1 Corinthians 12; 14.

that these mostly Gentile Christians participated in synagogue worship and thus heard Scripture read or performed there. The picture of Paul preaching in the synagogues comes from Acts, which was written at a later time, and that picture does not seem very probable on the basis of Paul's letters. Indeed Scripture reading in Christian worship is not mentioned until the early second century,[92] and the regular use of Scripture reading in services is first attested by Justin Martyr around the middle of the second century.[93] The only reading done during worship in Paul's churches was the reading—or rather performance—of Paul's letters.

Although Hebrew Scripture does not appear to be part of worship, it certainly informs Paul's basic view of God, history, and salvation. Such an understanding does not require extensive participation in manuscript culture. It could be, and for most Jews was, acquired orally through participation in the popular culture, through storytelling rather than manuscript reading. Paul, however, quotes and alludes to specific scriptural passages in his letters—which indicates participation in manuscript culture at some point in his history.[94] He is able to quote extensively from memory—since as a missionary for Christ, he is unlikely to have had access to Bible scrolls. The question then becomes, how central is Paul's textual use of Scripture? Is Scripture as written text central for Paul?

I would argue that it is not. In most of Paul's letters—1 Thessalonians, 1 Corinthians, 2 Corinthians, Philippians, and Philemon—if scriptural quotations appear at all, scriptural arguments are secondary, providing additional supporting evidence for positions already taken. It is only in Galatians and Romans that argumentation on the basis of Scripture is central. In Galatians, the necessity to argue from Scripture seems to have been forced upon Paul by his opponents. In a mixed oral/written media culture prestige is attached to appealing to an ancient, powerful written tradition, and the opponents in Galatia seem to have made this appeal. Paul responds, using Scripture often against its traditional meaning, arguing that Christians already have the Spirit—the written word would confine them.[95] The opposition to Paul on the part of some Jewish Christians is the reason for the

---

92. 1 Tim 4:13.

93. In *1 Apol.* 67:3; see Aune, "Worship, Early Christian," 977, 983; Graham, *Beyond the Written Word*, 123.

94. On Paul's use of Scripture, see, e.g., Hays, *Echoes of Scripture*; Scott, "Paul's Use of Deuteronomic Tradition."

95. See A. J. Dewey, *Spirit and Letter*; Kelber, *Oral and Written*, 140–83.

focus on Scripture in Romans; Paul must show that his understanding of the place of the Law is in accord with Scripture. Paul's more primary appeal, I believe, is an appeal to experience, his own and his churches' experience. The picture of Paul arguing on the basis of Scripture to prove Christianity is, of course, based on Acts, not Paul.

A contrast with Jewish use of Scripture is perhaps helpful at this point. The Pharisees were developing the Oral Torah, the oral interpretation of written texts, as a dominant mode of discourse. While the interpretation was oral, it was quite precisely interpretation of a written (and probably memorized) text. The manuscript—the text itself—was foundational and central for the oral interpretation. In contrast to this, for Paul, Christ is central. While Paul is clearly influenced by Jewish understandings of God, history, and apocalyptic, he seems little concerned with the text as text. Paul can and does appeal to Scripture when it is helpful to support his argument, but it does not appear to be the foundation for his understanding or the constant reference point. On the other hand, the way Paul uses Scripture as part of a larger rational theological argument about, say, the nature of justification, points ahead to later Christian debates focusing on what constitutes correct doctrine or belief, debates carried out in the manuscript medium, debates for which literacy was essential.

Summary

Paul and his congregations lived in a largely oral media world with minimal use of written texts or appeal to manuscript authority. Writing was used for long-distance correspondence (often with the adjunct of personal emissaries), but otherwise Christian life was oral, without even much reliance on Jewish Scripture. Paul's churches were not unique in their reliance on orality. As Antoinette Wire argues, the positions and activities of the Corinthian women oral prophets were characteristic of Hellenistic Christian communities prior to Paul. Christian worship and Christian mission could be and were carried on independent of writing. Christians were not yet a "people of the book." The hermeneutics of these churches were oral hermeneutics; authority was not yet vested in manuscripts. Yet Paul produced texts that later became authoritative texts; he began a way of arguing that was later developed extensively in Christian writings. The seeds of manuscript-based Christianity are found in Paul; they are not, however, dominant in Paul.

Orality remained the dominant medium for Christianity for some time to come.

Literary Continuations of Paul's Letters

In a world as oral as the first century was, intertextuality, the use of one text by the author of another text, need not mean actual copying (literary dependence), but may mean using oral memory of written texts to create new written texts. Paul's letters clearly constitute the beginning of an intertextual literary tradition that likely involves both memory and copying. The author of 2 Thessalonians made use of 1 Thessalonians. Ephesians is a classic case of intertextuality with its heavy use of Colossians and frequent allusions to most of Paul's letters. The author's use of several letters also suggests the beginning of a collection of Paul's letters. Furthermore, a Christian letter-writing tradition has begun: in due course, we have the Catholic Epistles, Clement of Rome writing to the Corinthian Christians, and Ignatius of Antioch writing to everyone. With Paul's creation of Christian texts, letters written to substitute for his personal presence, he begins a written textual tradition that rapidly develops a life of its own. This literary tradition continues not just in the letter genre but in other genres in the writings of both heterodox and orthodox Christians from the time of Irenaeus onward.[96] Paul may have preferred the Spirit to the letter; yet his letters began a literate tradition.

Continuing Oral Understandings of Paul

Paul may have begun a literate tradition; however, it was a long while before this literate tradition became the dominant one. The actual content of Paul's letters appears to be largely irrelevant to the understanding of Paul in the first and second centuries. While Paul's method of communicating at a distance is imitated, his thought is largely ignored. The oral memory of Paul seems to be far more central to Christian debate and life than what he or his successors wrote. If we consider the canonical Acts of the Apostles, the traditions of the Apocryphal *Acts of Paul*, and the Pastoral Epistles, we have three different and competing interpretations of Paul in the early second-century, none of which has anything to do either with the texts of

96. Babcock, *Legacies of Paul.*

23

the Pauline letters as texts or with the content of Paul's theology found in those letters.[97]

These differences in images of Paul are common knowledge among New Testament scholars and expounded in New Testament introductions.[98] I shall focus rather on the absence of references to the textual tradition of Paul's genuine letters in these writings. In neither the Acts of the Apostles nor the Pastorals is there any reference to Paul as letter writer. In none of these writings is there any quotation or allusion to Paul's letters, although there are quotations and allusions to the Septuagint and occasionally to the gospels.[99] In all these writings we see not the textual Paul of the letters but the oral Paul of Christian memory. Even the Pastorals, which use the device of the pseudonymous letter, neither view Paul as a letter writer nor appeal to his written authority. Second Timothy 1:11 reads, "I [Paul] was appointed a preacher and apostle and teacher." Second Timothy 4:13 instructs Timothy to bring the books (*ta biblia*) and the parchments (*tas membranas*). It is not clear what these refer to, but given the absence of any quotations or allusions to Paul's letters, parts of the Septuagint and gospels would seem more probable than Paul's letters.[100] Dennis MacDonald argues that the various Acts present a different Paul from the Paul found in his own letters because of their narrative genre based on the gospel genre.[101] Certainly narrative does dictate a different content emphasis; but the Pastorals, which are not narrative, equally ignore the letters of Paul.

The Paul of the late first- and early second-century texts is not the Paul we know from the letters.[102] I want to suggest that a major reason the letters were ignored was that Christianity still relied on oral memory and oral authority. Since the rhetoric of the letters, unlike narrative, is not easily re-

97. The same lack of reference to the content of the letters seems to be true of the writings of the Apostolic Fathers. See de Boer, "Which Paul?"; cf. Lindemann, "Paul in the Writings."

98. E.g., Duling and Perrin, *New Testament*, 223–59; 365–400; 484–93.

99. The only possible exception is Deut 25:4, "not to muzzle an ox that is treading grain," which is quoted both in 1 Cor 9:9 and 1 Tim 5:18. The passage in 1 Timothy hardly seems a reference to the Corinthian letter.

100. Given the reference to the reading of Scripture in 1 Tim 4:13, and the reference to books, the Pastorals have moved in the direction of manuscript-based authority. The Pastoral Epistles, however, do not yet appeal to Paul's own letters.

101. D. R. MacDonald, "Apocryphal and Canonical Narratives."

102. The letters of Paul are used from the mid-to-late second century on, both by the heterodox (Marcionites and Gnostics), and also by the orthodox. See Babcock, *Legacies of Paul.*

membered, the letters never became as well known among Christians. They did not become part of Christian oral literature, so to speak. Even the more highly literate and textually oriented of the New Testament writers such as Luke and the author of the Pastorals ignore Paul's letters. Only as the more literate Christian leaders turned away from oral memory and oral authority to manuscripts, does the Paul of the letters begin to creep into Christian discourse. The beginning of the shift to the centrality of manuscripts may perhaps be dated around the middle of the second century when we first see exact quotations from the gospels rather than paraphrases from memory.[103] Indeed, to leap through the centuries with a sweeping generalization, it was the invention of print and the spread of literacy to a broader segment of the population that ultimately created the context within which the thinking of Paul as encountered in the canonical letters could be central for the Protestant Reformation.

Part III: Some Implications

In spite of the fact that Paul composed written letters and quoted passages from written texts in those letters, Paul and his churches were fundamentally dependent on the oral medium and oral authority. Only gradually did the Christian churches shift to reliance on manuscripts, Christian texts. The endurance of the oral perspective can be seen in the textual treatments of Paul in the early second century. But by the mid-second century, both orthodox and a variety of heterodox Christian leaders are appealing to manuscripts rather than to oral tradition and authority.[104] The oral hermeneutics of the Pauline congregations were becoming the textual hermeneutics of the church fathers. This shift was facilitated by the emergence of an hierarchical, male, educated—thus literate—church leadership and then reinforced by such leaders' use of the manuscript medium. But for the first century or so of its existence, Christianity remained predominantly an oral phenomenon, relying on oral hermeneutics and appealing to oral authority. The Paul of this church was the Paul whose life and work could be recalled to memory, not yet the Paul chiefly apprehended through the letters.

---

103. Koester, *Synoptische Überlieferung*.

104. For centuries to come, the huge majority of Christians of course remained non-literate. However, their relationship to the churches changed as the leadership came to rely on the written medium, from which they were excluded.

The shift from oral hermeneutics and authority to manuscript hermeneutics and authority is not a neutral matter.[105] A full exploration of the consequences of the shift to manuscript media exceeds the scope of this chapter. In brief, writing affects both what content is included and how that content is presented.[106] How content is interpreted depends in part on whether it is read or performed orally.[107] Furthermore, reliance on manuscripts drastically restricts who has access to leadership positions. Our reconstruction of early Christianity has been largely based on manuscript (and print) understandings. We need much more research on orality and literacy and their interaction in the first centuries of the common era in general and in early Christianity in particular. As our knowledge grows, our reconstructions of the early church will increasingly need to be revised as we recognize how much difference it makes when we interpret texts in the context of a predominantly oral culture. The following is a list of some consequences and methodological implications we need to consider if we are to begin to take seriously the importance of the oral communication medium in the early churches.

1) Narrative can be remembered easily orally; therefore it was more central for early Christian development.[108] The stories about Paul were more formative for first- and early second-century Christians than Paul's written letters. This was true even for the literate, more elite Christians— Luke and the author of the Pastorals. It presumably was even more true for the nonliterate majority. The Paul of his own letters, our canonical Paul, was not very important in the first decades of Christianity, because the content of the letters could not be easily remembered. Just because a text was written and later became part of the New Testament canon does not mean that it was important to early Christians or influential to early Christian development.

2) Methodologically, we need to distinguish between two stages: first, the Christian use of writing in the service of orality (e.g., Paul's letters) and

---

105. See Kelber, *Oral and Written Gospel*; Ong, *Orality and Literacy*; Havelock, *Preface to Plato*; Boomershine, "Biblical Megatrends"; also the articles collected in J. Dewey, ed., *Orality and Textuality*.

106. J. Dewey, "Jesus' Healings of Women."

107. See chapter 6 and 10, below.

108. This has interesting implications for our understanding of the synoptic tradition: it suggests that the miracles and the parables may have been more important than the isolated sayings tradition—even if that material was written down earlier.

second, the Christian creation,[109] use of, and eventual reliance on writings as writings.[110] The first use of Paul's letters to communicate at a distance does not seem to be a major rupture in the fundamentally oral context. The reuse and collection of those letters for continued use in the church in situations quite independent of their original context is a move toward the primacy of manuscripts over orality, of fixed texts over contexts. Similarly the composition of Mark's gospel may still have been in the service of orality, as a script for storytelling.[111] Later, when authorized readings had to be taken from a collection of written gospels, then manuscripts had become primary. In our reconstructions of Christian history, we have tended to conflate these two stages, assuming that the reliance on the text was present from the moment of the text's initial composition. These are two separate events, separated by decades or more, and they need to be treated separately in our historical reconstructions.

3) In order to understand both Judaism and Christianity, it is helpful to compare how they used oral and manuscript media. Pharisaic Judaism seems to have taken the step to reliance on manuscripts earlier than Christianity. Thomas Boomershine describes Pharisaic Judaism as follows: "It adopted writing as an integral part of Biblical interpretation. But in that new paradigm the oral law remained primary. The oral tradition which produced the Mishnah and the Talmud was organized around memorization of oral law, the interpretation of the written law in relation to the living of individual and communal life, and the maintenance of face to face community."[112] Boomershine describes here a very typical way that literates in antiquity made use of texts in the service of orality. The oral law was a means of interpreting and using the written law. Precisely speaking, it was a use of specific written Scriptures. The Pharisees who engaged in this oral disputation were mainly relatively elite, educated, literate males. Pharisaic Judaism was much more textually grounded than Pauline Christianity,

---

109. Aune (*New Testament,* 205) has suggested that the Pastorals were initially composed to be part of a codex of Christian writings in order to supplement or correct other *writings* in the codex, rather than to address particular individuals at all.

110. In regard to the use of Jewish or Christian writings, we also need to pay attention to whether early Christians were actually using manuscripts, or whether they were drawing on oral knowledge of scriptural traditions.

111. See chapter 6, below.

112. Boomershine, "Biblical Megatrends," 146.

which, in Paul's own words, was based on the life of the Spirit rather than the letter of the law.[113]

It is perhaps reasonable to suggest, then, that where the influence of synagogues and Jewish teachers (either by Jews or by Christian Jews) on Christianity was greater, the importance of literacy, the emphasis on reading and interpreting texts, would also be greater. It is in Paul's letters to the Galatian and Roman Christians, where issues of relationship to Jews and Jewish Christians are at issue, that Paul makes greatest use of arguments from Scripture. The Torah seems most important in the more Jewish Gospel of Matthew than it does in the other Synoptic Gospels.[114] Christianity's later interaction with rabbinic Judaism may have pushed the early Christian groups towards greater reliance on the manuscript medium.

Eventually, from the late second century and after, Christian writers carried manuscript hermeneutics further than rabbinic Judaism did. Judaism retained a mixed oral-written hermeneutic in its development of the Oral Law. Christianity, on the other hand, moved away from oral understandings into abstract theological thought, making issues of doctrine and belief central.[115] This is a later Christian development, however, and should not be read back into the New Testament period.

4) The fact that our access to early Christianity is only through written texts means that our knowledge is biased in favor of the views of those of higher social status, the only ones who were literate. As noted earlier, literacy is an instrument of power and control in a society in which most people are not literate. In *Tristes Tropiques*, Lévi-Strauss writes: "The only phenomenon with which writing has always been concomitant is the creation of cities and empires, that is the integration of large numbers of individuals into a political system, and their grading into castes or classes . . . it seems to have favoured the exploitation of human beings rather than their enlightenment . . . My hypothesis, if correct, would oblige us to recognize the fact that the primary function of written communication is to facilitate slavery."[116] While Lévi-Strauss's view may be extreme, it is certainly true of Christianity that the shift to manuscript hermeneutics and manuscript-

---

113. See Kelber, *Oral and Written Gospel*, 140–83.

114. Mark is probably also addressed to a Jewish Christian audience—but to a peasant nonliterate audience (Rohrbaugh, "Social Location").

115. So Boomershine, "Biblical Megatrends," 147–48.

116. Quoted in Harris, *Ancient Literacy*, 38. Paul certainly interprets the written law in Galatians 3 as facilitating slavery.

based authority coincided with the shift to a hierarchal male leadership that upheld the patriarchal empire and family. As long as Christianity was based on oral authority, as it was in the early urban churches, full participation and leadership were open to all regardless of class and gender. Slaves, freedpeople, and women of all classes were able to become leaders; lack of literacy did not exclude one from leadership. As Christianity increasingly appealed to the authority of manuscripts in the second and following centuries, leadership became increasingly restricted to those with education, that is, to a small, male elite who were free and heads of households.

The shift from spirit-led oral leadership open to all regardless of status or education to hierarchical authority is most easily demonstrated with regard to gender. The shift from a more egalitarian "discipleship of equals" to a hierarchal structure in which obedience and fear were the proper behavior of subordinates including all women has been well documented by Elisabeth Schüssler Fiorenza, among others.[117] The connection with literacy is perhaps as easily seen. The active role of women in the oral church is obvious in the early period, as can be seen in 1 Corinthians and Romans 16.[118] Women's continued oral leadership is evident from the stories of the Apocryphal *Acts* and from the effort of relatively elite men to silence women's storytelling: "Have nothing to do with godless tales of old women."[119] Indeed a major aim of the Pastorals seems to have been to restrict the roles and authority of Christian women.[120] Of course at the time they were written, the Pastorals did not represent general church practice. Rather, they were prescriptive statements, evidence of how the author would like to see Christian women behave, and thus evidence that the opposite behavior was occurring. Women without husbands maintaining authority over them were gathering in houses and traveling from house to house teaching. Their teaching was oral, however, while the prescriptions of the Pastorals were in writing. As Christianity became manuscript based and developed its own canon, the writings of the literate male leaders restricting women's behavior became canonical, and the orally based teaching of Christian women was gradually lost and suppressed. Our New Testament writings are not fully representative of the world of early Christianity but are distorted in the interests of the relatively few who were literate.

117. Schüssler Fiorenza, *In Memory of Her*, 160–204, 243–315.

118. Wire, *Corinthian Women Prophets*; Schüssler Fiorenza, *In Memory of Her*.

119. 1 Tim 4:7.

120. D. R. MacDonald, *Legend and the Apostle*; J. Dewey, "Jesus' Healings of Women."

In summary, I would suggest that early Christianity was an oral phenomenon in a predominantly oral culture; the culture of the dominant elite, however, was a manuscript culture. This first-century oral Christianity was a diversified, nonhierarchical, and relatively egalitarian movement. Some early Christian communications were committed to writing, if they needed to travel a long distance, possibly if they were needed to aid memory, and if they accorded with the interests of those of higher status among Christians—the only ones who could write. Thus, early Christian texts are not necessarily representative or typical of early Christianity as a whole. As Christianity gradually shifted from orally based authority to manuscript-based authority in the second through the fourth centuries, these selective and biased writings gained authority to determine what was or was not Christian.

The restriction of power within Christianity to a small, educated male elite was greatly facilitated by their literacy in a society and church in which most were not literate. Media changes (in this case from orality to writing) affect not only hermeneutics (i.e., ways of thinking and deriving meaning) but perhaps, more important, relationships of power (i.e., patterns of dominance and submission). A religion that began with the claim, "There is neither Jew nor Greek, there is neither slave nor free, there is 'no male and female,'"[121] became a religion justifying the power structure of the dominant (literate) culture of the Roman empire. In reconstructing early Christian history we need to address these biases as best we can, as we strive for a fuller view of what early Christianity was like. Recognition of the chiefly oral perspective of early Christianity makes our task of reconstruction more difficult, but it also opens possibilities for richer understanding.

121. Gal 3:28.

2

The Gospel of John in Its Oral-Written Media World

Introduction

Contrary to our implicit belief, written texts were peripheral in antiquity. The first-century media world was primarily an oral world, with some influence and control exerted by writing. Of course, it was not a purely oral world: writing had been around for millennia, and alphabetic writing for several hundred years. Yet it remained one in which the overwhelming majority of people—perhaps 95 percent—were not literate at all, and those few who were literate employed writing to serve the larger functions of orality. This chapter describes some of the characteristics of the highly oral first-century world in order that we may grasp better the assumptions first-century people would bring to hearing, composing, performing, and—very occasionally—writing texts. For unless we are self-conscious about first-century orality, we are likely to bring out own print-based, highly educated, Western understandings to the texts still extant from antiquity. This chapter, then, is prolegomena to the interpretation of the Fourth Gospel, describing the first-century media world, rather than an analysis of the orality of the Fourth Gospel.

Literacy in Antiquity

The very definition of literacy is problematic: it can mean anything from the ability to write one's name to the ability to slowly decipher a simple text to the ability to read and write fluently. However, using even the most minimal definition (possession of any ability to read or write at all), cross-cultural analyses of agrarian and advanced agrarian societies estimate an overall literacy rate of only 2 to 4 percent.[1] Those ancients who were literate were disproportionately male, of high social status, and urban. Based on an exhaustive study of Greek and Latin literacy, William Harris concluded that the literacy rate for urban males only might be as little as 15 percent.[2]

The only group for whom full literacy would be customary were males of the elite ruling class, a group virtually unrepresented among first-century Christians. Some retainers of the ruling class were also literate, as were merchants involved in luxury trades. These groups also used slaves to read and write for them. Even for the elite, literacy was not a defining characteristic of what it meant to be a proper human: barbarians were those who spoke strangely. Not until the late seventeenth and eighteenth centuries, after the development of print and more widespread literacy, did literacy come to be understood as an essential part of civilized humanity.[3] Neither urban artisans nor peasants, male or female, would be literate, or indeed have any use for such a skill. The general lack of literacy among urban artisans and peasants suggests that writing and texts played a much less important role among early Christians than our assumptions derived from our experience of print culture and universal literacy would lead us to believe.

Knowledge about the uses of writing in antiquity confirms that texts were not central for early Christians. Writing was a utilitarian tool used mainly to communicate over distance and time, contexts in which orality was unreliable at best. The administrative letter was absolutely essential to the maintenance of the Roman empire because it enabled those in power to communicate with each other. For the populace in general, however, information was conveyed orally by public criers (*kērukes, praecones*) who were attached to all levels of government. The ruling elite also used writing for culture, philosophy, and literature, but in a way that reinforced orality. Reading and writing were both done out loud; words were formed for the ear rather than for the eye. Even the elite would not need to read or write, nor would they do so themselves very often. Rather, they would dictate to scribes, often slaves, and in turn be read aloud to by them, whether the material was administrative correspondence or Greek philosophy. Beyond that, writing would be used for luxury trade, either by traders or by scribes

---

1. Rohrbaugh, "Social Location," 115; Bar-Ilan, "Illiteracy," 56; see chapter 1, above.

2. Harris, *Ancient Literacy*, 267.

3. Harbsmeier, "Writing and the Other."

employed by them. Wills and marriage contracts would be in writing, but only for the few wealthy ancients.

For the overwhelming majority, apprenticeship agreements and letters to kin living at a distance would be the only instances in which writing usually was be employed, and the writing and reading would be done by someone else, probably a professional scribe. For this 95 percent of the people, illiteracy was neither a shame nor an inconvenience. They would know the traditions of their cultures well, primarily through listening to oral storytelling.[4] Those living in cities or larger towns would also have some experience of official readers reading aloud to them on public occasions. Yet writing did have an important influence on their lives: it maintained the empire under which they lived and the debt records that often mandated their fate. Artisans and peasants both esteemed writing as almost magical in its power and at the same time were suspicious of its power over them.

The limited spread and uses of literacy detailed above suggest that people could and did become Christian without any dependence on reading or writing. The early Christian texts are central to our understanding of early Christianity; indeed, they provide virtually our only access to that time. They were, however, much more peripheral to early Christians, who relied on the spoken word. Christians began to create texts early: Paul wrote letters to communicate at a distance, which he could do only by writing. Throughout the first century, these texts were an aid to oral communication and reception and not yet fundamental to Christian understanding or developing beliefs and practices.

Oral, Manuscript, and Print Cultures: Transitions and Divides

Christianity began as an oral movement. Jesus himself was entirely an oral teacher. As a village artisan, he would not be literate.[5] He would be familiar with the scriptures primarily through hearing the oral stories of the popular tradition, and he probably occasionally heard them read aloud by some scribe or official. Most first-century Christians would only have heard the gospel told; only very rarely, if at all, would they have had Hebrew scriptures or the Christian writings read to them. A few Christians began to write texts early, Paul in the middle of the first century, most of the re-

---

4. See chapter 8, below.

5. Only Luke presents Jesus as literate, which is probably due more to Luke's assumptions about his hero than to historical reality.

mainder of the New Testament authors by the end of the century. But these texts functioned as aids to orality, and probably were not widely known or used. The shift towards greater use of writings and greater authority attributed to them begins to happen in the early to middle decades of the second century, when we get the first references to Scripture being read in Christian worship and the first exact quotations from the gospels rather than paraphrases from memory. However, even at this point, the writings were used by the few who could read or write to augment orality, and—increasingly, with the formation of canon—to control the oral tradition; they were not yet an integral part of day-to-day Christianity.

For most of the twentieth century, scholars assumed that the medium did not make much difference, that oral material slid effortlessly into written texts with little change. Then, in 1983, Werner Kelber challenged this assumption. Using the seminal work of Eric Havelock and Walter Ong, he argued forcefully in *The Oral and the Written Gospel* that there was a great divide between early Christian oral communication and the written Markan text, which emerged "out of the debris of deconstructed orality."[6] Since then, scholars have recognized that the first-century oral and written media were more blended. Vernon Robbins has suggested that we develop a more precise taxonomy of progression towards greater dependence on writing. He proposes the categories of oral culture, scribal culture, rhetorical culture, reading culture, literary culture, print culture, and hypertext culture.[7] In this paradigm, the first century would be partially scribal (Palestine) and partially rhetorical (the Greco-Roman world). In a rhetorical culture, "oral operations (presentation and hearing) and literary operations (reading and writing) were (1) inescapably interlocked, and (2) . . . communal activities."[8] Robbins spells this out: "In practice this means that writing in a rhetorical culture imitates both speech and writing, and speech in a rhetorical culture imitates both speech and writing."[9]

All New Testament texts show some evidence of both oral and writing practices. All are composed for the ear, not the eye, and thus utilize many of the oral compositional practices that facilitate comprehension and memory. And all have found their way into writing, whether they were composed in writing, dictated by an individual or group, or transcribed from

6. Kelber, *Oral and the Written Gospel*, 95.

7. Robbins, "Oral, Rhetorical and Literary," 77–82.

8. Cartlidge, "Combien d'unités," 14.

9. Robbins, "Oral, Rhetorical and Literary Cultures," 80.

oral memory. However, they may be located along a continuum from more literate to more oral. Of the New Testament authors, the author of Hebrews was able to write eloquently according to the educated rhetorical standards of his day. Luke clearly had considerable skills in writing, although not at the level demonstrated in Hebrews. Paul had considerable rhetorical ability, but not the educated standards of either the author of Hebrews or Luke. In all probability, he dictated his letters, and part of his style was due to the scribes. The Gospels of Mark and John are at the oral end of the continuum, showing abundant evidence of oral composition procedures and little if any evidence of the incorporation of writing conventions. Their composers may or may not have been literate.

Existence of texts, however, does not entail reliance on texts even by the most literate within the society. To us, writing—print, books—seems more convenient and more authoritative than the spoken word. For the ancients, oral memory and performance seemed more authoritative than writing. Manuscripts were inconvenient, perishable, and above all expensive, much too expensive for most small poor Christian communities to own. Furthermore they were difficult to read since there were no spaces between words and no punctuation. One really had to know what a manuscript said before one was able to read it aloud to a group. In addition, manuscripts were scarce; in the first century, there probably existed few copies of any of the writings that later came to constitute the New Testament.

Manuscripts are immensely more stable than oral performance, but they are much less stable than those of us accustomed to print usually think. No two manuscripts are identical. Changes continue to occur through copying and recopying, deliberate change, scribal error, omission, and incorporation into the text of glosses. Writing did not produce fixity of wording, nor was it expected to. Even after the development of print and the Reformation, at the Council of Trent, when the Roman Catholic Church declared the Latin Vulgate to be the authoritative version of Scripture, the Council did not specify which particular text of the Vulgate, or even choose among the major Vulgate traditions. Exact wording was still not at issue.

The written texts, once they came into existence, would continue to interact with orality in the life of Christian communities. In such a heavily oral/aural world as that of the first centuries and in the social milieu of early Christianity, the written texts would rarely have been read aloud. Rather they mostly would have been performed from memory. In such contexts, there is a great deal of feedback or cross-influence between oral and literate versions of particular stories. A written version of a story would be recycled orally through performance from memory and in interaction with new audiences, naturally changing in the process. Then it would get written down again, with or without changes added by the transcriber or author, and again recycled into oral performance, and so on. Such a process is the norm, not the exception, for oral traditional material in a culture of very limited literacy.

This continued interaction of oral and written is important for our understanding of early Christianity. First, we have no idea of how close our texts of the Fourth Gospel (based mostly on fourth- and fifth-century manuscripts) are to the first-century renditions of the Fourth Gospel, but we can be sure that there has been considerable change. Second, for the large majority of Christians of the first centuries, the only versions of the gospels they probably ever heard were oral, which almost certainly deviated a good bit from the written versions and from each other. While literate bishops and scholars may have argued theological niceties in writing, most Christians continued to experience the gospel entirely orally.

In summary, then, there was no great divide between the oral and the written word in the first century, no great gulf between those who could read and those who could not in first-century culture. Overall, the communications system of antiquity for the literate and nonliterate alike was still thoroughly imbued with orality. Conventions of orality undergirded all composition, performance, and reception whether a particular performance was entirely oral or dependent in some ways upon writing.

There may, however, be a great divide between the Christians of the first century and those of us trained in modern silent print. In his seminal study of the interaction of oral and written in scriptural religions, William Graham writes:

> In the West at least, the really major displacement of oral modes of thought and communication came only as a postprint phenomenon . . . In terms of changes in modes of consciousness as well as sheer material change, the great chasm in forms of communication turns out to be not that between literate societies and nonliterate societies but . . . the gulf between our own modern Western, post-Enlightenment world of the printed page and all past cultures (including our own predecessors in the West), as well as most contemporary ones.[10]

10. Graham, *Beyond the Written Word*, 17, 29.

Thus, if we wish to understand the New Testament texts in terms of their own media environment, we must self-consciously turn from our instinctive assumptions about texts derived from our print culture, and learn about oral and oral-written cultures. I turn now to a description of some of the characteristics of orality that may be helpful in understanding and interpreting the Fourth Gospel and other ancient texts.

Characteristics of Orality

When we think of written texts, we think of exact wording. We think in terms of print, where there are multiple copies of the same text, identical both in content and in spacing on the page. This was not so with written texts, let alone oral stories, in antiquity. Oral stories are never fixed. Some oral storytellers insist that they repeat the story identically, but electronic recordings easily demonstrate that they do not. Tradition is multiform. The audience always affects the performance. Changes—minor and major—are inevitably made, depending on the storyteller, the context, and the audience. It is true that oral cultures can remember some material extremely accurately. As late as the 1960s, the Ibadan cattle market in Nigeria handled some seventy-five thousand cattle every year, with all sales on credit, for a debt of one hundred thousand pounds at any one time, all without aid of writing, banks, or courts.[11] A small and carefully trained group among the South Sea Islanders learned chants with detailed, accurate navigational information.[12] However, this sort of accuracy is atypical, and only occurs where something critical is at stake—the navigator who got the chant wrong might well never return. Too, even here, the aim was usefulness, not accuracy or fidelity for its own sake.

Present usefulness strongly affects the transmission of oral tradition, which is continually adapting to changed conditions. This is true even—or perhaps especially—of traditions that are important for the constitution of groups, as the gospels were for early Christian communities. In such cases, materials are expanded, omitted, and adapted to fit the current situation. The classic example of this phenomenon is the Gonja oral tradition in Ghana.[13] When the historical legends of the founder of the Gonja state were first recorded around 1900, the founder had seven sons, each a ruler

11. Cohen, "Social Organization," 8–9, cited in Finnegan, *Literacy and Orality*, 149.

12. Couch, "Oral Technologies," 595–97.

13. Goody and Watt, "Consequences of Literacy," 33.

of one of the territorial divisions. When the legends were recorded again some sixty years later, the story told of only five sons, since there were now only five divisions. The legend had adapted to accommodate the new political reality. Only because the earlier version was preserved in writing do we know the earlier historical reality. "Historical facts in the remembered past are under constant pressure from the needs of the present. The memory adapts, transposes them, or eliminates them altogether, when they are no longer useful."[14] (Actually, things not seen as relevant for the present are also forgotten in print culture. For example, the very active women's movement in mid- to late-nineteenth-century England was not part of the English history taught throughout most of the twentieth century. In print culture, however, texts remain to be rediscovered if they again become relevant to the present—as in this instance, when a new wave of feminism arose in the 1970s. In print, this issue was only temporarily forgotten, not permanently lost as it would be in an oral culture.) Oral tradition is not fixed but continues to adapt to the present contexts, whatever they may be.

Composition, reception, and transmission exist as one event in oral culture. An oral storyteller generally makes up the story as he or she tells it; that is, the person works not with a memorized script but with tradition and a story line. Even in the first century's rhetorical culture, it is unlikely that the Fourth Gospel would have been read aloud from a scroll or codex in hand. Rather it would have been retold on the basis of prior hearing or reading of the text. A good storyteller could hear the Fourth Gospel told once and be able to retell it. The gospel as we have it is short enough to be told in one storytelling session, so it was probably often heard in its entirety in one and a half to two and a half hours. In addition, length is one of the most variable elements in oral narrating: a storyteller will shrink or expand a story from as little as ten minutes to a couple of hours, depending on the receptivity of the audience. So audiences undoubtedly heard both expanded and contracted versions of the Fourth Gospel.

The oral performance event exists as a face-to-face happening in some particular social context. It primarily involves sound, but actually engages all the senses. Much of meaning and impact of the performance is conveyed, not by the words alone, as on a printed page, but by all the other visual and aural affects that are part of the experience—gesture, movement, facial expression, inflection, pitch, and volume. Thus oral culture may be considered high-context culture: much of a story's effect and power, as well

14. Clanchy, "Remembering the Past," 166.

as cues to interpretation of it, are to be found in the context, not in the words themselves—which are all that remains to us today.

The context is relevant in three ways. First, an oral/aural story builds on traditions known to the performer and the audience. As John Miles Foley has shown, reference in oral literature is generally metonymic, recalling the larger tradition rather than some specific objective reality.[15] Thus, for example, Homer's reference to "swift-footed Achilles" functions not so much to tell the audience that Achilles was quick on his feet as to recall to the hearer the whole complex of ideas and motifs associated with Achilles. Insofar as we no longer know the tradition among first-century Christians, we are at a disadvantage in interpreting the text.

Second, in an oral/aural story, much is conveyed not through the words but through the other aspects of performance. A written transcript of an oral story loses much of its power. Ruth Finnegan writes that when she heard and recorded Limba stories in the field, she was impressed by "by their subtlety, imaginativeness, creativity, drama and human qualities," but when she transcribed them back in England, they seemed lifeless and dull, since so much of the performance was not in the words themselves.[16] Elements of characterization were often completely lost, since they were conveyed in the oral rendition. In modern print culture, we embed much more information in the text itself because we know the text will be read in isolation from other factors. In dealing with ancient texts, we no longer have access to information that came from the performance context, not the written words.

Third, an oral/aural story is adapted to the particular context/audience in which it is being told. Writing about North Turkic tribal singers, Wilhelm Radloff says, "If wealthy and noble Kirgiz are present, [a singer] knows how to skillfully weave in praises of their dynasties, and he sings about those episodes which he expects will stir the nobility's applause in particular. If only poor people are in his audience, he includes some bitter remarks about the arrogance of the noble and wealthy."[17] This suggests that performances of a gospel would have been adapted to the social levels and cultural contexts (Jewish, Gentile, or what have you) of the particular audiences, and that what we have in our texts is only one particular version. We are again at a disadvantage in understanding oral/aural texts because

---

15. J. M. Foley, *Singer of Tales*, 53–59.
16. Finnegan, "What Is Orality," 134–35.
17. Radloff, "Samples of Folk Literature," 85.

we no longer share or understand their contexts, which were a large part of the experience, and because we no longer have the full, live experience. Furthermore, since texts (both oral and written) were composed to facilitate performance and memory (memory of both the performer and of the audience), we often do not know how to interpret common features of the text, features that are no longer characteristic of printed texts.

These features, the compositional characteristics of oral/aural composition have been well described by Havelock and Ong. Havelock interprets Plato's attack on poetry or mimesis in *The Republic* as an attack on the oral mindset. He suggests that the content of oral/aural literature has three characteristics. First, it is made up of *happenings* (*gignomena*): events in time, episodes, little stories, or situations. Teaching is embedded in these happenings, rather than being presented as general rules organized topically. Second, it consists of the *visible* (*horata*): happenings that can easily be visualized in the mind's eye. The performer and the audience can picture them, and thus more easily remember them. Third, it consists of the *many* (*polla*): episodes placed side by side, not integrated with one another. The happenings are not joined to one another in a hierarchical or tight chronological structure of cause and effect but are simply placed alongside one another paratactically.[18] In print, we tend to insist upon specifying the relationship of one clause to another, one event to another. Oral media simply place them side by side, so that the story consists of many instances, not a single structured whole.

Ong presents a good summary of the typical features of oral composition style.[19] Oral compositions tend to be additive, rather than subordinating some things to others. The normal way of connecting clauses, sentences, and whole episodes is paratactic: "and next," "and then." Oral compositions tend to be aggregative rather than analytic or linear. Ong uses the opening verses of Genesis to illustrate this shift in our ways of thinking/writing. The 1610 Douay translation preserves the additive style of the Hebrew, with nine introductory *and*s. The 1970 New American Bible translation preserves only two of the *and*s, eliminates two altogether, and translates the other five as a *when*, a *while*, a *thus*, and two *then*s.[20]

---

18. Havelock, *Preface to Plato*, 180. *Parataxis* is the rhetorical term for this sort of parallel, coordinating (rather than subordinating) arrangement of elements.

19. Ong, *Orality and Literacy*, 37–52; 141–44.

20. Ibid., 37.

Oral clauses, sentences, and whole episodes are not organized in an analytic or chronological way but occur in clusters arranged in symmetrical fashions of various sorts: simple parallel (A-B-C, A-B-C), chiastic (A-B-C, C-B-A), and concentric (A-B-C, D-C-B-A) structures. They tend to be redundant or copious—to our print sensibilities, very repetitive—but always with variations, in order to assist memory. "The basic method for assisting the memory to retain a series of distinct meanings is to frame the first of them in a way which will suggest or forecast a later meaning which will recall the first without being identical with it . . . Though the narrative syntax is paratactic . . . the narrative is not linear but turns back on itself in order to assist the memory to reach the end by having it anticipated somehow in the beginning."[21]

Thinking tends to be situational rather than categorical, concrete rather than abstract, with teaching embedded in story. The plot of the story, however, tends to be loose, even formless in comparison to the tightly woven plots characteristic of print culture, building toward a climax only by accumulation of episodes. Compositions are close to human experience, told in a narrative about people, usually gathered around a major hero or group of heroes. They tend to be agonistically toned, so polemical that they often strike people from print cultures as verbal abuse. Finally, they are presented as empathetic and participatory, rather than objectively distanced. Performer and audience alike identify with characters in turn, fighting, weeping, and rejoicing with them, experiencing what they experience.

While Ong stresses this empathetic and participatory nature of oral/aural narrative, Havelock points out that the oral mindset is strongly emotional.[22] The performer identifies with the content, and appeals to the audience's emotions, and the audience in turn identifies with the performance. This emotional subjectivity is necessary to facilitate memory, both of the performer and of the audience. Thus, the focus for both performer and audience is on the experience of the performance event, not on information learned or reinforced. The point is the emotional impact, not the knowledge gained. True, modern audiences still value experience—if we are lost in a good novel or, somewhat more communally, in watching a film in a movie theater. On the whole, however, we think of the printed word as a tool to give us information about something outside of the printed page. As

21. Havelock, "Oral Composition," 183.
22. Havelock, *Preface to Plato*, 20–34.

biblical scholars we want to know something about the beliefs of the Johannine community, or the sources the Fourth Evangelist used. As people in church pews, we read for cognitive information on what to believe and how to act. We rarely approach the gospel narratives as experiences that may transform our relation to the world (although we may experience worship this way). Yet this is how the gospels would have been experienced in the first century.

As argued earlier, oral tradition is multiform and always changing. This is the way memory works. Modern studies of the brain show that memory is not exact. Similar memories overlay earlier memories and get conflated with each other, so that what we believe are clear memories of one particular event can generally be shown to be composite memories of several events. So also with memories about Jesus and his sayings. If Jesus had trained his disciples in verbatim memorization, exact memory would be more likely, but a nonliterate oral teacher would have no concept of either *verbatim* or *memorization*.

Studies of the brain also show that memory solidifies quickly. In an Emory University study on student memories of where they were when the space shuttle *Challenger* exploded, the difference between what the students reported the day after the event and what they remembered two and a half years later was huge.[23] None remembered exactly where they were and what they were doing when they found out, and 25 percent were wrong on all the details: where they were, what they were doing when they heard, and how they found out. When these same students were asked again, six months after the second interview, their memories were consistent with what they had reported the second time. Whether right or (more often) wrong, these memories had solidified into a clear and visually vivid picture.

Though oral tradition is much more communal then the individual memories investigated in the above study, it also has a tendency to solidify, not into an exact memory, but into clear complexes of stories and sayings. Furthermore, as noted earlier, stories and traditions tend to coalesce into a larger story centered around a hero. Havelock writes, "The tighter . . . the group structure . . . the more urgent is the need for the creation of a great story which shall compendiously gather up all the little stories into

---

23. Neisser and Harsch, "Phantom Flashbulbs." Cited in Lewis, Amini and Lannon, *Theory of Love*, 134–35; Crossan, *Birth of Christianity*, 61–63.

a coherent succession, grouped round several prominent agents who shall act and speak with some over-all consistency."[24]

As largely oral subgroups with "tight group structures," Christian groups within the empire would have needed such a "great" or inclusive story. Contrary to most scholars' assumptions, it is extremely likely that connected narratives—or a single changing connected narrative—about the life and death of Jesus began to be told very early, probably earlier even than Q was written down, as the oral tradition coalesced. Jan Vansina, an authority on oral history, argues that this process happens quickly. He writes: "When accounts of events have been told for a generation or so the messages then current may still represent the tenor of the original message, but in most cases the resulting story has been fused out of several accounts and has acquired a stabilized form. The plot and sequence of episodes changes only gradually after this."[25]

Thus, the conclusion of the form critics that the individual stories traveled independently until they were combined in larger complexes in writing is almost certainly wrong. That is not how oral tradition typically works, even in a culture that has writing, as the first century did. Given most early Christians' level of culture and limited literacy, and given the ease with which such a story could be remembered and retold orally, a coherent overall narrative is likely to have emerged in entirely oral form. It is extremely probable that a multiform general story about Jesus—his ministry, death, and postdeath—had already coalesced in oral form by the middle of the first century, and that such an oral narrative underlies both Mark and the Fourth Gospel. Also, given the evidence we have about frequent communication and interchange among Christian communities, it is also likely that versions of such a connected oral narrative were widely, if not universally, known wherever there were Christians. Certainly there would be variations on this story by different storytellers in different communities and different nascent theologies, and the social class and gender of the tellers and audiences would also affect the story. Nonetheless, knowledge of oral tradition suggests that such a larger comprehensive narrative would have existed and been generally known.

24. Havelock, *Preface to Plato*, 175.
25. Vansina, *Oral Traditions*, 17.

The Fourth Gospel

Recognition of the highly oral/aural nature of the first century adds to our already great difficulty in reaching historical certainty. At the same time, though, an understanding of some of the ways that this media culture operated can aid us in interpreting the texts that we do have. In the remainder of this article, I shall indicate seven questions in Johannine studies that knowledge of the oral media world may help us understand. I am not attempting to interpret the Fourth Gospel and its prehistory in light of the first-century media world; rather I am naming areas where I think orality studies have a contribution to make.

1) *Does knowledge of orality help us to determine what goes back to Jesus?* As noted earlier, memory alters, conflates, and adapts to present situations. This is as true for the Synoptic Gospels as for the Fourth Gospel. Both are far removed from the days of Jesus. The workings of memory and the process of solidification of oral tradition must make us question the historical reliability of all the gospels. Furthermore, closeness to oral style in a written text does not necessarily make the text earlier or any closer to what actually happened than a written text. The degree of orality is not in itself a useful criterion for sifting historicity out of gospel texts.

2) *Was there a larger oral narrative underlying the Fourth Gospel?* I argued earlier that individual oral stories do not simply continue to circulate independently until they are put in writing, as form criticism supposed. Rather, they tend to aggregate into larger, somewhat coherent narratives focused on the hero or heroes. Such an oral narrative is likely to underlie the gospels. The substantial differences between the Fourth Gospel and the Synoptics lead me to ask whether there were two different and more or less comprehensive oral narratives in existence: one that lies behind the Gospel of Mark, and another that lies behind the Fourth Gospel. Is the Fourth Gospel evidence for a somewhat different oral traditional story? I doubt this can be proved or disproved, but it is quite probable. The two stories might originate from different geographical centers: Jerusalem for the Fourth Gospel and Galilee for the Synoptics.[26] Furthermore, nondominant groups normally both know the traditions of the dominant group and have their own—often critical—versions of tradition.[27] The community of the Fourth

---

26. These oral narratives would differ from those proposed by Crossan, since each would cover both the life and death of Jesus (Crossan, *Birth of Christianity*).

27. Scott, *Domination*.

Gospel seems to have understood itself as a minority among Christians; therefore it might well have developed its own alternate oral narrative.

3) *Was there a written Signs Source?* Many scholars posit that there was a written source, containing many of the miracles or signs of John 1–12, which the Fourth Evangelist used in composing the gospel. Knowledge of first-century media culture suggests that such a written source is improbable. Unlike isolated sayings or discourse material, miracle stories are narrative and thus easy to remember. In a culture in which very few could read and writing materials were expensive and cumbersome, and in which memory was well developed, it seems unlikely that anyone would go to the trouble to write a Signs Source. The inconsistencies and sudden shifts in the Johannine narrative that the posited Signs Source explains can equally be explained as the result of oral composition, writing, or interaction of oral and written versions. Listening audiences tolerate (or do not even notice) inconsistencies, even different theologies, much more easily than we with our print-formed minds do. Furthermore, the colloquial nature of the Greek of the Fourth Gospel suggests that its author was not highly educated, and thus probably not a fluent reader. He would more likely have garnered his information from hearing than from working with a written source. Recognition of the first-century oral/aural culture argues against the existence of a Signs Source.

4) *Was there a pre-Johannine Passion narrative?* I think we have far too little evidence to posit a pre-Johannine written Passion narrative, for the same reasons that I think a Signs Source is improbable. If a larger oral narrative does indeed underlie the Fourth Gospel, then some of the peculiarities of the Fourth Gospel's Passion narrative could easily derive from it. However, the ability to isolate particular parts of John 18–20 seems highly problematic to me. First, it seems to assume a fixity and reliability of both the text of the Fourth Gospel and of the proposed source that are simply not characteristic of texts in antiquity. Second, our tools for separating source from redaction often rely on subtle analytic distinctions that the additive and aggregative nature of oral narrative and most first-century writing simply did not make.

5) *What is the relation of the Fourth Gospel to the Synoptics?* Scholars continue to argue different positions on the Fourth Gospel's relation to the Synoptics. Some argue for literary dependence on Mark (or the Synoptics), others for complete independence, others for some mediating position that the Fourth Evangelist was acquainted with Mark but did not use it as a

source. The conditions of first-century oral and manuscript transmission make the last seem most probable to me. There are occasional echoes of Mark that are so specific and idiosyncratic that it seems to me most likely that the Fourth Evangelist heard Mark performed at some time, which in itself is quite probable. However, his limited use of Mark suggests that a text of Mark was not in front of him nor fully in his memory as he was composing. Furthermore, as noted earlier, the level of his Greek suggests greater reliance on oral memory than use of written texts.

6) *How oral or written in style is the Fourth Gospel?* As noted earlier, speech imitates writing and writing imitates speech in this oral-manuscript media world. One frequently cannot tell with any great degree of certainty whether a text we now have was composed orally in performance and then (or later) transcribed, or whether a text was initially created in writing. As certain conventions of writing become the norm, they are often incorporated into oral performances. A speaker who is thoroughly familiar with the oral tradition can compose in oral style as they write or dictate. All ancient writers were writing for the ear, and those with less formal education were likely to rely heavily on oral compositional techniques. Further, even if the Fourth Gospel had been created entirely orally or entirely in writing, the ongoing interchange between written text and oral performance would likely have left residues in the manuscripts that have survived. I would like to include a few observations here.

Our text of the Fourth Gospel gives clear evidence of considering itself to be a writing. In John 20, it concludes: "Although Jesus performed many more signs for his disciples to see than could be written down in this book, these are written down so you will come to believe that Jesus is the Anointed One, the son of God—and by believing this have life in his name" (SV)[28] The later appendix of John 21 concludes: "This is the disciple who is testifying to all this and has written it down" (SV).[29] The question I would raise is, was the narrative conceived of as a writing from the beginning, or were these conclusions added on in the process of oral and written transmission of the material? The Johannine conclusions suggest, though they do not prove, that the Fourth Gospel was initially conceived as a writing.

The style of the Fourth Gospel is heavily oral. The Greek uses mainly simple clauses and frequent instances of present tense where written convention would normally require a past tense. However, the style is slightly

28. John 20:30–31.
29. John 21:24.

less oral than Mark's.[30] Mark connects almost all episodes simply with an "and" (*kai*). The Fourth Evangelist uses a fair number of *and*s, but he also regularly uses "the next day," "after this," and other similar connectors. However, they remain simple connectors: "and next," "and next," and so on.

According to Havelock's categories, the narrative is made up of happenings visible and many. In contrast to those in the Synoptics, the episodes are long, evolving into dialogue and often monologue—that is, the episodes conclude with relatively long sections of teaching or discourse material. As is characteristic of orality, teaching is embedded in or tagged onto the events; the discourses are not presented as freestanding teaching. This is true even of the last discourses of John 13–17. Furthermore, as in oral narrative, dialogue is restricted to two characters at a time (e.g., the sequential dialogues of the Samaritan woman, Jesus, and the disciples, or the sequential dialogues around the blind man).

In addition, both these episodes and their following dialogues are on the whole visualizable. The ensuing monologues are not easy to remember by visualizing them. However, the added cues provided in live performance likely clarified such issues as who the speaker or narrator is in John 3:31–36. And the gospel is definitely made up of the many: many miracles, many dialogues and discourses, which could well be described as repetitions with variation. It involves, not a tight linear plot, but the unfolding of similar events and discourses.

Much more work needs to be done on the discourse material to understand better its relation to oral and written media. Did the discourses evolve only in writing with little or no prior existence orally? Or were they oral, perhaps the work of Christian prophets speaking to the community?[31] Then, is the confusion and repetition of the discourses due to the difficulty of remembering them orally and embedding them in a connected narrative? Or, as a third possibility, were they composed in writing perhaps more systematically then we now have them, and did they become confused and conflated as the gospel got recycled orally? Or, perhaps most probable, did the discourses begin orally in much shorter form, and get expanded in succeeding written versions? All these are possible. Analysis of the text may shed some light on the discourses' oral and/or written characteristics.

One feature of the Fourth Gospel that has puzzled scholars and readers is the tension between the present and future eschatologies contained

---

30. See chapter 5, below.

31. As suggested by David Rhoads in a personal communication.

in the narrative. Given the first-century media world, this phenomenon can be explained easily in either of two ways. First, oral-type narrative can embrace what seems to us as contradiction; it tends to create a both-and world, both "you are already saved if you believe," and "there is a last day." Second, this tension in eschatologies could be the result of the sequence of transmission, from oral performance to written text to oral performance, and so on, that characterized the use of the Fourth Gospel over the second and probably much of the third century. Updated or corrected material would naturally be added in as the gospel was adapted to its present use, without the old necessarily dropping out. In a totally oral media world, the old would probably be lost altogether. In a manuscript world, the text maintains some stability, so the old is more likely to remain.

What we have in the Fourth Gospel, then, would seem to be a writing that remains very close to the oral-performance world, but that is also indebted to writing. Its composer probably did not use any written sources but may well have built on a preexisting oral narrative. This person was certainly immersed in much of the oral tradition and had at least heard Mark.

7) *How does oral reception of the Fourth Gospel affect interpretation?* Again, what I present here is not a full exploration but rather some preliminary suggestions. First, as noted earlier, we need to take less seriously the inconsistencies and disjunctions of the text. We need to take more seriously the both-and nature of oral/aural thought, and to see how we can integrate rather than analyze and separate the different strands of thought found in the gospel. Second, we need to remember that the oral culture was heavily agonistic. First-century audiences probably took much less seriously the negative portrayal of the "Jews" and of other Christian groups simply because they expected discourse to be polemical. Third, and most important, in order to assist memory, both the performer and the audience identify with each character in turn. For the episode of the woman at the well, they would identify with Jesus and with the Samaritan woman, the disciples, and the villagers, thus experiencing each character sympathetically in turn. This process of identification would also extend to the "Jews," and here also might ameliorate to some extent the negativity of their portrayal. More work is needed around how oral reception differs from the experience of reading silent print.

Conclusion

I have presented some of the major features of the first-century oral-written media world that contrast with the assumptions we bring to reading from our training in Western print culture. I have also suggested some ways that recognition of the high degree of orality may impact our study of the Fourth Gospel and its prehistory. Orality studies are still in their infancy, and much needs to be done to understand and apply them to New Testament studies. Yet I think we have learned enough to know that consideration of the communication medium does make a difference in interpretation. On the one hand, orality makes our reconstructions of early Christian history even more problematic and uncertain; on the other hand, orality also gives us new ways of investigating and new insights into our texts.

PART 2

Oral Patterning in Mark and Implications for Interpretation of Mark

3

The Literary Structure of the Controversy Stories in Mark 2:1—3:6

Introduction

It has long been agreed that the five controversy stories of Mark 2:1—3:6 (the healing of the paralytic, the eating with tax collectors and sinners, the question about fasting, plucking grain on the sabbath, and the man with the withered hand) constitute a collection of conflict stories compiled either by Mark or by some earlier collector.[1] In this chapter, I argue that these five stories have not merely been collected in one place because of similarities in form and content, but they have been constructed in such a way as to form a single literary unit with a tight and well-worked-out concentric or chiastic structure: A B C B' A' (Mark 2:1–12, 13–17, 18–22, 23–28; 3:1–6). If these passages do indeed constitute a coherent *literary* unit, recognized by Mark as such, then a consideration of the literary structure will aid in understanding the individual elements within Mark 2:1—3:6 and will aid in determining its meaning and place in the overall structure of the Gospel of Mark. First, the chiastic structure of the five stories will be established using formal, linguistic, and content criteria. Then the question of whether the structure is Markan or pre-Markan will be considered.

---

1. Albertz, *Die synoptischen Streitgespräche*, 5–16; Dibelius, *From Tradition to Gospel*, 219; Taylor, *St. Mark*, 91–92.

Establishing the Structure

To begin with, the author of the Gospel of Mark intended 2:1—3:6 to be viewed as a literary unit or subunit within the gospel. He set the section into a frame. The first chapter of Mark ends with Jesus's healing the leper, and the leper spreading the news "so that Jesus could no longer openly enter a town, but was out in the country; and people came to him from every quarter" (1:45b). Chapter 2 opens with a complete break: "And when he returned to Capernaum" (2:1). The first thing Mark has Jesus do, after not being able openly to enter a city, is to enter a city. But Mark 3:7 picks up again right where 1:45 left off: "Jesus withdrew with his disciples to the sea, and a great multitude from Galilee followed; also from Judea and Jerusalem and Idumea, and from beyond the Jordan and from about Tyre and Sidon, a great multitude, hearing all that he did, came to him" (3:7–8). Jesus once again *is* outside of the cities, and people are coming to him from every quarter; the places are now specifically named. The evangelist has blocked off the controversy section by means of a frame.

The five pericopes appear to be combined in a chiastic pattern according to content: A, the healing of the paralytic, contains a healing of the resurrection type; B, the eating with tax collectors and sinners, concerns eating; C, the question about fasting, fasting; B', plucking grain on the sabbath, eating again; and A', the man with the withered hand, contains another miracle of the resurrection type. The chiastic pattern is also to be seen in details of form and language.

The first and fifth stories, A and A', are constructed along parallel lines. They begin with virtually identical introductions: A: *kai eiselthōn palin eis,* "and having entered again into" (2:1) and A': *kai eisēlthen palin eis,* "and he entered again into" (3:1). Both occur indoors: in one case a house, in the other a synagogue.

Both stories have the same form: a controversy apophthegm embedded into a healing miracle.[2] This is a mixed form and relatively uncommon.[3] The miracles are both of the resurrection type, not exorcisms; the paralytic and the withered hand are each restored. The verb *egeirō* is used three times in the story of the paralytic, and once in the parallel story of the

---

2. Contrary to the opinion of Rudolf Bultmann, who views Mark 3:1–5 as an "organically complete apophthegm" not utilizing the style of a miracle story (*Synoptic Tradition*, 12; 209).

3. Ibid., 209.

withered hand in the rather odd expression *egeire eis to meson*, "get up to the middle" (3:3), which serves to bring the verb into the story.

In both stories the controversy apophthegm is embedded into the miracle and set off from it by means of the repetition of Jesus's address to the man being healed: *legei tō paralytikō* in Mark 2:5 and 10; *legei tō anthrōpō* in Mark 3:3 and 5. In neither story do the opponents of Jesus openly state their opposition: in the first, A, Jesus knows that they debate in their *hearts*; in the last, A', Jesus is grieved at their hardness of *heart*. These are the first uses of *kardia* in the gospel,[4] and the term is not used again until 6:52 where it is the disciples' hearts that are hardened. In both A and A', Jesus responds to unspoken opposition with a counterquestion in good rabbinic-controversy style: "Which is easier to say . . . 'Your sins are forgiven'; or to say, 'Rise, take up your pallet and walk'?" (2:9, RSV) and "Is it lawful on the sabbath to do good or to do harm?" (3:4, RSV).

Then, by means of Jesus's speaking again to the one being healed, stories A and A' revert to the miracle form. The miracle is completed, and the reaction of the onlookers described: "the impression the miracle creates on the crowd."[5] The content of the reactions is not parallel but antithetical: to the healing of the paralytic, "So that they were all amazed and glorified God, saying 'We never saw anything like this!'" (2:12, RSV); to the healing of the withered hand, "The Pharisees went out, and immediately held counsel with the Herodians against him, how to destroy him" (3:6, RSV). The reaction in 3:6 is hostile, not admiring, but it seems nonetheless to fill the slot in the miracle form of the response of the audience.

Thus A, the healing of the paralytic, and A', the restoration of the withered hand, are constructed in a parallel manner as shown by form, by content, and by assorted linguistic details. I would propose that 3:1–6 has been composed by Mark in order to balance the story of the paralytic and to complete the Sabbath-controversy pattern (see below).[6] The parallelism of structure, in any case, seems beyond accidental.

The middle three pericopes—B, eating with tax collectors; C, fasting; and B', plucking grain on the Sabbath—contain several features which set them off from A and A'. None contains a miracle and all contain wisdom sayings or proverbs. In A and A' the cast of characters consists of Jesus, opponents, and the sick man. In B, C, and B' the cast consists of Jesus,

---

4. Used twice in the first story.

5. Bultmann, *Synoptic Tradition*, 225.

6. Cf. Grob, *Einführung*, 38–39.

opponents, and disciples. In all three, either Jesus or his disciples are questioned about their behavior; Jesus does not take the initiative as he did in the two healing stories.

The setting of B and B' within the overall structure of the controversy section is somewhat more complex. Not only are these pericopes parallel to each other in structure, but B is also set in relation to A, and B' to A'. Story A, the healing of the paralytic, deals with the issue of forgiveness of sins. Story B, the eating with tax collectors, has to do with Jesus's association with sinners. These two stories are joined by the catchwords *hamartia* and *hamartōloi*.[7]

Stories B' and A', on the other hand, are both concerned with the Sabbath law. In B' the Pharisees ask why the disciples do what is not lawful on the Sabbath (2:24). In A' "they" are watching to see if Jesus will heal on the Sabbath (3:2), and Jesus asks if it is lawful on the Sabbath to do good or evil (3:4). These last two controversies are joined by the catchwords *tois sabbasin* and *exestin*.

Though in content B points back to A (the subject of sin), and B' ahead to A' (the subject of Sabbath law), in structure and form B is parallel to B'. Story B opens with Jesus out of doors, beside the sea, calling Levi from his tax office, calling a sinner who is in the middle of sinning (2:13–14). It closes with a proverb, "Those who are well have no need of a physician, but those who are sick," followed immediately by the implied christological saying, "I came not to call the righteous, but sinners" (2:17, RSV).

Story B' similarly begins out of doors, in the fields, with the disciples breaking the Sabbath law by working, plucking grain (2:23). It ends with the proverb, "The Sabbath was made for man, not man for the Sabbath" followed immediately by the christological saying, "So the Son of Man is lord also of the Sabbath" (2:27–28, RSV). The content in B and B' is different, but the structure or form is the same. In both cases the final proverb and saying justify the initial action.

The central sections of both B and B', however, are concerned not with sinners or Sabbath, but rather with *eating*. In story B, Jesus enters a house (just as story A took place in a house) and eats with tax collectors and sinners (2:15–16). The verb *esthiō* is used twice in the present tense. In B', Jesus refers to the scriptural incident of David entering the house of God (as A' takes place in a synagogue), eating the bread of the presence and giving it also to "those with him" (2:25–26). *Esthiō* is used twice in the aorist. In

7. Sundwall, *Zusammensetzung*, 15.

story B, Jesus and his disciples eat with tax collectors, something not lawful in light of the laws of ritual cleanliness.[8] In B', David and his followers ate that which was lawful only for priests to eat (Mark 2:26).

In story B, the eating is an integral part of the pericope; Jesus is questioned on his behavior in eating with tax collectors and sinners. Yet the response, "I came not to call the righteous, but sinners" (2:17b, RSV), may refer not only to the call to table fellowship[9] but also to the call of Levi in 2:14. The relevance of the example of David's action to the breaking of Sabbath laws in story B' is debatable,[10] and the story reads more smoothly without the insertion of vv. 25 and 26. I suggest, therefore, that Mark (or an earlier collector) has inserted this Old Testament reference into B' because of its parallelism in content to story B—Jesus's eating with sinners—in order to balance his chiastic structure.[11] And in light of the chiasm, David's action may justify not so much the breaking of the Sabbath law, but Jesus's behavior in story B: David broke the law when he had need (*chreian eschen*, 2:25); Jesus asserted that it was the sick who had need of a physician (*chreian echousin*, 2:17).

The literary interrelationships and correlations of the first two and the last two stories seem sufficiently numerous and precise to establish that Mark 2:1—3:6 is a well-worked-out, deliberate chiastic structure. This leaves C, the question about fasting, as the middle section of the structure by definition. Story C is set apart from the pattern of the other stories. Each of the other four stories has an explicit setting; C is completely without any indication of setting. In the other four, the opponents are named; in story C, they are not specified.[12]

C itself consists of three separate units: 2:18–19, a controversy apophthegm about fasting, with Jesus's response to the effect that it was a time for joy, not fasting; 2:20, the christological allegorization of the "bridegroom"

---

8. If a tax collector even enters a house, all that is in the house becomes unclean, not merely what he has touched (Mishnah, *Tohoroth* 7:6).

9. Bultmann, *Synoptic Tradition*, 18.

10. Daube, *New Testament*, 67–71.

11. The prevailing view has been that 2:27–28 was added to 2:23–26 (Bultmann, *Synoptic Tradition*, 16–17; Taylor, *St. Mark*, 218). Recently, however, Hultgren ("Sabbath Pericope") and Kuhn (*Ältere Sammlungen*, 74–77) have argued that vv. 25 and 26 are an insertion into an earlier unit consisting of 2:23–24 and 2:27, with verse 28 as another insertion into the pericope.

12. The verbs *erchontai* and *legousin* in 2:18b are best understood as impersonal plurals, meaning in effect, "Jesus was asked." See Turner, "Marcan Usage."

and the justification of the fasting practice of the early church;[13] and 2:21 and 22, two apparently unattached sayings on the incompatibility of the old and new, which in their present context justify the new over against the old. The restatement of the apophthegm counterquestion, "Can the sons of the bride chamber fast while the bridegroom is with them?" into the statement "As long as they have the bridegroom with them they cannot fast" (2:19, RSV) may have been done in order to produce a double saying to balance the two new-old sayings,[14] with v. 20, the allusion to Jesus's death, in between. This pattern—double saying, allusion to the crucifixion,[15] double saying—in itself seems quite probable. But then the whole of v. 18, contrasting the fasting practices of the disciples of John and of the Pharisees with the disciples of Jesus, would balance the phrase "new wine is for fresh skins" (2:22c). This phrase, however, is not parallel in form to v. 18, and is also of doubtful textual validity. Story C does not appear to be, as one might like, a precise chiastic structure itself, set within the larger chiastic structure.

In terms of content, C fits very well as the center of the chiastic structure. It is concerned with fasting, set between B and B', which are concerned with eating. Verse 20, with its allusion to the crucifixion, is the center not only of C but of the entire controversy section. It is set over against the two outside stories, A and A', with their resurrection-type healings. According to Nils Lund's laws of chiastic structure, there is often a "shift at the center" where an antithetic idea is introduced.[16] The death of Jesus is alluded to for the first time here. Also according to Lund, identical ideas are often distributed in the extremes and center of a chiastic system: so here the extremes and center are concerned with resurrection-death-resurrection (the verbs *egeirō* in A and A' and *apairō* in C) while the remainder of the system is concerned primarily with eating-fasting-eating.

Along with the chiastic structure of the five subunits there exists also a linear development of hostility in the opponents: from silent criticism to the questioning of Jesus's disciples to the questioning of Jesus himself to

13. These two units appear already merged in the *Gospel of Thomas*, logion 104. The last unit appears as logion 47.

14. The restatement is not necessary to establish the allegory that the bridegroom is Christ, since both Matthew and Luke drop the restatement but keep the allegory (Matt 9:15; Luke 5:34–35).

15. Crucifixion, of course, is not explicitly mentioned. The much milder verb *apairō* is used here and in the parallels, Matthew 9:15 and Luke 5:35, its only occurrences in the New Testament.

16. Lund, *Chiasmus*.

watching him, and finally to plotting to destroy him. The opponents are designated in order as the scribes, the scribes of the Pharisees, the Pharisees, and finally the Pharisees with the Herodians. The attack of the opponents becomes increasingly overt in the sequence of stories. This may be a deliberate literary device used to lend a time-sense, a sense of progression, to an otherwise content-structured unit.

Thus the five controversy stories of Mark 2:1—3:6 form a tightly constructed literary unit, predominantly chiastic in principle: the first two stories have to do with sin, and the last two with the Sabbath law; the first and last stories deal with resurrection-type healings, the second and fourth with eating, and the middle one with fasting and crucifixion. This pattern is seen not only in content but in the details of structure, form, and language.

It would appear, furthermore, that the overall chiastic structure of Mark 2:1—3:6 has influenced the form of the individual pericopes within the section. The story of the man with the withered hand (A', 3:1–6) may have received its precise form so that it would parallel the healing of the paralytic (A, 2:1–12). The incident of David eating the showbread (2:25–26) may have been added not to fill out the pericope in which it is placed, but to balance another pericope altogether. The fact that stories B and B' each end with a proverb followed by a christological saying may not be the result of the independent development of each pericope but the result of the literary activity of the redactor setting the two pericopes in relation to each other, adding or deleting material as necessary.[17] The settings—in a house in stories A and B, in a house of God and a synagogue in B' and A'—are not necessarily ideal settings produced by the community for each saying, but may in part be the invention of the evangelist creating a literary whole out of separate incidents. The compiler of Mark 2:1—3:6 appears to have been more than a redactor, indeed a genuine author. If the form of individual pericopes has indeed been influenced by the incorporation of the pericopes into a larger literary structure, then to determine the form criticism and history of tradition of a pericope, one needs to consider not only the isolated pericope but also its setting in larger literary units.

---

17. For instance, there has been considerable debate as to whether Mark 2:27–28 is a unit, and if not, which verse was added later. See Hultgren, "Sabbath Pericope," 38–43. One must also consider the possibility that Mark has added one or the other saying in order to balance the proverb/christological saying in v. 17. Or perhaps, more probably, Mark may have added verse 17b in order to balance v. 28 and to tie the incident of eating with sinners to the call of Levi in v. 14.

Investigating the Origin

Such a structure as found in Mark 2:1—3:6 does not occur by accident. Either Mark worked out the literary structure himself, or the entire section virtually as it now stands was created by some earlier writer or collector, and Mark incorporated the unit as a whole. On literary and theological grounds it would seem that the present structure is due to Mark. This does not, of course, exclude the idea that Mark was using earlier tradition or even an earlier collection of traditions to construct his section.

As a composer, Mark often sandwiched blocks of material.[18] The setting off of material by means of a frame seems a natural extension of Mark's sandwiching technique. Therefore, the framework around 2:1—3:6 is quite as likely to indicate a Markan construction as to indicate insertion of an already extant block of tradition. That Mark was sufficiently master of his material to create a fairly elaborate chiastic pattern has been shown by Lafontaine's and Beernaert's chiastic literary analysis of Mark 8:27—9:13,[19] a section whose construction is generally agreed to be Markan.[20]

Albert Vanhoye, in his study of the Passion Narratives in the Synoptics, demonstrates that it is Mark's habit to underline contrasts, a literary device used for a theological purpose. "Mark is not afraid to stun us; rather, he seeks to do so. He brings out contrasts, he underscores the paradox: the Cross is scandalous, it none the less reveals the Son of God."[21] The controversy section as a whole also emphasizes contrasts: eating/joy vs. fasting/mourning; resurrection vs. crucifixion. Viewed in this manner, the allusion to the crucifixion does not come surprisingly early in the Markan scheme, as scholars have often suggested,[22] but it is for Mark a suitable literary climax. Theologically also, it is consonant with Mark's emphasis on the theology of the cross. Jesus's ministry is shown to be under the shadow of the cross from the beginning.

The controversy section fits naturally into the structure of Mark's gospel. Mark, after he showed the enthusiastic response of the crowds to Jesus in chapter 1, then demonstrated the hostility that these actions of Jesus

---

18. E.g., Mark 3:20–35; 5:22–43; 6:7–30; 11:12–25; 14:53–72.

19. Lafontaine and Beernaert, "Structure de Marc." For the use of chiasm in oral and written literature, see Lohr, "Oral Techniques," 424–27.

20. Dibelius, *From Tradition to Gospel*, 230; Taylor, *St. Mark*, 98; Johnson, *St. Mark*, 147, 154, 159; Haenchen, "Komposition," 81–109; Perrin, *Redaction Criticism*, 66.

21. Vanhoye, *Structure and Theology*, 8–9.

22. Albertz, *Die synoptischen Streitgespräche*, 5; Taylor, *St. Mark*, 211–12.

aroused, which eventually resulted in his death. The conclusion in Mark 3:6, "the Pharisees went out and immediately held counsel with the Herodians against him, how to destroy him," serves not only as a conclusion to the story of the withered hand but also to the entire controversy section. To *this* result Jesus' actions lead.

Thus Mark employed the conflict stories theologically to place Jesus's life in the context of his death, and he used them in his narrative construction to show how Jesus's death historically was to come about. The controversy section appears to fit in with Mark's literary technique and with his theology; indeed, it is a good example of both.

The one fact not accounted for by the assumption of a Markan construction from previously independent units of tradition is the occurrence of the title Son of Man[23] in stories A and B. The title is not used in the suffering-eschatological sense that Mark employs from 8:31 on.[24] Nor does its double use fit into Mark's literary pattern, as the allusion to the crucifixion does. The double appearance of the title may imply that Mark is reworking a previous collection of conflict stories. Or, it may simply be the result of variation within repetition.

Heinz-Wolfgang Kuhn, in his recent study of earlier collections used by Mark, arrives at the same result via the methods of form criticism, especially the determination of the *Sitz im Leben* in the community. He concludes that there was an earlier collection of four units: the healing of the paralytic, the eating with the tax collectors (without 2:13–14), the question about fasting, and the plucking of grain on the Sabbath without its Old Testament reference.[25] Since all four concern Jewish praxis and are settled by appeals to christological arguments,[26] they serve the needs of the community against Jewish Christians who accept the full power of the earthly Son of Man.[27] Verse 28, "the Son of Man is lord *also* of the Sabbath," concludes the entire collection, referring to the Son of Man's authority to forgive sins in the first story.[28]

23. *If* it is to be considered a title in this section; see Hay, "Son of Man." For two interpretations that understand the use of "Son of Man" in 2:10 and 2:28 as part of Mark's own theology, see Perrin, "Creative Use"; and Elliott, "Man and Son of Man," 50–58.

24. Another of the arguments of Albertz (*Die synoptischen Streitgespräche,* for a pre-Markan collection.

25. Kuhn, *Ältere Sammlungen,* 74, 86, 87.

26. Ibid., 82, 83.

27. Ibid., 73, 81, 83–85, 96.

28. Ibid., 29.

Kuhn interprets Mark's insertions of the Old Testament reference (2:25–26) and the story of the withered hand (3:1–5) as a reinclusion of Jewish-type arguments,[29] the insertion of the call of Levi (2:13–14) and the conclusion in 3:6 as evidence of Mark's historicizing tendency.[30] The earlier collection explains the appearance of the title Son of Man and also the "too early hints of Jesus about his death" in verse 20.[31]

Kuhn's reconstruction of the earlier collection, with its explanation of the occurrence of the title Son of Man in Mark's controversy section, is admirable. However, his explanations for the Markan expansions are inadequate. More probably, Mark has reworked the material in order to create his chiastic literary structure, which in turn brings out his meaning. Further, v. 20, the allusion to the crucifixion, is not a leftover from earlier tradition but the center of Mark's literary structure and the heart of his message: Jesus's life is to be seen as the way of the cross.

Mark was a writer of considerable literary skill, if not of elegant Greek; it is only by paying attention to the literary structure he created that we can hope to interpret his gospel properly. Moreover, since the literary structure has in part determined the shape of the individual pericopes, it is also necessary to consider it when studying the form or history of the tradition of an individual pericope.

29. Ibid., 74, 77, 86.
30. Ibid., 86, 87, 223.
31. Ibid., 87

4

Mark as Interwoven Tapestry

Forecasts and Echoes for a Listening Audience

Introduction

Of making outlines of the Gospel of Mark there is no end, nor do scholars seem to be wearying of it. Yet we have been unable to agree on a structure or outline for Mark. Over thirty years ago, James M. Robinson observed, "The detailed explanation of the Marcan order continues to be obscure."[1] Fourteen years ago, Paul Achtemeier wrote, "a satisfactory solution to the problem of the outline of Mark . . . remains to be found."[2] Today, in spite of intense redactional and literary work on Mark, these statements remain true.

There is, of course, some agreement among scholars. In a survey of seventeen outlines ranging from Benjamin Bacon's and Karl Ludwig Schmidt's to the present, I found that 82 percent thought there was a distinct section in the middle of the gospel, beginning at either 8:22 or 8:27 and ending at 10:45 or 10:52. Seventy percent, but not the same 70 percent in each instance, agreed that there was a break at 1:14 or 1:16 after the prologue in Mark 1; in Mark 3 at either verse 7 or verse 13; and at the beginning of the Passion Narrative at Mark 14. Less than one-fourth saw any break at Mark 13, the little apocalypse, or at Mark 16, and there was no consistency about where or whether to break in Mark 6.[3] While some posited transitional

---

1. Robinson, "Mark's Understanding," 393 n. 3.

2. Achtemeier, *Mark*, 1st ed., 40.

3. Bacon (*Beginnings of the Gospel*, 9–11): 3:7, 6:14, 8:27, 11:1, 14:1; Schmidt (*Rahmen der Geschichte*, xi–xvi): 1:14, 2:1, 3:7, 6:14, 8:27, 10:46, 14:1; Lohmeyer (*Evangelium des Markus*, 7–8): 3:7, 6:30, 8:27, 11:1, 14:1; Kümmel (*Introduction*, 61–62): 1:14, 6:1, 10:1, 11:1, 14:1; Taylor (*St. Mark*, 107–11): 1:14, 3:7, 6:14, 8:27, 11:1, 14:1; de la Potterie ("De compositione evangelii Marci," 135–41): 1:14, 3:7, 6:6b, 8:27, 10:46, 14:1; Schweizer

pericopes between sections, others did not—that is, some saw 1:14–15 as transitional between 1:1–13 and 1:16 on, while others saw a new beginning at either 1:14 or 1:16.[4] Overall, the degree of consensus is not impressive.

A few scholars have suggested that the disagreement over Mark's outline may be due to the gospel narrative itself. Achtemeier attributed the disagreement either to the insufficient work of scholars or to the way Mark composed the narrative.[5] Howard Clark Kee argued that it is the narrative: "It would appear that Mark no more lends itself to analysis by means of a detailed outline developed by simple addition of components than does a major contrapuntal work of music . . . [rather] multiple themes . . . are sounded throughout this document," which Kee likens to a fugue.[6]

Most scholars, however, have continued to try to define Mark's structure. For example, in his book *Jesus the Teacher: A Socio-Rhetorical Interpretation of Mark*, Vernon Robbins has attempted to determine the exact transition points scholars debate over in Mark 1, 3, 6, and so on. He has identified a three-step progression which recurs in the gospel.[7] Extending over two or three pericopes, it shows Jesus first going to a new place with his disciples; second, engaging in some sort of interaction (with the disciples or others); and third, summoning his disciples for special purposes.[8] The progressions are transitional passages, which "unfold the identity of Jesus and reveal the means by which Jesus' system of thought and action

---

(*Good News*, 7–10): 1:14, 3:7, 6:6b, 8:27, 11:1; Perrin (*New Testament*, 147): 1:16, 3:13, 6:7, 8:27, 11:1, 13:5b; Trocmé (*Formation of the Gospel*, 83–4): 3:13, 6:14, 8:22, 11:1, 14:1; Pesch (*Markusevangelium* 1:32–39): 3:7, 6:30, 8:27, 11:1, 14:1; Lang ("Kompositionsanalyse," 12–13): 1:14, 3:7, 8:22, 10:46, 14:1; Williamson (*Mark*, vii–ix; 1–7): 1:16, 3:13, 6:7, 8:22, 11:1, 14:1, 16:1; Hedrick ("What Is a Gospel?" 267–68): 1:14b, 4:1, 4:35, 5:21, 7:24, 7:31, 8:13, 9:30, 10:1, 11:11, 11:27, 13:1, 14:1; Standaert (*Commentaire*, 23–28): 1:14, 6:14, 11:1, 16:1; van Iersel ("Locality, Structure and Meaning," 45): 1:16, 8:27, 11:1, 15:46; Robbins (*Jesus the Teacher*, 25–48): 1:14, 3:7, 6:1, 8:27, 10:46, 13:1, 16:1; Achtemeier (*Mark*, 2nd ed., 39–40): 3:7, 6:7, 8:22, 11:1, 14:1.

4. In particular, de la Potterie, Perrin, van Iersel, Robbins, and Williamson posit transitional passages (see n. 3).

5. Achtemeier, *Mark*, 1st ed., 40. However, in his 2nd edition, Achtemeier ventures his own outline (see n. 3).

6. Kee, *Community of the New Age*, 64, 75.

7. Robbins, *Jesus the Teacher*, 19, 45–46. See also Robbins, "Summons and Outline," 97–114.

8. Robbins, *Jesus the Teacher*, 25. The instances are 1:14–20, 3:7–19, 6:1–13, 8:27–9:1, 10:46—11:11, and 13:1–37 (25, 27–45).

is transmitted to disciple-companions."[9] In my opinion, Robbins's progression includes too wide a range of material to be considered a repetitive form. For example, the call of James and John, the entry into Jerusalem, and Jesus's entire apocalyptic speech in Mark 13 are all third steps of progressions. But the very fact that Robbins can posit such a pattern suggests how recurrent certain motifs in Mark are.

While Robbins has attempted to build upon what consensus there is on Mark's structure, Charles Hedrick has rejected it altogether.[10] He questions the use of theology, that is, content, to arrive at structure, which is what he considers scholars to have done. Rather, scholars must first seek Mark's formal or narrative indicators of structure before they use theology or content. He finds "the only evident overall framework given to these independent episodes and the sub-groupings of material" in Mark 1–13 is geographical.[11] The pericopes are linked with spatial indicators of where Jesus goes, by the sea, in the synagogue, and the like, which in turn are grouped into larger geographical units—in Galilee, a trip to Tyre and Sidon, and so forth.[12] On the basis of the geographical subgroupings, Hedrick outlines Mark into fifteen sections that do not necessarily coincide and sometimes conflict with the more content-oriented divisions noted above. Thus Hedrick rejects 8:27–10:45 as a Markan structural unit because it interrupts the composition of 10:1–11:11 as a travelogue to Jerusalem, and it ignores the clear geographical break between 9:50 and 10:1.[13]

Certainly Hedrick is correct to observe that Mark has used geographical indicators to connect and group individual episodes, creating a geographical outline for the Gospel. But if there is a geographical structure, must it coincide with theologically based structures as well? (By structure I simply mean an observable surface organization of material.) Both Robbins and Hedrick—and most other scholars—assume that Mark must have a single linear outline or structure, whether elegantly rhetorical or rather

---

9. Robbins, *Jesus the Teacher*, 45.

10. Hedrick, "What Is a Gospel?," 255–68.

11. Ibid., 257.

12. Hedrick is disturbed by the story of the death of John the Baptist in Mark 6, which violates his geographical/sequential order, and he explains it on grounds of Mark's theological needs (ibid., 261–62). It seems to me more likely that Mark is following the oral composition practice of including information only at the point it becomes relevant to the story. See Havelock, *Preface to Plato*, 179.

13. Hedrick, "What Is a Gospel?," 265.

haphazard;[14] they recognize recurring themes, but nonetheless they attempt to ascertain the major division points. But is this assumption valid? I would argue that either Kee's metaphor of a fugue or Sherman Johnson's metaphor of an oriental carpet with crisscrossing patterns[15] is a better model for understanding the structure of the Gospel of Mark than linear outlines.

Mark's problem, after all, was not to divide the gospel into separate sequential units. Rather, Mark's task was to interweave and integrate disparate and episodic material into a single narrative whole, to bridge breaks rather than to create them. Mark is telling a story for a listening audience, not presenting a logical argument. Arguments may be clouded by the lack of a clear linear outline, but stories gain depth and enrichment through repetition and recursion.

In this chapter I argue that the Gospel of Mark does not have a single structure made up of discrete sequential units but rather is an interwoven tapestry or fugue made up of multiple overlapping structures and sequences, forecasts of what is to come and echoes of what has already been said. I shall then suggest that such a nonlinear, recursive compositional style is characteristic of aural narrative and suggest a few implications.

First, the fact that scholars cannot agree on Mark's outline is itself a strong argument against such a structure. We can agree on the five speeches in Matthew or the geographic spread of Christianity in Acts, but not on Mark. Second, recent literary work on the gospel has highlighted gospel interconnections. I cite two works in particular: Norman Petersen lays out the numerous retrospective and prospective references to be found throughout the gospel.[16] David Rhoads and Donald Michie show what a consistent narrative world Mark creates with the episodic material.[17]

Since it is impossible to map the various structural sequences in the whole of Mark in a single article, I shall concentrate on those portions of the gospel where scholars most frequently place breaks: that is, in Mark 1, 3, 8, 10–11, and 14. For if I can show that these pericopes are parts of different overlapping sequences or outlines, my case that the gospel does not consist of a single linear structure will be made.

---

14. Van Iersel ("Locality, Structure and Meaning," 45–54) and Scott ("Chiastic Structure," 17–26) have suggested chiastic rather than linear outlines for Mark. But like the linear outlines, the chiastic structures posit clear division points in Mark's structure.

15. Johnson, *St. Mark*, 24.

16. Petersen, *Literary Criticism*.

17. Rhoads and Michie, *Mark as Story*.

Interconnections, or repetitions and anticipations, are anything and everything that remind a hearer of other parts of the narrative. A list of the ways episodes or series of episodes can be interconnected would include theme; manifest content; particular aspects of content such as setting, geography, or characters; form-critical type, and rhetorical devices such as key and hook words, *inclusio*, intercalations and frames, and parallel and chiastic repetitions.[18] These means may be used to structure a single episode, to interrelate a few episodes, or to interconnect an entire narrative.

To the extent that the various means (theme, content, settings, form, word repetition) form *congruent* patterns of repetition, the structure of the episode, section, or gospel will be clearly defined, delimited, and recognized by the hearer. To the extent that the various means exhibit differing or even conflicting patterns of repetition, the effect on the hearer/reader will be one of interweaving or overlapping progression rather than of discrete outlineable structure, and scholars will create different outlines depending on which means they emphasize.

Mark 1:14–15

The first place scholars tend to divide Mark's outline is before or after 1:14–15, "Now after John was arrested, Jesus came into Galilee, preaching the gospel of God, and saying, 'The time is fulfilled, and the kingdom of God is at hand; repent, and believe in the gospel'"(RSV). Certainly these verses point forward in the narrative. Schmidt described them as a summary report (*Sammelbericht*), giving an overview of the individual episodes that follow.[19] Indeed, Jesus will be in and about Galilee for eight chapters. They are not, however, a specific introduction to what immediately follows: the calling of disciples and the healings of Mark 1. They point farther ahead: the kingdom of God is particularly the subject of the parable discourse of Mark 4; eschatology and faith are recurrent themes throughout the gospel. The handing over of John points ahead to the handing over of Jesus and (in turn) the disciples at the end of the gospel.

The verses also refer back.[20] They belong rhetorically to the preceding verses. As Leander Keck has argued, the word *gospel* in 1:14–15 forms an

18. For a description of the rhetorical devices, see J. Dewey, *Markan Public Debate*, 31–34; 132–36.

19. Schmidt, *Rahmen der Geschichte*, 33.

20. Donahue (*Are You the Christ?*, 207–8) has observed that the *Sammelberichte* are

inclusio with Mark 1:1, delimiting 1:1–15 as a rhetorical unit.[21] Within this unit, v. 14a forms its own *inclusio* with v. 9a around Jesus's baptism in the Jordan and time in the desert: 1:9a, "Jesus came from Nazareth of Galilee"; 1:14a, "Jesus came into Galilee." Word form and word order are the same.

The fact that vv. 14 and 15 point ahead in content to Jesus's whole ministry, but belong rhetorically to 1:1–13, suggests that they are transitional verses. But the content of 1:1–13 also recurs after v. 15, suggesting continuity in narrative development rather than a major break. The voice from heaven speaks again at the transfiguration in Mark 9, recalling the baptism. And in spite of his arrest, John the Baptist continues to be brought to the hearers' attention: his disciples fast in 2:18; people compare Jesus to him in Mark 6 and 8; his death is recounted in Mark 6; he is alluded to as Elijah in Mark 9; and Jesus likens his own authority to John's in Mark 11. In summary, while 1:14–15 does mark the beginning of Jesus's public ministry, there is no sharp division between what precedes and what follows. Rather there are multiple verbal and content connections, repetitions and anticipations, echoing backwards and forwards in the narrative.

Mark 3

Scholars tend to see a major break in Mark either after 3:6, "The Pharisees went out, and immediately held counsel with the Herodians against him, how to destroy him"; or after 3:7–12, Jesus's withdrawal to the sea and healing of many; and before 3:13–19, the naming of the Twelve. Mark 3:7–12 is, of course, another of Schmidt's *Sammelberichte*. We are accustomed to think of such passages as different in character, less colorful than the particular episodes, and thus a break in the rhythm, which might represent a break in structure.[22] Yet I doubt a listening audience would sense a break. Taking an analogy from film, the effect is rather that of drawing back for a distant shot between sequences of closeups.[23] The passage is not set off in kind.

---

a Markan compositional technique of anticipating and recapitulating at the same time.

21. Keck, "Introduction to Mark's Gospel," 352–70.

22. Perrin explicitly used the *Sammelberichte* in constructing his outline of Mark (Perrin, "Towards an Interpretation").

23. The fact that the summary statements function as typical episodes is quite clear from David Rhoads's videotape *Dramatic Performance of the Gospel of Mark*.

Considering only the two adjacent pericopes, there is a complete content break—and no hook words—between 3:6, the culmination of a series of conflicts between Jesus and his opponents, and 3:7, which stresses Jesus's popularity with the people. Nonetheless, 3:7–12 has many connections both backwards and forwards in the narrative. First, in Mark 1, Jesus's fame spread throughout Galilee; here it has extended well beyond it to the north and south. Second, the pericope is part of a sequence of lakeside episodes. (In Jesus's first time by the sea, he calls the four brothers as disciples [1:16–20]; the second time by the sea, the whole crowd comes to him [2:13]; here, the third time, the boat is prepared for Jesus; and the fourth time [4:1], Jesus actually teaches the crowd from the boat.) This pericope is the third element in a sequence of interrelated lakeside episodes.

Third, the healing and exorcising motifs in 3:7–12 have multiple anticipations and responsions in the narrative. As well as specific healings both before and after this pericope, there was a distant shot of Jesus healing many at 1:32–34, and there will be another distant shot in Mark 6. The desire of the sick to touch Jesus points ahead to the story of the woman with the flow of blood in Mark 5.[24] Mark 3:11 contains the middle of the three acclamations by demons: in 1:24, the demon calls Jesus "the holy one of God"; here they say, "You are the son of God"; and in 5:7, the demon calls him "Jesus, son of the Most High God." Jesus's command for silence recalls Jesus's rebuke to the demon in the synagogue (1:25) and the narrator's report that he would not let the demons speak (1:34). Further, Jesus's command for silence from the demons emphasizes his control over demons in preparation for the debate over Satan casting out Satan later in Mark 3.[25] Thus, 3:7–12 seems to be one scene in an ongoing development of intertwined episodes, not a new beginning or a specific transition between two clearly distinct sections.

Likewise, the following pericope, the naming of the Twelve, furthers the development of an ongoing thread in Mark: that of the call and mission of the disciples. Jesus calls the four brothers in 1:16–20, and the audience learns they are to be fishers of people. In 2:15, Mark first uses the word *disciples*. In this passage, 3:13–19, Jesus appoints the Twelve to be with him, to preach and to cast out demons. And finally at 6:7 Jesus sends the disciples out to preach and heal. This pericope is the third in an ongoing series of episodes rather than a new section.

24. Taylor, *St. Mark*, 225.
25. Ibid.

Of course, what has led many scholars to posit a break at 3:6 is the abrupt shift from the Pharisees' plotting of his death to Jesus's overwhelming popularity in 3:7 and following. There is a break between the two adjacent episodes but not a major division in the longer narrative. Rather, Mark has bracketed the five conflict stories of 2:1—3:6 with a frame stressing Jesus's fame. In 1:45, after the cure of the leper, the leper tells the news "so that Jesus could no longer openly enter a town, but was out in the country; and people came to him from every quarter." Mark 2:1, the very next verse, begins, "And when he returned to Capernaum"; that is, the first act Jesus is shown doing after not being able to enter a town is entering a town. But 3:7–8 resume where 1:45 left off: "Jesus withdrew with his disciples to the sea, and a great multitude from Galilee followed; also from Judea and Jerusalem and Idumea and from beyond the Jordan and from about Tyre and Sidon a great multitude, hearing all that he did, came to him." In 1:45 people came to Jesus from every quarter. In 3:7–8 the quarters are specifically named. This resumption of the earlier narrative in effect brackets the controversies for later development, while resuming the story of Jesus's popularity.[26]

The techniques of resuming the narrative from an earlier point and the related use of frames seem characteristic of Markan compositional means. For example, in 4:10–13, the disciples ask about the parables in v. 10; vv. 11–12 contain Jesus's saying on the mystery of the kingdom of God; and v. 13 begins Jesus's answer about the parable as if there had been no intervening saying. The intercalations are another variation on this device.[27] In fact the resumption of 1:45 at 3:7 makes 2:1—3:6 one long intercalation.

Further, although there are no explicit death threats against Jesus again until 11:18, there are recurrent episodes showing the scribes' and Pharisees' hostility to Jesus. In 3:22, the scribes from Jerusalem accuse him of being possessed by demons. In Mark 7 the Pharisees and scribes from Jerusalem question him about unwashed hands; in 8:11 and again in 10:2, the Pharisees come testing him. John's death and the Passion predictions would also serve to remind the listening audience of the danger to Jesus's life. Opposition to Jesus is not forgotten. Mark 3 does not, then, present any clear break and new beginning. Rather there are multiple interconnections and overlapping sequences backwards and forwards in the narrative.

26. J. Dewey, *Markan Public Debate*, 105–6.
27. Donahue, *Are You The Christ?*, 78–84, 241–43.

Mark 8

Since there is so little agreement about where the dividing point in Mark 6, if any, should come, it seems unnecessary to establish that there is no major break there. This brings us to Mark 8, and the pericopes of the healing of the blind man of Bethsaida and Peter's recognition of Jesus as the Christ. These are particular stories, not *Sammelberichte* as earlier. Even so, the material presents abundant anticipations and responsions.

The healing at Bethsaida in 8:22–26 and the healing of Bartimaeus at Jericho in 10:46–52 are often viewed as a frame to the "way section" in which Jesus teaches about the way of the cross.[28] And they do bracket the material. They are the only healings of blindness in the gospel; one takes place at Bethsaida in the north and the other at Jericho near the southern end of the journey. Symbolically, the first is only accomplished in two stages, indicating the following teaching is difficult, while the second is instantaneous, and Bartimaeus follows Jesus on the way.

But these healings are involved in other structures, in addition to framing the way material. Indeed, for listeners, the healing of the blind man at Bethsaida would first of all recall the earlier healing of the man who was deaf and mute in 7:31–37. Both are healings by physical means using spittle (and the only such in Mark); both contain commands to silence. The vocabulary overlap is extensive.[29] Indeed, the similarities are such that Bultmann considered them variants of the same story.[30] Since the hearers have recently heard two stories of the disciples afraid on the boat (4:35–41; 6:45–52), and two stories of miraculous feedings of thousands (6:30–44; 8:1–10), a second difficult healing using spittle would not be unexpected. The healing at Bethsaida is the third item in a sequence of doublets.[31] It would not strike the hearer as an introduction to a new section.

In addition, the two spittle healings relate symbolically to the material between them, another boat episode in which the disciples discuss bread (8:14–21). The spittle healing in Mark 7 deals with hearing; the one in Mark 8, with seeing. In between, Jesus asks the disciples, "Having eyes do you not see, and having ears do you not hear?" (8:18). The healing of the blind

---

28. See for example Perrin, "Towards an Interpretation," 7–13; La Potterie, "De compositione evangelii Marci," 139–40.

29. See Taylor, *St. Mark,* 368–69.

30. Bultmann, *Synoptic Tradition,* 213.

31. For a valuable discussion of Mark's use of doublets, see Fowler, *Loaves and Fishes,* 91–114.

man at Bethsaida is thoroughly intertwined with the preceding material; it would not strike the listener as a new beginnning.

Furthermore, the healing at Bethsaida anticipates not only the Bartimaeus story in Mark 10 but also the healing of the boy with an unclean spirit in 9:14–27. In both (and only in these two) Jesus does the healing in two stages. In neither healing does the restored person or the watching crowd do anything as the result of the healing. But in the healing in Mark 9 (the third of this series), the spirit is not one of blindness but rather of deafness and muteness, which harks back to the healing of the man who was deaf and mute in Mark 7.[32]

Thus the four healings of 7:31—10:52 ring the changes on restoring hearing, speech, and sight. They seem to punctuate—or frame—discipleship material: first, the difficult healing of the man who was deaf and mute, followed by evidence of the disciples' blindness in the feeding of the four thousand and the discussion about bread in the boat; second, the two-stage healing of the blind man at Bethsaida, followed by Peter's recognition of Jesus as the Christ and his rejection of the way of the cross; third, the healing of the boy with the unclean spirit, followed by teaching on servanthood; and finally, the healing of Bartimaeus, who follows on the way. Thus the healing of the blind man at Bethsaida participates in a number of overlapping sequences or structures. It is the third in a series of doublets, it is the second in a series of four related healings that alternate with teachings, and it is the opening frame around the way section.

The second pericope considered a major new beginning in Mark 8 is Peter's recognition of Jesus as the Christ and the first Passion prediction of 8:27–33. These verses certainly are a major climax and turning point in the narrative, as most interpreters of Mark have stated.[33] The disciples have finally recognized who Jesus is, and the emphasis shifts to teaching the way

---

32. 9:17 (*pneuma alalon*), 9:25 (*to alalon kai kōphon pneuma*); 7:32 (*kōphon kai mogilalon*).

33. If 8:27–33 is indeed a climax and turning point, this suggests that although all pericopes probably have multiple interconnections in the narrative, some pericopes may be more important to the structure or plot than others. I would argue that some, including this one, are important. However, I am not sure how much my decision reflects my education in a print culture and my training in Markan scholarship, and how much the Markan narrative. For a listening audience, the pericope being heard at the moment is for the moment the most important one, and an aural narrative has enough repetition for listeners to follow, even if some miss hearing crucial pericopes. I suspect we need to learn to think somewhat differently about narrative turning points, about plot in aural narrative.

of the cross. But would an audience sense any break or shift here as they listen? Questions of Jesus's identity have already been raised, and miracles continue to occur with some frequency until 10:52.

For this pericope is also well intertwined with the larger narrative. It obviously points ahead to the second and third Passion predictions (9:30–31; 10:32–34); it also recalls earlier material. The question of who Jesus is would certainly remind the hearer of the episode in 6:14–16 where Herod and the crowd considered Jesus's identity. Not only do the answers to the question of who Jesus is repeat the earlier list, but the larger sequence of the two passages is similar.

First, both list the possibilities: in 6:14–15, "Some said, 'John the baptizer has been raised from the dead'; . . . But others said, 'It is Elijah.' And others said, 'It is a prophet, like one of the prophets of old.'"; in 8:27–28, "'Who do people say that I am?' And they told him, 'John the Baptist; and others say, Elijah; and others, one of the prophets.'"[34] Second, in each someone recognizes Jesus: in 6:16, "But when Herod heard of it he said, 'John, whom I beheaded, has been raised.'"; in 8:29, "And he asked them, 'But who do you say that I am?' Peter answered him. 'You are the Christ.'"

Third, in each there is an indication of death: in 6:17–29, the vivid story of Herod's execution of John the Baptist; in 8:31, Jesus's prediction that he will be killed. Finally, both also include resurrection, although not in the same sequence: in 6:16, Herod thinks that Jesus is John raised from the dead; in 8:31, Jesus prophesies "and after three days rise." Indeed, these two pericopes are so similar that 8:27–33 is likely to strike the audience as the continuation of the series of doublets begun in chapter 4, not as the beginning of a new section.

What we find, then, for Mark's structure or outline for the posited break in Mark 8 are overlapping sequences: the sequence of recognition and Passion predictions, which begins in Mark 6; the sequence of healings of deafness/muteness and blindness that begins in Mark 7; and a sequence of doublets, which began in Mark 4. In Mark 8, there is neither a clear-cut dividing point to be found nor a single passage to be identified as *the* transitional one between two sections. Mark eases the listener into the way material.

---

34. Indeed, Mark can use the short expression, "one of the prophets," in 8:28, because he has already spelled out "like one of the prophets of old" in 6:15.

Mark 10–11

The next posited break comes at the end of the way material, either at 10:46, the healing of Bartimaeus, or at 11:1, the entry to Jerusalem. Again there are patterns of interconnection, anticipations, and responsions. The Bartimaeus narrative (10:46–52) needs little further discussion. It is the closing frame for the way material. It is the last in the series of healings of blindness and deafness already discussed; its use of *hodos*, "way" (10:46, 52) links the pericope to the just-concluded way material, providing a key word link between the healing and teaching sequences described earlier. The pericope also anticipates what follows by introducing Davidic imagery.[35]

Finally, the pericope is in the middle of the journey to Jerusalem, the travelogue that begins at 10:1. This journey is increasingly foregrounded in the narrative: in 10:32, "They were on the road, going up to Jerusalem . . ."; in 10:46, "And they came to Jericho; and as he was leaving Jericho . . ."; in 11:1, "And when they drew near to Jerusalem, to Bethphage and Bethany, at the Mount of Olives . . ."; and in 11:11, "And he entered Jerusalem, and went into the temple . . ." Thus the story of Bartimaeus serves as the end or frame for the way material, as the introduction to the Jerusalem events, and as a midway stopover on the road to Jerusalem. The hearer would not perceive a break in the narrative.

The second option for a major break in this part of the narrative is at 11:1–11, the entry into Jerusalem. Its interconnections are as follows: it is, as we have just seen, the concluding pericope of the Jerusalem travelogue. Verses 1–6, the sending of the two disciples to fetch the colt, anticipate the story of the preparation for the Passover meal in 14:12–16. Verses 7–10, recounting the entry cry, "Blessed is the kingdom of our father David that is coming," continue the Davidic imagery of the preceding Bartimaeus story but also recall the earlier kingdom of God material.

Finally, 11:11, the first entry into the temple, forms a narrative frame around the Jerusalem public ministry with 13:1–2, the final exit from the temple. The frame is similar to that around 2:1—3:6, in which 3:7 resumes the crowds coming to Jesus of 1:45. Mark 11:11 reads, "And he entered Jerusalem and went into the temple; and when he had looked round at everything, as it was already late, he went out to Bethany with the twelve." Mark 13:1 resumes with the disciples' reaction to seeing the temple: "Look, Teacher, what wonderful stones and what wonderful buildings!" Thus in

---

35. Robbins, "Healing of Blind Bartimaeus."

Mark 10–11 also there is not a clear dividing point in the narrative, but rather overlapping sequences and intertwined content.

Mark 14

The final break posited by many scholars in Mark is at 14:1, the beginning of the Passion Narrative. It is a break in sequential action. In 13:37, Jesus is on the Mount of Olives with four disciples; in 14:1, the narrator informs the audience that it is two days before Passover and the chief priests and scribes are plotting. Such breaks are rare in Mark. In the sequential action that started with the beginning of Jesus's public ministry in 1:14, there has only been one other break before this: the flashback to Herod and the death of John the Baptist in Mark 6.

There are, however, elements of intertwining as well. Verses 1 and 2 contain the final of the three repetitions in which the chief priests and scribes seek to destroy Jesus but fear the crowd; they recall 11:18 and 12:12. They are also the opening frame for the intercalation of the anointing of Jesus by the woman at Bethany (14:3–9).

And, in their turn, the anointing story and the story of the woman who gave her mite to the temple treasury (12:41–44) form a frame around the apocalyptic discourse of Mark 13. These two stories about women frame Mark 13 much as the two healings of blind men frame the way material of Mark 8–10.[36] In both stories, Jesus praises the woman for her act. These are the only stories in Mark in which individuals are praised. In both, Jesus's saying is introduced with "Truly, I say to you"; in neither does the woman speak. The stories are joined by the hook word "poor," used twice in each story. The widow's mite in the first contrasts with the expensive nard in the second. Also, each story forms a contrast with its immediate setting: the widow with the scribes, who act for show, and the woman with Judas, who betrays. Both stories point ahead to Jesus's death. The widow gives "her whole life" while Jesus says that the woman has anointed his body for burial. Thus the anointing narrative in Mark 14 both recalls the earlier story and points ahead to the tomb where women again will be the actors.[37]

Again, as at other suggested breaks in Mark's structure, there are overlapping structures or sequences—in this case overlapping frames. Mark 11:11 and 13:1–2, the first entry into and the final exit from the temple,

36. J. Dewey, *Markan Public Debate*, 154–55.
37. See Cassel, "Strategy and Irony."

frame the Jerusalem public ministry. Mark 12:41–44 and 14:3–9, the widow's mite and the anointing at Bethany, frame the apocalyptic discourse. And Mark 14:1–2 and 14:10–11, the chief priests' plot and Judas's betrayal, frame the anointing at Bethany. Such a use of interlocking frames enables Mark to anchor the apocalyptic discourse firmly into the narrative. It is very difficult to fit Mark 13 into a linear structural outline—so difficult that Trocmé posited a precanonical Mark ending at 13:37, and Pesch, one that excluded Mark 13.[38] But it is quite easy to see how Mark 13 is embedded into the narrative by means of a series of interlocking frames. And frames serve both to include and to set off material.

Conclusion

In conclusion, none of the commonly posited breaks in Mark's outline are straightforward dividing points or simple transitions between adjacent sections. Rather, they, like other pericopes in Mark, participate in a number of sequences. There is no single linear outline for scholars to identify. Rather, the image of a fugue or of an oriental carpet is more descriptive of Mark's structure. Mark is indeed an interwoven tapestry. Yet a fugue may be the better metaphor, for Mark certainly contains development and dramatic climax as well.

Mark's compositional procedure of overlapping sequences corresponds very closely to Eric Havelock's understanding of oral methods of narrative development: "The basic principle . . . can be stated abstractly as variation within the same."[39] Oral composition "operates on the acoustic principle of the echo."[40] This principle operates not only for single episodes or small clusters of episodes but for entire narratives. Havelock spells out the oral chaining method in more detail:

> The same compositional principle [the echo principle] extends itself to the construction of the tale as a whole; it will avoid sheer surprise and novel invention . . . The basic method for assisting the memory to retain a series of distinct meanings is to frame the first of them in a way which will suggest or forecast a later meaning which will recall the first without being identical with it. What is to be said and remembered later is cast in the form of an echo of

38. Trocmé, *Formation of the Gospel*, 216–40; Pesch, *Naherwartungen*, 65–66; 70–73.

39. Havelock, *Preface to Plato*, 147.

40. Havelock, "Oral Composition," 182.

> something said already; the future is encoded in the present. All
> oral narrative is in structure continually both prophetic and retro-
> spective . . . Though the narrative syntax is paratactic—the basic
> conjunction being 'and then,' 'and next'—the narrative is not linear
> but turns back on itself in order to assist the memory to reach
> the end by having it anticipated somehow in the beginning.[41]

It is hard to conceive of a better description of the gospel's narrative technique. Mark does not have a clear linear structure; rather it consists of
forecasts and echoes, variation within repetition, for a listening audience.[42]

In closing, I would like to make a few observations:

(1) I am not saying that Mark lacks dramatic development. What I
am saying is that the development follows different principles from a linear
analytic model. In her analysis of geopolitical, topographical, and archi-
tectural space in Mark, Elizabeth Malbon suggests that "each of the three
suborders indicates breaks in the flow of the narrative action, but not precisely at the same points. A break in one suborder may be anticipated in a
second suborder and recapitulated in a third."[43] This, I would argue, is true
not only of space but of all aspects of the gospel. There are developments
in the flow of narrative action—developments in christology, in discipleship, in relations with authorities. But they do not occur at the same points;
rather, developments in one will anticipate or recapitulate developments in
others. A scholar's outline of Mark tells us more about which aspect of the
gospel narrative is the scholar's focus than it does about Mark's structure.
The Markan narrative is one in which any part always echoes what has gone
before and prepares for what is to come. It does not have the tightly plotted
structure we are accustomed to in modern print narrative and keep seeking
in Mark.[44] Therefore I suggest we may gain a better understanding of the
gospel and its individual pericopes by focusing on the interconnections, on
the repetitions, and the variations in the repetition, than by analyzing its
divisions.[45]

---

41. Ibid., 183.

42. In chapter 5, below, I present a more extended argument for oral compositional
techniques in Mark.

43. Malbon, *Narrative Space*, 142.

44. On plot in oral narrative, see Ong, *Orality and Literacy*, 141–43.

45. See for example Rhoads, "Jesus and the Syrophoenician Woman."

(2) I am also not arguing that the Gospel of Mark was composed orally. It may have been, but there also seem to be indications of writing. I am arguing, however, that it was still very close to oral composition, and that it was certainly composed with the needs of a listening audience in mind. Therefore, we need to pay more attention to oral hermeneutics in studying the gospel.[46] Instead of studying plot development according to the tight linear norms of the print novel, we need to be open to the much looser and more additive aural plot structure. For instance, the teaching on suffering in the middle of Mark was probably heard as added to the earlier emphasis on miracle, rather than as replacing or contradicting it. We need to look at character development both in terms of an audience's identification with characters during oral performance and in terms of the use of bad examples as a standard oral teaching technique. The negative portrayal of the disciples would probably have been taken much less seriously by a first-century listening audience than by modern scholars accustomed to printed texts. By studying Mark in light of oral hermeneutics, we should reach a better understanding of how first-century hearers heard the gospel.

(3) Finally, although the first-century audience for Mark, with few exceptions, was not composed of readers but hearers of Mark's gospel, *we are readers*. It is perfectly legitimate for us to approach the gospel with all our sophisticated tools and theories of literary analysis, provided we remember that these are our interpretations, not first-century understandings of the gospel. As long as the Gospel of Mark matters to us, the need for interpretation continues.[47]

---

46. *Contra* Kelber, *Oral and the Written Gospel*, I would argue that the Gospel of Mark is still closely aligned with oral understandings. Robert Fowler ("Reading Matthew Reading Mark," 10–11) has also suggested the relevance of research on orality and textuality to our understanding of Mark.

47. See Kermode, *The Genesis of Secrecy*.

5

Oral Methods of Structuring Narrative in Mark

IN RECENT DECADES, SCHOLARS such as Walter Ong and Eric Havelock have developed an understanding of differences in oral and written composition and hermeneutics.[1] In his seminal work *The Oral and the Written Gospel*, Werner Kelber has applied this knowledge to early Christian development. He argues persuasively for the significance of the shift from oral to written media for early Christianity, stressing the radical discontinuity between the two media. Kelber sees in the Gospel of Mark the disruption of the oral synthesis, a new textuality arising "out of the debris of deconstructed orality."[2] While in no way questioning the importance of the media shift for early Christianity, I will argue that the Gospel of Mark *as a whole*, and not just in its individual episodes,[3] shows the legacy of orality—indeed, that its methods of composition are primarily oral ones.

Oral-Written Composition

Before turning to the analysis of Mark, a few preliminary observations are in order. Kelber has emphasized the discontinuity between oral and written media. Yet, in a manuscript culture with high residual orality, there is considerable overlap between orality and textuality. First, the gospel was heard; its reception remained aural. Thus oral techniques of composition are to be expected in the gospel even if it was composed in writing. It had

---

1. See Ong, *Presence of the Word*; Ong, *Interfaces of the Word*; Ong, *Orality and Literacy*; Havelock, *Preface to Plato*; Havelock, "Oral and Written Word"; and Havelock, "Oral Composition."

2. Kelber, *Oral and the Written Gospel*, 95.

3. As Kelber argues in ibid., 44–89.

to be structured so that a listening audience could follow it. Walter Ong notes that even as late as the Renaissance, the listening audience had to be kept in mind while writing. He cites the instance of an author revising an unsuccessful work "to make it more episodic and thus better fitted for oral reading to groups."[4] The needs of a listening audience would be even more central in the first century, in the social milieu of early Christianity.

Second, while an author may compose in writing, he or she can draw on techniques from the oral medium. Oral techniques continue to influence writing.[5] Ong states the principle that "a new technology of the word reinforces the old while at the same time transforming it."[6] At first, writing was basically a transcription of oral performance, since no other compositional methods were yet known. Then writing would exaggerate oral techniques, employing even more *topoi* or creating even more extensive and elaborate structural patterns, since it enabled a composer to do better what he or she was already doing. Only very gradually do techniques proper to the new medium take over.[7] On these grounds, oral compositional techniques are also to be expected in Mark.

So, assuming that the Gospel of Mark was composed in writing, one would still expect it to have oral characteristics. Obviously, the presence of oral compositional devices does not prove that Mark was orally composed. It does mean, however, that we must take oral hermeneutics into account for understanding the gospel.[8] In this article, I will compare Mark to the structural characteristics of oral narrative, as described primarily by Eric Havelock, the foremost student of the shift from oral to written media in Greek culture. My aim is to show that oral compositional means pervade

4. Ong, *Orality and Literacy*, 158.

5. The reverse is also true: Oral composers will come gradually to use some techniques first developed in writing. According to Ong, a somewhat more orderly linear account becomes possible, even demanded, in oral composition after it has been developed and assimilated through writing (*Interfaces of the Word*, 87). Further, oral lives may begin to present a single continuous story of a hero's life and death if this is the standard for written lives, even though as Albert B. Lord points out, such comprehensive lives are not generally found in primary oral cultures (Lord, "Gospels as Oral Traditional Literature," 39–40).

6. Ong, *Orality and Literacy*, 153.

7. Ong, *Interfaces of the Word*, 61–62; Ong, *Presence of the Word*, 239–40.

8. A major reason for Kelber's rejection of oral hermeneutics for Mark is the gospel's focus on Jesus's death in contrast to the oral emphasis on life and presence (*Oral and the Written Gospel*, 184–211). Yet the *Iliad* shows that a central concern with death is quite possible in an oral-media world.

the larger gospel narrative, and then to suggest a few implications for understanding the gospel.

Oral Mimesis

In his *Preface to Plato*, Havelock argues persuasively that Plato's attack on poetry, or mimesis, in the *Republic* is in fact an attack on the whole oral mindset still pervasive in fourth-century Athens. According to Havelock, what Plato rejects about mimesis is what is characteristic of oral media. So one way to approach the issue of oral structuring techniques in Mark is to compare the gospel to Plato's understanding of mimesis. If Mark shares the characteristics of mimesis rejected by Plato, then Mark too shares characteristics of oral media. I will first summarize Plato's description of mimesis (as interpreted by Havelock), and then compare Mark to it.

For Plato, poetry or mimesis includes far more than what we understand as poetry. Plato rejects not only poetic style but also the entire content of epic and drama, the performer's identification with the content, his or her appeal to the audience's emotions, and the audience's identification with the performance.[9] Plato considers the content of mimesis to be merely *doxa* or opinion, which has three limitations. It is made up of happenings (*gignomena*), not abstract thought; the happenings are visually concrete (*horata*); and they are many (*polla*), that is, pluralized, not organized according to cause and effect.[10] For Plato, then, mimesis is only "an illusion of reality" and "a phantom of virtue," the "stark antithesis" of knowledge or science (*epistēmē*); it is utterly "alien" to thinking (*phronēsis*).[11]

Doxa Consists of Happenings

Plato's description of *doxa* fits the Gospel of Mark well. Mark certainly consists of "happenings," "events in time," "episodes," "little stories or

---

9. Havelock, *Preface to Plato*, 20–35. Of course, Mark is not in elegant hexameters. However, poetic meter is not central to Plato's argument against mimesis, which relates more to content and to the fact of oral performance. Furthermore, most oral poetry apart from the Greek had much simpler and freer rhythms, and oral prose narratives exist in many cultures (ibid., 130 n.13). See also Finnegan, *Oral Poetry*, 24–28, for a discussion of the difficulty of distinguishing prose and poetry in oral literature.

10. Havelock, *Preface to Plato*, 180.

11. Ibid., 238–39.

situations."[12] Havelock writes, "Information or prescription, which in a later stage of literate culture would be arranged typically and topically, is in the oral tradition preserved only as it is transmuted into an event."[13] The embedding of teaching in event is characteristic of Mark. For example, unlike Matthew 6, with its general instructions on fasting and prayer, Mark includes such teaching only in the context of events: the dispute over why Jesus's disciples do not fast (2:18–20) and the episode of the discovery of the withered fig tree (11:20–25).

Mark 4 and Mark 13 perhaps stretch the limits of oral memory's ability to preserve instruction apart from event. However, Mark 4 is made up of parables, little stories that can be remembered. Further, our text shows evidence of the composer's difficulty in handling it: it begins with Jesus teaching the crowd from a boat on the lake (4:1–2a), shifts to private discourse to explain the seed and the sower (4:10), and yet ends with Jesus still teaching the crowd from the boat, without any transition (4:33–36). Listening audiences, who cannot refer back to earlier passages, tend to be more tolerant—or unaware—of such lapses.

Mark 13, the apocalyptic discourse, does not consist of parables. It is, however, largely narrative, albeit narrative of future events, and as Lambrecht had shown, it is intricately patterned with much chiasm, ring composition, and verbal echoing, all of which facilitate memory.[14] Twice the real audience is addressed, in "let the reader understand" (v. 14, RSV) and in "what I say to you I say to all: watch" (v. 37, RSV). We know from contemporary study that oral performers often make direct addresses to their live audiences.[15] Scholars have generally assumed that "reader" in v. 14 refers to the person reading Mark's gospel, who is being encouraged to understand the reference to Daniel's "abomination of desolation" correctly.[16] This interpretation is difficult to sustain, since the gospel is hardly designed for, or likely to appeal to, the limited first-century reading public. I suggest that "reader" refers not to the reader of Mark but to the public reader of Daniel. Bultmann also suggests this possibility, noting that the words "to read" and "reading" are used particularly for public reading in

12. Ibid., 174, 180.

13. Ibid., 174. I note in passing that it may be the difficulty of remembering sayings material apart from events that accounts for the early writing of Q.

14. Lambrecht, "Structure de Mc, XIII."

15. See, e.g., Başgöz, "The Tale-Singer."

16. E.g., Taylor, *St. Mark*, 511–12; Lane, *Gospel according to Mark*, 467.

the synagogue or congregation.[17] Thus Mark's use of "reader" in v. 14 is not a stumbling block to an oral understanding of the gospel. The second aside, "What I say to you, I say to all," serves to extend the teaching embedded in the event from the four disciples who are part of the episode, and to apply it to the listening audience. Teaching in Mark is conveyed through events or happenings.

"Doxa" Consists of the Visible

For oral remembering, episodes must be visual, that is, pictured in the mind's eye. Havelock writes, "In their separate and episodic independence from each other they are visualized sharply, passing along in an endless panorama."[18] The episodes in Mark are easily visualized. This is true not only of individual units with much concrete detail, such as the healing of the paralytic or the flight of the demons into the pigs—passages that likely had a prior existence in oral tradition. It is also true of the summary statements, the *Sammelberichte* identified by Karl Ludwig Schmidt, which we generally assume are Mark's own written contribution.[19] We tend to think of such passages as less colorful and as different in kind. Yet heard as part of a succession of incidents, they are easily visualized. For example, Mark 2:13, "And he came out again beside the sea, and the whole crowd came to him and he taught them," suggests a vignette of Jesus addressing a crowd on rather barren ground against a backdrop of blue water. The general healing passages, such as Mark 3:7–12 and 6:53–56, would be visualized as crowd scenes with people jostling about and pushing to get their sick to Jesus. To draw an analogy from film, the effect is that of drawing back for a distant shot between sequences of closeups. When one hears the Gospel, the passages do not seem set off in kind; they too are "visibles."[20]

"Doxa" Consists of the Many

Plato's third complaint about opinion is that it is made up of the many, not the one; that is, it is pluralized. Ong describes this feature as the additive

---

17. Bultmann, "*anaginōskō, anagnōsis*," 343–44.

18. Havelock, *Preface to Plato*, 180.

19. So Kelber, *Oral and the Written Gospel*, 51.

20. The fact that the summary statements function as scenes is quite clear from David Rhoads, *Dramatic Performance of the Gospel of Mark*.

and aggregative character of oral narrative.[21] To illustrate the difference between a translation that takes orality into acount and one that does not, Ong contrasts the 1610 Douay version of the opening of Genesis, which preserves the additive style of the Hebrew, with the New American Bible from 1970, a more contemporary translation:

> *Douay:* In the beginning God created heaven and earth. And the earth was void and empty, and darkness was upon the face of the deep; and the spirit of God moved over the waters. And God said: Be light made. And light was made. And God saw the light that it was good; and he divided the light from the darkness. And he called the light Day, and the darkness Night; and there was evening and morning one day.

> *NAB:* In the beginning, when God created the heavens and the earth, the earth was a formless wasteland, and darkness covered the abyss, while a mighty wind swept over the waters. Then God said, "Let there be light," and there was light. God saw how good the light was. God then separated the light from the darkness. God called the light "day" and the darkness he called "night." Thus evening came, and morning followed—the first day.[22]

In place of the nine introductory *and*s of the Douay/Hebrew, the modern translation has only two *and*s, with a *when*, a *while*, a *thus*, and two *then*s.[23] With our sensibilities formed in a print culture, we read analytic relationships into the additive oral narrative.

In oral narrative *and* links not only clauses and sentences but also whole pericopes. Havelock writes that the oral tradition is "remembered and frozen into the record as separate disjunct episodes each complete and satisfying in itself, in a series which is joined together paratactically. Action succeeds action in a kind of endless chain. The basic grammatical expression which would symbolise the link of event to event would be simply the phrase 'and next.'"[24] The Markan narrative is certainly a series of independent episodes joined by *and*. Of the thirteen pericope introductions

---

21. Ong, *Orality and Literacy*, 37–39.

22. Ibid., 37.

23. Ibid., 37.

24. Havelock, *Preface to Plato*, 180.

in Mark 1–2, eleven begin with *kai*.[25] Only Mark 1:1, the opening of the gospel, and 1:14, the beginning of Jesus's public ministry, do not.[26]

Furthermore, the sequence of paratactic episodes is generally not determined by attaching subordinate to main acts, or by connecting cause and effect.[27] Ong writes, "One of the places where oral mnemonic structures and procedures manifest themselves most spectacularly is in their effect on narrative plot, which in an oral culture is not quite what we take plot typically to be," for it makes no attempt at climactic linear development.[28] Certainly there is no attempt in Mark to develop a gradually intensifying conflict between Jesus and the authorities, rising to a climax only at the arrest and crucifixion. The hostility first rises to a climax in 3:6, where the Pharisees and Herodians plot to kill Jesus. It is then forgotten about for eight chapters (although there are occasional conflicts between Jesus and the authorities), until in 11:18 and 12:12 the authorities, the chief priests, elders, and scribes seek to kill Jesus. The level of conflict then appears to decrease in the remaining controversies in Mark 12, ending with a scribe and Jesus praising each other in 12:32–34; but in 14:1, the authorities again seek Jesus's life, and the actual plot to arrest him is finally set in motion. Contemporary Markan scholars, long accustomed to the linearity typical of print narrative, have tended to attribute Mark's order (or lack of order) either to his "simple" writing style or to his incorporation of sources. In all probability, it is the natural consequence of his oral narrative technique.

If the episodes in oral narrative are not grouped according to cause and effect (that is, in linear plot development), neither are they necessarily arranged in chronological order. "The poet will report a situation and only much later explain, often in detail, how it came to be."[29] The past is brought into the narrative only at the point at which it becomes relevant to some episode being narrated.[30] Thus, in Mark, we are told the story of John the Baptist's arrest and death only in Mark 6, in explanation of how Herod could think Jesus was John raised from the dead—not at Mark 1:14, when John's arrest is noted. Here again the Markan narrative follows oral

25. As indicated by English titles in the United Bible Society Greek text.

26. Here also modern versions tend to reduce sharply the number of *and*s. The relatively literal RSV keeps six of the eleven *and*s in Mark 1–2; the NEB keeps none.

27. Havelock, *Preface to Plato*, 182–83.

28. Ong, *Orality and Literacy*, 141; 142–43.

29. Ibid., 142.

30. Havelock, *Preface to Plato*, 179.

ordering principles. It is made up of the many; it does not subordinate the many to the one.

Thus, Mark may be said to consist of *doxa*. The narrative consists of events that are visible and many. It is not ordered logically in terms of cause and effect or plot development or chronologically in terms of time, as those accustomed to print expect. As *doxa*, its contents and their ordering are those characteristic of oral narrative.

Acoustic Echoes

Not only does Mark conform to the limitations of *doxa*, but its methods of narrative development also correspond to those found in oral compositions. Havelock writes, "The basic principle . . . can be stated abstractly as variation within the same."[31] Oral narrative "operates on the acoustic principle of the echo."[32] Ring composition (*inclusio*) is endemic in oral narrative, marking the boundaries of individual episodes and of much longer sections. Ong notes that individual episodes and clusters of episodes are narrated in balanced patterns in either parallel or chiastic order.[33] Havelock comments that when we notice these correspondences at all, we tend to call them patterns, a visual concept; rather, he says, we should think of them as acoustic responsions.[34]

Scholars have been noticing patterns—or acoustic responsions—in Mark for some time now. The Markan sandwiches are a form of ring composition. Scholars have suggested more elaborate concentric or parallel rhythms for several sections of Mark, among them 1:16–45; 2:1—3:6; 4:1–34; 8:27—9:13; 12:1–40; 13:56–37.[35] It should be noted that these sections are relatively brief, each covering five or six pericopes—a length during which an oral performer can easily manipulate both structural and verbal parallels. Mark, even in writing, is still conforming to the restrictions of oral composition. Although the proposed structures are not all equally convincing, the very fact they can be posited is an indication of the quantity of thematic and verbal echoes to be found in the gospel.

31. Ibid.,147.

32. Havelock, "Oral Composition," 182.

33. Ong, *Orality and Literacy*, 34.

34. Havelock, "Oral Composition," 183.

35. For references, See J. Dewey, *Markan Public Debate*, 144. See also Standaert, *Composition et genre littéraire*, 174–262.

The longer narrative is also formulated on acoustic responsion. Ong speaks of oral narrative as episodes strung "together in . . . intricately managed patterns."[36] Havelock spells out the oral narrative chaining method in more detail:

> The same compositional principle [the echo principle] extends itself to the construction of the tale as a whole; it will avoid sheer surprise and novel invention . . . the basic method for assisting the memory to retain a series of distinct meanings is to frame the first of them in a way which will suggest or forecast a later meaning which will recall the first without being identical with it. What is to be said and remembered later is cast in the form of an echo of something said already; the future is encoded in the present. All oral narrative is in structure continually both prophetic and retrospective . . . Though the narrative syntax is paratactic—the basic conjunction being "and then," "and next"—the narrative is not linear but turns back on itself in order to assist the memory to reach the end by having it anticipated somehow in the beginning.[37]

Such a description applies remarkably well to the Markan narrative. In *Literary Criticism for New Testament Critics*, Norman Petersen lays out the numerous prospective and retrospective references in Mark, as evidence for Mark deliberately plotting the narrative.[38] It also would seem to be evidence that Mark has plotted the narrative employing typical oral techniques. He has not ordered the material logically or chronologically but rather by anticipation and responsion so that what is new is framed in terms of what is already known.

The plethora of backward and forward echoes that constitute the narrative of Mark become more evident (to us) if we consider those places where scholars have posited breaks in Mark's outline. Scholars have failed to reach consensus on the exact outline or structure of Mark, though not for lack of trying. I have argued that this is because Mark does not have a single linear structure; rather the structure consists of overlapping repetitive sequences.[39] All of the portions of Mark in which scholars frequently place breaks—Mark 1, 3, 8, 10–11, and 14—actually participate in several different overlapping sequences, echoing both backwards and forwards in

---

36. Ong, *Interfaces of the Word*, 284.

37. Havelock, "Oral Composition," 183.

38. Petersen, *Literary Criticism*, 49–80.

39. See chapter 4, above.

the narrative. Since virtually every scholar posits a major new beginning at either 8:22, with the blind man of Bethsaida, or at 8:27, with Peter's recognition of Jesus as the Christ, I will use Mark 8 as an example of these multiple echoes and variation within repetition.

The Echo System in Mark 8

It has become commonplace to view the healing at Bethsaida in 8:22–26 along with the healing of Bartimaeus at Jericho in 10:46–52 as a frame to the "way section" in which Jesus teaches about the way of the cross,[40] and so these healings are. They are the only healings of blindness in the gospel.[41] The pericopes begin identically: "And they are going into Bethsaida" (8:22, author's translation); "And they are going into Jericho" (10:46).[42] Bethsaida and Jericho are near the northern and southern points of Jesus's journey to Jerusalem. Symbolically, the Bethsaida healing is only accomplished in two stages, indicating the following teaching is difficult, while the Jericho healing is instantaneous and Bartimaeus follows Jesus on the way. So the healing at Bethsaida does point ahead in the narrative, or in Havelock's terms, the Bartimaeus healing is an echo and variation on the Bethsaida healing.

Yet for the person listening to Mark, the most obvious thing about the healing of the blind man in the Bethsaida story is not its newness, pointing ahead, but its retrospective echo to the healing of the man who was deaf and mute in 7:31–37. Both begin "They are bringing to him . . . and begging him that he might . . ." (7:32; 8:22, author's translation). Both are healings by physical means using spittle (and the only such in Mark). The verbal echoes are extensive throughout.[43] Indeed the similarities are such that Bultmann considered them to be two versions of the same episode.[44] The hearers are hardly likely to miss the echo.[45]

40. E.g., Duling and Perrin, *New Testament*, 248–49.

41. *Typhlos* occurs twice in the Bethsaida story, three times in the Bartimaeus story, and nowhere else in Mark.

42. While pericopes beginning with Jesus coming or going somewhere are common, the only other instances of *erchomai eis* in a pericope introduction are 3:20 (*kai erchetai eis oikon*) and 11:27 (*kai erchontai palin eis Hierosolyma*). The phrase *kai ēlthon eis* also occurs twice, in 5:1 and 9:33.

43. A convenient comparison of the Greek may be found in Taylor, *St. Mark*, 368–69.

44. Bultmann, *Synoptic Tradition*, 213.

45. Albert Lord, the oral critic par excellence, who concluded the Synoptic Gospels were oral variants, was particularly struck by the presence of doublets in the Gospels as

The next healing in Mark, after Bethsaida, is the healing of the boy with the unclean spirit in 9:14–27. This healing echoes both of the prior healings and also the exorcisms that appear earlier in Mark. The healing of the boy with the unclean spirit, like the one at Bethsaida, is done in two stages. In neither of these episodes does the restored person or the watching crowd do anything as the result of the healing. The difference is that the boy's unclean spirit is not one of blindness but rather of deafness and muteness, which harks back to the healing of the man who was deaf and mute in Mark 7.[46]

In addition, this third healing, of the boy with the unclean spirit, anticipates the final healing, that of Bartimaeus. These two healings are by spoken word, not physical action as the earlier two, and both involve faith.[47] Finally, the Bartimaeus healing echoes the first, the healing of deafness and muteness, in that both have responses in which someone disobeys Jesus's command. In Mark 7:36, "they" were commanded to silence but preached all the more; in Mark 10:52, Bartimaeus was commanded to depart but immediately followed Jesus on the way. Thus these four healings ring the changes on restoring hearing, speech, and sight. Here there is certainly variety within repetition, characteristic of oral narrative, without any definite starting or ending point.

Similarly, Peter's recognition of Jesus as the Christ, the second passage considered a major new beginning in Mark 8, echoes backwards and forwards in the narrative. These verses form a climax to the preceding eight chapters. In them, the disciples finally recognize who Jesus is, something the hearer was told in Mark 1:1. These verses begin the way section, which continues through to the Bartimaeus healing. They lead immediately into the first Passion prediction, which obviously anticipates the second and third predictions.

Yet for the listener, the most obvious feature of these verses would be their echo of Mark 6:14–16, where Herod decides that Jesus is John the Baptist raised from the dead. Not only are most of the suggestions about who Jesus is the same, but the structural sequence of the two passages is also similar. (Structural sequence is, of course, the basis of oral memory.)

---

evidence for their oral composition ("Gospels as Oral Traditional Literature," 76).

46. 7:32, *kōphon kai mogilalon*; 7:37, *tous kōphous poiei akouein kai alalous lalein*; 9:17, *pneuma alalon*; 9:25, *to alalon kai kōphon pneuma*. These are the only uses of *kōphos, alalos,* and *mogilalos* in Mark.

47. 9:24, *pisteuō boēthei mou tē apistia*; 10:52, *he pistis sou sesōken se*.

First, each lists the possibilities for who Jesus is: in 6:14–15, "John the baptizer," "Elijah," "a prophet like one of the prophets of old"; in 8:28, "John the Baptist . . . Elijah . . . one of the prophets." Second, in each someone recognizes Jesus: in 6:16, Herod says, "John, whom I beheaded, has been raised"; in 8:29, Peter says, "You are the Christ." Finally there is the theme of death: in 6:17–29, Herod's execution of John the Baptist; in 8:31, the prediction that the Son of Humanity will be killed.

As in the healing of the blind man at Bethsaida, what leads forward to new material in the narrative is formulated as an echo of what has been said already. Mark certainly seems to have followed the oral method analyzed by Havelock for the tale as a whole: the way to show a "series of distinct meanings is to frame the first of them in a way which will suggest or forecast a later meaning which will recall the first without being identical to it."[48] In summary, Mark indeed possesses Havelock's characteristics of oral narrative. It is made up of happenings easily visualized and not arranged in a logical order. Rather, the happenings appear in an endless chain of association, based on the echo principle.

Interpreting Mark Orally

The fact that the Gospel of Mark fits the characteristics of oral narrative argues that it was composed for a listening, not a reading, audience. This suggests that we need to take the dynamics of orality much more seriously in interpreting the Gospel of Mark and in reconstructing early Christian history. A few suggestions follow:

1) *The Negative Portrayal of the Disciples.* As Ong has repeatedly stressed, oral narrative tends to be "agonistically toned," that is, strongly polemic.[49] Accustomed to an adversarial atmosphere, a first-century audience hearing the gospel would probably take the negative portrayal of the disciples much less seriously than contemporary Markan scholars do.[50] Instruction often was conveyed to an audience through "warning examples of how not to behave."[51] Achilles in the *Iliad* provides an excellent example of

---

48. Havelock, "Oral Composition," 183.

49. Ong, *Orality and Literacy*, 43–45; Ong, *Presence of the Word*, 195–207.

50. See esp. Weeden, *Mark: Traditions in Conflict*; Kelber, *Oral and the Written Gospel*, 186.

51. Havelock, *Preface to Plato*, 48.

how not to behave to win a war. Yet Alexander the Great quite consciously took Achilles as his model as he campaigned to conquer the world.

Also, in understanding the role of the disciples, we need to consider the process of identification with the characters that occurs in oral performance.[52] The identification occurs in succession—that is, the performer and the audience would identify in turn with Jesus and then with the disciples.[53] Since oral narrative consists of the many not logically connected, it can tolerate different viewpoints in a way print culture cannot. As Ong rephrases Lévi-Strauss, "the oral mind totalizes," it does not analyze.[54] Acceptance of Jesus need not mean rejection of the disciples. We need to rethink the question of the role of the disciples in Mark in light of oral processes. Perhaps we will reach greater agreement on their significance in the story.

2) *The Open Ending of Mark.* Several scholars have argued that the gospel as a whole is a parable writ large.[55] The parable works best in an oral setting where the performer in interaction with the audience can make sure the point of the parable is grasped—whether accepted or rejected. In the written tradition, parables became allegories and moral examples; they lost their parabolic force. Perhaps something similar happened with the Gospel of Mark. As long as the gospel was performed orally, the open ending might function very well before a live audience. Yet when the gospel became treated as a writing and its parabolic function was no longer understood, its open ending would be ambiguous and intolerable, and the longer endings would be needed to bring resolution.[56] We need also to rethink the Markan ending in light of oral processes.

3) *Oral Narrative in the Early Church.* In this chapter I have argued that Mark was composed in writing for a listening audience. Yet the prevalence of oral compositional techniques suggests to me that we need to ask

52. Havelock, *Preface to Plato*, 44–45; 145–64.

53. For the reader identifying with the disciples, see Tannehill, "Disciples in Mark"; and Tannehill, "Gospel of Mark." For the reader identifying with Jesus, see Petersen, "'Point of View'"; and Tolbert's 1978 "Response to Robert Tannehill." For a literary argument that the reader identifies with both, see J. Dewey, "Point of View."

54. Ong, *Orality and Literacy*, 175.

55. See Kelber, *Oral and the Written Gospel*, 117–29 and 215–20; as well as Malbon, "Mark: Myth and Parable," and the literature they cite.

56. Several scholars have recently suggested that the ending at Mark 16:8 is a call to readers to complete the narrative and follow Jesus. See, e.g., Petersen, "'When Is the End.'" Yet as Ong points out in "The Writer's Audience," writers have had to educate readers over time to participate appropriately in their writings. It is questionable that a first-century *reader* would have been able to follow an ending such as 16:8.

again if Mark is a written transcription of oral narrative, or—perhaps more probable—if Mark is building on an oral storytelling tradition.[57] The Gospel of Mark possesses both oral methods of connecting individual episodes and a very high degree of inner consistency among the episodes.[58] To accomplish this, it seems more likely that Mark is building on an existing oral narrative tradition of some sort, not connecting the disparate episodes of the synoptic tradition for the first time. The form-critical assumption that there was no story of Jesus prior to the written gospels, only individual stories about Jesus, also needs to be reconsidered in the light of our growing knowledge of oral narrative.

4) *First-Century Media Model.* Finally, or perhaps first of all, we must develop a media model for the Gospel of Mark and early Christianity in general. We need a better understanding of how oral and written media work both together and in opposition to each other in the early Christian mixed media situation. I agree with Werner Kelber that we need to take into account the shift from oral to written media in understanding Christian development. The Gospel of Mark (whether as written composition or as transcription of oral story) is only the first step in the transition to a written hermeneutic, a process that took decades if not centuries.

57. Since Johann Gottfried Herder in the eighteenth century, Thorleif Boman, Albert B. Lord, and Thomas E. Boomershine have argued for Mark as an oral composition. For specific references, see Kelber, *Oral and the Written Gospel*, 77–78. See also Keck, "Oral Traditional Literature," for a summary of scholarship on early Christian storytellers.

58. For literary consistency in Mark, see Rhoads and Michie, *Mark as Story*, and the literature cited there.

6

The Gospel of Mark as an Oral/Aural Event

Implications for Interpretation

Introduction

Today many Christians experience the Gospel of Mark as a communal and aural event: they hear short portions of the gospel read aloud at Sunday morning worship. What they know of Mark comes from hearing it in a communal context, but they hear only isolated snippets, not the whole story. In the last two decades, on the other hand, scholars have rediscovered the literary unity of Mark and now locate its meaning, not in individual passages, but in its narrative whole.[1] However, scholars tend to read and analyze the text on the basis of individual, silent readings of printed texts.

Ancient Christians neither heard isolated snippets of Mark nor read the entire gospel silently in isolation. In antiquity, people in groups would have heard the gospel performed in its entirety. This was true for ancient literature in general. "There is virtually no evidence to contradict the assertion that private, silent reading and writing simply did not exist in the period. Texts were produced to be read aloud in a communal setting."[2] But a written text was not even necessary. Brian Stock writes: "What was essential for a textual community, whether large or small, was simply a text, an interpreter and a public. The text *did not have to be written*; aural

---

1. E.g., Rhoads and Michie, *Mark as Story*; Tolbert, *Sowing the Gospel*; Fowler, *Let the Reader Understand*; Anderson and Moore, *Mark and Method*.

2. Cartlidge, "Combien d'unités," 406 n. 37.

record, memory, and reperformance sufficed."[3] In many recitations or performances of a non-elite narrative such as the Gospel of Mark, there was probably simply an oral performer who had heard the story performed, who in turn retold the story in interaction with a group of listeners. In this chapter I wish to address some implications of understanding Mark as an oral performance for a live audience rather than as a written text.[4] First, however, our assumptions, based on our Western experience of widespread literacy and print media, require some preliminary remarks about literacy in antiquity.

Orality and Literacy in Antiquity

Only a small minority of persons in the ancient world would have been literate. Using cross-cultural data on agrarian and advanced agrarian societies, scholars estimate that between 2 and 4 percent of ancient Mediterranean people were literate.[5] Literacy would be higher in cities and among males, perhaps as high as 15 percent for urban males.[6] But except for men among the ruling elite,[7] literacy in antiquity was unlikely to mean the ability to read and write fluently. Even among literates not many would be literate enough to read easily a relatively long narrative text such as Mark. Sometimes literacy meant simply the ability to sign one's name. Few if any early Christians belonged to the elite group for whom full literacy was normal. Furthermore, papyrus was very expensive,[8] and a scroll the length of Mark would have been well beyond the resources of most early Christian groups.

Thus, if more than a very few people had any acquaintance with the gospel, their acquaintance would have to have been from oral performance.[9]

---

3. Stock, *Listening for the Text*, 37 (italics added).

4. In this chapter I use *oral* to emphasize the aspect of composition or performance, and *aural* for that of reception. At times I use both in order to stress both aspects.

5. Malina and Rohrbaugh, *Social-Science Commentary*, 3; Rohrbaugh, "Social Location," 115; Bar-Ilan, "Illiteracy," 56.

6. Harris, *Ancient Literacy*, 267.

7. Percentages as always are elusive. The governing classes rarely exceed 2 percent of the population in an agrarian society (Lenski and Lenski, *Human Societies*, 219; Duling and Perrin, *New Testament*, 56; Rohrbaugh, "Social Location," 117). Since some of the higher-status merchants and retainers may have participated in elite culture, a somewhat higher percentage may have been fully literate.

8. Harris, *Ancient Literacy*, 194–95.

9. The fact that Mark survived to be included in the canon suggests that it had wide

Oral performance was a very common phenomenon in the ancient world, as it is in other cultures today where widespread literacy is not the norm.[10] A composition the length of our text of Mark would take an hour and a half to two hours to tell, a quite customary duration for oral performances. Furthermore, good storytellers could easily learn the story of Mark from hearing it read or hearing it told.[11] Oral performance and reception for the transmission of the Gospel of Mark is not at all improbable; it would in fact have been the typical means.[12]

The Gospel of Mark shows evidence of its close connection to the world of oral performance and reception. I have argued elsewhere that Mark was composed for a listening audience using techniques of oral composition.[13] Recently, Richard Rohrbaugh has argued that Mark's intended audience consisted primarily of nonliterate peasants. Indeed the connection of Mark to the oral world is so great that we need to ask the question, was it initially composed in writing (either by the author himself or herself or by the author dictating to a scribe, the more common method of composition), or was it initially composed and transmitted orally and only eventually put into writing?[14] That question, however, is a historical one, going beyond the scope of this article. Here my focus is on implications that oral performance and reception of Mark in a largely oral culture have for our understanding of the gospel.

---

popularity. Otherwise, after it was absorbed into Matthew and Luke, it would have been lost, as Q was lost. See chapter 10, below.

10. Scobie, "Storytellers"; Sjoberg, *Preindustrial City*, 286–89.

11. See Ong, *Presence of the Word*; Ong, *Interfaces of the Word*; Ong, *Orality and Literacy*; Howe, "Cultural Construction of Reading."

12. On the first-century media world and its significance for understanding early Christian texts, see Kelber, *Oral and the Written Gospel*; Kelber, "Modalities of Communication"; Boomershine, "Jesus of Nazareth"; J. Dewey, ed., *Orality and Textuality*.

13. See chapters 4 and 5, above; see also Botha, "Mark's Story."

14. Most scholars assume the gospel was initially composed in writing. Kelber, in *Oral and the Written Gospel*, saw its composition as a radical disruption of early Christian orality. Since Johann Gottfried Herder in the eighteenth century, Thorleif Boman, Albert B. Lord, Thomas E. Boomershine and Pieter J. J. Botha have argued for Mark as an oral composition. (For references see Kelber, *Oral and Written Gospel*, 77–78, and Botha, "Mark's Story.") I suspect there is a more complex interaction of oral and written composition involved in the creation of Mark. For a good discussion on issues the oral/aural culture poses for our understandings of synoptic development, see Kelber, *Oral and the Written Gospel*, 1–43; and Kelber, "Jesus and Tradition"; for the formation of Mark, see Keck, "Oral Traditional Literature."

Literary analyses of Mark over the last two decades have greatly increased our understanding of the gospel. Some have studied the narrative of Mark in light of first-century literary conventions of biographies or romances.[15] Others have applied modern literary-critical methods directly to the Markan text: general literary criticism of plot, character and surface structure,[16] reader-response criticism,[17] structuralist criticism,[18] and post-structuralist criticism.[19]

All of us have employed close reading of the printed text in our analyses. We have had access to the Markan text in ways that were impossible for ancient audiences. Modern readers can stop and reflect on the text at any point; ancient hearers could not. We can reread and check back; they could not. We read the text silently and alone; they heard it spoken in community. Even ancient performers, if they had had contact with a written text at all, were more likely to have learned it from hearing it read aloud, than from reading it themselves. We need now to ask: What difference or differences do our different modes of reception make? How would ancient composers have gone about composing differently from modern writers? How would ancient audiences have heard differently? What conventions of composition and of reception would such a highly oral/aural culture as that of first-century Christians have had? Of course, not all cultures with the same communications media are going to have the same conventions;[20] nonetheless, oral performance and reception are likely to require some understandings substantially different from our modern reading assumptions—differences that affect interpretation and perceived meaning.

New Testament scholars are just beginning to explore the issues of how the oral/aural/textual media of antiquity influenced composition and reception of particular ancient texts.[21] Even anthropology and folklore

15. For a biography perspective, see Robbins, *Jesus the Teacher*; for a romance perspective, see Tolbert, *Sowing the Gospel*.

16. E.g., Rhoads and Michie, *Mark as Story*; Malbon, "Narrative Criticism"; Malbon, "Echoes and Foreshadowing"; J. Dewey, *Markan Public Debate*.

17. E.g., Fowler, *Let the Reader Understand*; and Fowler, "Reader-Response Criticism."

18. E.g., Malbon, *Narrative Space*.

19. E.g., Moore, "Deconstructive Criticism"; and Moore, *Mark and Luke*. The references cited are examples; many additional works could be adduced.

20. Boomershine, in "Jesus of Nazareth," argues that post–70 CE Christianity and Judaism developed very different communications systems within the broader mix of ancient orality and textuality.

21. Kelber's *Oral and the Written Gospel* remains the basic work for New Testament

studies, the social-science loci for studies of oral literature, have not yet done much research on oral reception.[22] Thus, the following discussion is of necessity exploratory, in some instances suggesting areas for further research. Furthermore, in order to clarify some of the implications of orality, the following may overstate the disjunction between aural reception and silent, print-reading reception. But this discussion is a first step, and one that needs to be taken.

Characteristics of Oral Narratives

Oral narratives, including written narratives performed orally for nonliterate audiences, tend to differ in characteristic ways from print narratives written for silent, individual reading. Walter Ong summarizes these characteristics as follows: content is combined in additive rather than subordinating relationships; the structure is aggregative rather than analytic or linear; the content is also repetitious or 'copious,' close to the human world, agonistically toned, and empathetic and participatory rather than objectively distanced.[23] Recognition of some of these characteristics, particularly the additive and aggregative structures and the participatory character, helps us to interpret various aspects of Mark that have puzzled and divided scholars and literary critics of the gospel.

Additive and Aggregative Composition

First, additive and aggregative composition results in nonlinear plotting or—from our print perspective—lack of a climactic linear plot.[24] Havelock describes the oral/aural method of composition as the echo principle: "What is to be said and remembered later is cast in the form of an echo of something said already; the future is encoded in the present. All oral narrative is in structure continually both prophetic and retrospective . . . Though the narrative syntax is paratactic—the basic conjunction being 'and then,' 'and next'—the narrative is not linear but turns back on itself in order to

scholarship. However, although he correctly grasped the differences in the two media, at that time Kelber had greatly overestimated their separation—and the written textuality of Mark—in the ancient media world.

22. Though the articles collected in Boyarin, *The Ethnography of Reading*, provide a good beginning.

23. Ong, *Orality and Literacy*, 37–49.

24. Ibid., 141–44.

assist the memory to reach the end by having it anticipated somehow in the beginning."[25] Awareness of these structural characteristics helps us to make sense of Mark. On the one hand, the gospel consists of independent, often repetitive, episodes loosely connected without the linear climactic plot development we are accustomed to from modern novels and short stories. On the other, it exhibits elaborate interweaving and development of themes.[26] Judged for effectiveness in oral communication, Mark may be seen as a sophisticated and adept composer, rather than a somewhat inept compiler who, in the words of Bultmann, was "not sufficiently master of his material."[27]

Understanding the additive and aggregative manner of composition also helps to make sense of the apparent tension between miracles and persecution in Mark. Today most scholars seem to read Mark with eyes trained on the internal consistency and linear plot development character-istic of print narrative. Since healings are numerous in the first half of the narrative, become rare after 8:26, and end entirely at 10:52, while suffering is increasingly foregrounded in the narrative after 8:27, modern scholars read Mark as rejecting healing, miracle-based power in favor of suffering.[28] But in additive and aggregative narratives new information does not negate earlier information; it is added to it. Persecution at the hands of the powers of the world is added to the miracles of healing, sea crossings and feedings of thousands. The oral/aural logic is both/and, both miracles (which are to be prayed for in confidence, 11:22–25) and persecution (which is to be expected, 13:9–11). According to the narrative, both miracles and persecu-tion are the lot of both Jesus and the disciples.

Agonistic Tone

A second characteristic of oral/aural narrative that helps us to interpret Mark is its agonistic tone. Ong writes: "Many, if not all, oral or residu-ally oral cultures strike literates as extraordinarily agonistic in their verbal

---

25. Havelock, "Oral Composition," 183. Scholars using electronic media also create echoes. Some sentences of this chapter strongly echo chapters 4 and 5, above.

26. See chapters 4 and 5, above; see also Malbon, "Echoes and Foreshadowing."

27. Bultmann, *Synoptic Tradition*, 350.

28. E.g., Kelber, *Oral and the Written Gospel*; Tolbert, *Sowing the Gospel*; Fowler, *Let the Reader Understand*. This is, of course, an oversimplification of their arguments. A few do not see suffering superseding miracles (e.g., Kolenkow, "Beyond Miracles"; Donahue, "Neglected Factor"; Dowd, *Problem of Suffering*.

performance . . . Bragging about one's own prowess and/or verbal tongue-lashings of an opponent figure regularly in encounters between characters in narrative."[29] What we perceive as negative treatment of the disciples in Mark may be considered agonistic. The disciples have trouble understanding Jesus and his teaching; they finally fail, deserting, denying and betraying him. The female disciples, introduced into the narrative once the male disciples have fled, remain faithful through the crucifixion and burial, but in their turn they fail at the empty tomb. Furthermore, the Markan Jesus at times treats the disciples rather agonistically: for example, in 7:18, "Then are you also without understanding?"; in 8:17–18 and 21, "Why do you discuss the fact that you have no bread? Do you not yet perceive or understand? Are your hearts hardened? Having eyes do you not see, and having ears do you not hear? And do you not remember? . . . Do you not yet understand?"; and in 8:33, "Get behind me, Satan!" Bragging is also found: in 14:29 and 31, Peter literally brags, "Even though they all fall away, I will not . . . If I must die with you, I will not deny you"—which, of course, he fails to fulfill.

Modern scholars in general tend to take the negative portrait and the agonistic dialogue very seriously. Often they interpret the Markan disciples referentially, so that Mark aims to discredit the original disciples, their successors or some group in his own community.[30] Even if they do not make historical inferences, literary critics often see the conflict as fundamental enough to exclude the possibility of restoration of the disciples after they have deserted Jesus in Mark's narrative world.[31] Yet it is doubtful that ancient listening audiences would have interpreted the Markan disciples so negatively. Finding an adversarial atmosphere normal, they would not take the conflict as seriously, and they probably would not give the disciples' portrait much referential weight.[32]

Furthermore, ancient hearers were accustomed to instruction by means of bad examples, "warning examples of how not to behave."[33] As Havelock points out, "It should be noted that the examples which tend to predominate are in fact those in which the instruction fails to be car-

29. Ong, *Orality and Literacy*, 43–44.

30. E.g., Weeden, *Mark: Traditions in Conflict*; Kelber, *Oral and the Written Gospel*.

31. Tolbert, *Sowing the Gospel*; Fowler, *Let the Reader Understand*.

32. Of course, how they would in fact interpret the Markan disciples would also depend on what traditions they knew about the actual disciples, information to which we have no access.

33. Havelock, *Preface to Plato*, 48.

ried out: the action that supervenes becomes 'heroic' or 'tragic' (or in the Hebrew case 'sinful') but no less effective as a warning as it preserves and conserves the underlying 'lesson.'"[34] The negative portrayal of the disciples may well have seemed to audiences merely part of a normal story.[35]

Participatory Character

Third, the implications of the participatory character of oral/aural performance and reception are particularly important for our understanding of Mark. Participation is at the heart of oral performance. Participation is not just on the part of an audience who responds to a fixed text, but also on the part of the performer who constantly adapts his or her performance/ text to the audience.[36] Walter Ong writes that "public verbal performance in an oral culture is participatory and essentially integrative. Speaker and audience and subject matter are raveled together in a kind of whole."[37] Thus, for the performer and the audience alike, the emphasis is on the experience of the performance event, not on new information learned from the performance. Oral culture "tend[s] to be performance-oriented rather than information-oriented."[38] Communication is often "an invitation to participation, not simply a transfer of knowledge from a place where it was to a place where it was not."[39] Thus, biblical scholars' practice of reading of the gospel for the information it gives us about the historical Jesus, or the Markan community, reads against the gospel's genre convention of inviting participation in its story.

Here modern literary critics, analyzing Mark as a silent printed text, are closer to the genre function of the gospel than historical critics are, because they analyze the gospel as they would narrative fiction. John Barth writes, "you hear it said that the novelist offers you an attitude toward life and the world. Not so, except incidentally or by inference. What he offers you is not a *Weltanschauung* but a *Welt*; not a view of the cosmos, but a

---

34. Havelock, *Muse Learns to Write*, 77.

35. Given that ancient rhetoric shares this agonistic character, we probably also take too seriously the evidences of conflict in Paul's letters.

36. Ong, *Interfaces of the Word*, 69.

37. Ibid., 282.

38. Ong, *Orality and Literacy*, 171. Ong finds this true even within more oral subgroups in highly literate cultures.

39. Ong, *Interfaces of the Word*, 118.

cosmos itself."[40] Modern fiction, like oral narrative, creates a world that invites the reader in. What is true of print narrative today was even more true of oral narrative performance, where the audience participated in the creation of the cosmos. David Barr writes about those who heard the book of Revelation in worship: "[They] live in a new reality in which lambs conquer and suffering rules. The victims have become the victors. They no longer suffer helplessly at the hands of Rome; they are now in charge of their own destiny and by their voluntary suffering they participate in the overthrow of evil and the establishment of God's kingdom."[41] Similarly, hearing the Gospel of Mark performed is the experience of becoming part of a world in which both miracles and persecution are real. The hearers enter a world in which the courage to move forward in following the Markan Jesus—in spite of and through human failure as experienced through the disciples—becomes a possibility, even a reality. The oral/aural story does not primarily convey historical information; it gives meaning and power to a way of life, to a cosmos become real in performance.[42]

In the oral performance event, participation becomes "empathetic identification."[43] According to Havelock, identification is necessary among nonliterates to enable both the performer and the audience to remember:

> You threw yourself into the situation of Achilles, you identified with his grief or his anger. You yourself became Achilles and so did the reciter to whom you listened.[44] . . . The minstrel recited effectively only as he re-enacted the doings and sayings of heroes and made them his own, a process . . . [of] making himself 'resemble' them in endless succession . . . His audience in turn would remember only as . . . they became his servants and submitted to his spell . . . Psychologically it is an act of personal commitment, of total engagement and of emotional identification.[45] [T]he whole experience becomes a kind of dream in which image succeeds image automatically without conscious control on our part, without

40. Barth, "How to Make a Universe," 17.

41. Barr, "Apocalypse as Symbolic Transformation," 50.

42. Of course, we may wish to read Mark for what we can learn about history. That is a legitimate enterprise, but not one that is likely to lead us to a better understanding of the gospel itself.

43. Ong, *Interfaces of the Word*, 18.

44. Havelock, *Preface to Plato*, 45.

45. Ibid., 160.

> a pause to reflect, to rearrange or generalize, and without a chance
> to ask a question or raise a doubt.[46]

Similarly, the audience at a performance of Mark's gospel, insofar as the narrative came alive for them, would identify sequentially with the various characters and events of the narrative. In the process of successively identifying with the different characters as they are portrayed in performance, the audience would identify alternately with the reality of miracle-based power and with the reality of suffering/persecution. They would also identify alternately with Jesus and with the disciples. In these ways, the audience's processes of identification would reinforce the both/and effect—both healing and persecution, the acceptance of both Jesus and the disciples—which the additive and aggregative nature of oral/aural narrative has engendered.

The process of identification in oral performance among nonliterates or highly aural cultures is central for the interpretation of oral/aural texts. Consideration of some theories of identification may help us to clarify the aural processes of participation. My aim here is not to provide a theoretical framework adequate to the complexity of types and levels of identification. Rather, it is to see if a theory, used heuristically, can help illuminate the differences between identification for oral and written media.[47] The observations of Ong and Havelock are descriptions based on ancient and modern oral literatures. Susan Sniader Lanser has developed a theory of narrative identification that, at first, seems promising in dealing with such literatures.[48] In her study of narrative levels in print narratives, she argues that the reader identifies with the narrator in regard to values but with the narratee or character addressed in regard to situation. In reading the gospel, then, the reader would identify with both Jesus and the disciples: with Jesus's values, on the one hand, and with the disciples' behavior, on

---

46. Ibid., 190. Havelock is speaking of the metrical composition of the *Iliad*, which Mark lacks. Nonetheless the process of mimesis—the term Plato uses for the act of composition, the performance, and the audience response—seems to refer to the quality of continual emotional identification and not to the style of the narrative (ibid., 22–25; 44–45; 145–64).

47. We can, of course, still experience an oral performance of Mark today. But our experience will be, at least in part, conditioned by our assumptions and perceptions formed by our highly literate training. We remain, if you will, literate hearers. Nonetheless, we can in such a way more closely approximate the ancient experience. The modern experience of performing Mark can also help us to understand oral processes (see Rhoads, "Performing the Gospel").

48. Lanser, *Narrative Act*.

the other. The theory explains how the reader can identify with both Jesus and the disciples: the reader as reader identifies with each in a different way.[49] If Havelock is correct, however, about successive identification with each character in turn for oral narrative, Lanser's model does not apply to hearing the Gospel of Mark. Her model would require the hearer to distinguish between values and behavior rather than to identify fully with each character.

More helpful is the work of Hans Robert Jauss on associative identification.[50] In theorizing on the aesthetics of reception, Jauss posits five levels of identification of the audience with the hero. His first level, associative identification, fits the oral-performance situation very well: "By 'associative identification' we mean a type of aesthetic conduct which is realized at its purest by the assumption of a role in the closed imaginary world of a play-action. Play-action, however, does not here refer to a presentation for spectators. What the associative identification of the players does, rather, is suspend the opposition between presentation and contemplation, between actors and spectators."[51] Jauss locates associative identification in situations of "Game/Competition (Ceremony)"[52]—that is, situations of ritual, celebration, and what he calls 'play-action.' In particular, he cites the example of medieval religious dramas. These are generally occasions of oral performance, which Ong also connects to celebration and play.[53] For Jauss, associative identification is characterized by the suspension of the opposition "between work and audience, between actors and spectators,"[54] and by "placing oneself in the roles of all other participants."[55] For Jauss, associative identification can help create or reinforce shared group values:

> And since the player . . . can be a judge as well as an interested party, participation in the play-action leads beyond the acknowledgement of others' roles, and of the other party, to an acknowledgement and comprehension of the justice that prevails in the game . . . The constructive role that the associative identification games play in the formation of social groups thus resides in the

49. J. Dewey, "Point of View."

50. Jauss et al., "Levels of Identification."

51. Ibid., 299.

52. Ibid., 298.

53. Ong, *Presence of the Word*, 30.

54. Jauss, "Levels of Identification," 296.

55. Jauss et al., "Levels of Identification," 298.

fact that the player can develop his own identity to the same extent that he, in the game, adopts the attitudes of others and exercises himself in modes of communication which, as expectations of behavior, can preorient social life.[56]

Associative identification functions to preserve memory and "can be employed by a class or institution of society in order to represent its ideal image of order."[57] Associative identification enables the hearer to experience a new and better cosmos.

Jauss's understanding of associative identification is very similar to the ways in which Ong and Havelock describe what happens when a performer (literate or nonliterate) interacts with a nonliterate audience. The hearer of Mark would identify fully, in terms of values and behavior, with both Jesus and the disciples. The process of sequential or associative identification explains the both/and of miracles and persecution; it enables us to understand how the audience could identify with both Jesus and the disciples rather than choose between them. With our ways of identifying formed in print culture and directly or indirectly influenced by Aristotle's thought, today we may read Mark according to Jauss's fourth level of identification, Aristotle's cathartic identification with the suffering hero: "the spectator is . . . placed in the position of the suffering or hard-pressed hero in order to undergo, by way of tragic emotional upheaval or comic release, an inner liberation."[58] Indeed, cathartic identification with the sufferings of Jesus may be a natural way to read Mark as a modern print narrative, and such a way of reading may undergird interpretations of Mark as exalting suffering over healing. But hearing the gospel fosters associative identification, which helps to integrate both healing and suffering.

But hearing or experiencing Mark in associative identification presents the biblical scholar with new questions. If the audience truly identifies with all characters in turn, what is the effect of their identification with the Jewish leaders who recur throughout the narrative? How is the process of associative identification affected by the performer's evaluation of characters as sympathetic or hostile—or is it? Furthermore, how is the process of identification affected by the audiences' preconceptions and prior knowledge about characters in the story? How do differences of class, gender, psychology, and so forth among individual members of an audience hearing

56. Ibid., 299–300.

57. Ibid., 302.

58. Ibid., 310.

Mark affect each person's reception of the gospel? How does the shared context of the performance event affect the reception of the audience as a whole?[59] To what extent do the views of the audience in fact control the performer's presentation of characters as sympathetic or negative? Kelber writes, "If a message is alien to an audience, or a matter of indifference, or socially unacceptable, it will not be continued in the form in which it was spoken. It will either have to be altered, that is, adjusted to prevailing social expectations, or eliminated altogether."[60] That is, how does the audience's influence over the performer affect the narrative standards and evaluations presented by the performer?

Answers to these and similar questions are beyond the scope of this article. The questions indicate areas that will benefit from new, cross-disciplinary research. The need to ask these questions suggests that a greater understanding of the reception of oral performance—of the processes of participation and identification—may lead scholars to quite different 'readings' of the Gospel of Mark. Our full recognition of the orality/aurality of Mark may transform our interpretations of it.

The participatory character of oral performance also helps us to understand the apparently unfinished ending of Mark. The gospel ends abruptly at Mark 16:8, with the women fleeing the tomb, saying nothing to anyone. From what we can infer from the scanty manuscript evidence, the written gospel soon acquired longer endings that bring closure to the story. I suggest that in the situation of oral performance, with its sequential or associative identification of the audience with the events of the story, the unresolved ending at 16:8 functioned as a summons to the audience to follow Jesus in the way of discipleship, enjoying healings and risking persecution, failing and succeeding "on the way."[61] The ending would call the audience to continue the story, expecting both successes and failures.[62] The lack of closure helps to involve the hearer in the continuation of the

59. Oral performance in highly oral/aural cultures tends to take place in a high-context society, in which much is shared and assumed by the audience and the performer—in contrast to our low-context literate culture, where much more information needs to be embedded in the written text (Malina and Rohrbaugh, *Social-Science Commentary*, 9–13).

60. Kelber, *Oral and the Written Gospel*, 28–29.

61. For the gospel ending "on the way," see Malbon, *Narrative Space*.

62. The oral function of the ending is similar to that of a parable. See Kelber, *Oral and the Written Gospel*, 117–29 and 215–20, as well as Malbon, "Mark: Myth and Parable," and the literature they cite.

story. As the process of associative identification blurs the boundaries of identification, so it also blurs the boundaries of actor/spectator, and, with an open ending such as Mark 16:8, it also blurs the boundaries between story and everyday reality. As the female disciples replace the male disciples when they are portrayed fleeing at Jesus's arrest, so the audience replaces the women, and the story goes on.

Literary critics have suggested that this open ending is a challenge to readers to do better than the characters in the narrative.[63] I suggest that, as the narrative functioned orally, the audience would not compare themselves to the internal characters. A comparison requires distance between the characters and the audience, a clear distinction between actor and spectator; without distance, analysis and comparative evaluation are not possible. Associative identification stresses participation, indeed merging with the internal characters, thus leading to a continuation of the story into everyday life.

Instability of the Text: A Final Implication

In the foregoing, I have tried to suggest ways that investigating Mark as oral performance/reception in a highly oral and aural culture may affect our interpretation of the gospel. Recognition of the gospel's oral and aural context alters our understanding of the relationship of miracles and persecution, our interpretation of the negative portrayal of the disciples, of the identification of the audience with the story, and finally, of the ending of the narrative.

In conclusion, I would like to suggest one more important implication of the oral setting of the gospel, the one perhaps most disconcerting to biblical scholars. When we recognize how oral and aural the media world of early Christianity was, we also have to recognize the destabilization of the text itself. In oral/aural cultures, before there is any written text, or when a written text is recycled back into oral circulation, there is no fixed text that is used in oral performance. According to Ong, oral memory "is never verbatim . . . the general story varies little from one telling to another. But the words always do."[64] Furthermore, performances vary radically in length, in terms of what is included and what is excluded. Ong writes: "A real audience controls the narrator's behavior immediately. Students of mine from

---

63. E.g., Petersen, "'When Is the End'"; Tolbert, Sowing the Gospel.

64. Ong. Presence of the Word, 24.

Ghana and from western Ireland have reported to me what I have read and heard from many other sources: a given story may take a skilled or 'professional' storyteller anywhere from ten minutes to an hour and a half, depending on how he finds the audience relates to him on a given occasion . . . The teller reacts directly to audience response. Oral storytelling is a two-way street."[65] A recognition of the oral/aural milieu of early Christianity informs us that actual performances of the Gospel of Mark almost certainly differed substantially, one from another. The Gospels of Mark that first- and second-century Christians heard probably varied a good deal from each other and from the text we use today.

The question of the relationship of our written Markan text to oral performances of its story is a complicated and debated historical issue that cannot be argued in full here.[66] In brief, given the nature of oral memory and tradition,[67] it is likely that the original written text of Mark was dependent on a preexisting connected oral narrative, a narrative that already was being performed in various versions by various people. If this is true, then we have in writing just one textual rendition of a living tradition,[68] one that at the time may have had little if any impact on the ongoing oral narrative tradition. In such oral contexts, the very concept of an original or authentic version makes little sense. Kelber writes of the Jesus tradition: "The concepts of original form and variants have no validity in oral life, nor does the one of *ipsissima vox*, if by that one means the authentic version over against secondary ones. 'In a sense each performance is "an" original, if not "the" original.'[69] Moreover, if each utterance constitutes an authentic speech act, then the question of transmission can never be kept wholly separate from composition."[70] This observation would be equally true of the tradition of

---

65. Ibid., 69.

66. Refer to note 15 above, for references. I agree with Kelber, *Oral and the Written Gospel*, that there is no natural evolution from orality to textuality. I would argue, however, that there was a complex and varied interaction between orality and textuality in the first centuries of the common era. Thus, contra Kelber, I do not view Mark as a disruption of an oral synthesis, creating a new textuality "out of the debris of deconstructed orality" (ibid., 95).

67. Per Keck, "Oral Traditional Literature"; and Vansina, *Oral Tradition as History*.

68. If one takes account of Secret Mark, we have perhaps evidence for two textual versions; and if there were two texts, then perhaps there were more before the canon became fixed.

69. Here Kelber is quoting Lord, *Singer of Tales*, 101.

70. Kelber, *Oral and the Written Gospel*, 30; see also Kelber, "Jesus and Tradition."

the Gospel of Mark. Each performance of Mark would be an original performance, and there would be no meaning in saying that one performance is truly Mark while another is not.

If, on the contrary, Mark was first composed in writing out of disparate pieces of tradition,[71] then one can argue that there was an original Mark, an original written creation. We would not know, however, how closely our text, whether UBS[3] or UBS[4], resembles original Mark since our manuscript evidence is much later than 70 CE. Does our text actually represent Mark's original version, or does it reflect later oral tellings? Eusebius wrote, "They say that this Mark was the first to be sent to preach in Egypt the Gospel which he had also put into writing."[72] Regardless of his accuracy about how Christianity got to Egypt, and Mark's role in bringing it there, Eusebius does attest to the continued importance of the storyteller even when a written text is available. And the storyteller who performs orally will alter his or her story from performance to performance; different storytellers will present different performances.[73] Furthermore, textual transmission is likely to have been heavily influenced both by oral performance traditions and the preferences of the literate people who were using manuscripts.

All we can say with certainty is that our text likely represents only one version among many, one version that may or may not be characteristic of the Markan performance tradition. We do not know if, in our modern sense, there was an original Mark, and, if there was, precisely what original Mark looked like. Nonetheless, our written text is the only text we have. Whether we are doing literary analyses of the text as an object to be read, or trying to reconstruct its meanings in the context of oral performance/reception, it is the text that of necessity we must use. Let us use it; but let us remember how differences between literate and oral/aural worlds affect how we understand Mark. Let us remember that it represents one version among many. Let us remember we do not know how typical it is, and that we do not know which audience it reflects at what time. With all its uncertainties—especially with all its uncertainties—the Gospel of Mark remains a fascinating narrative.

---

71. Per Kelber, *Oral and the Written Gospel*, 90–139.

72. Eusebius, *Ecclesiastical History*, 2.16.1.

73. As scholars using computers, we may be regaining some appreciation of the fluidity of texts.

7

The Gospel of Mark as Oral Hermeneutic

Introduction

In 1983, when Werner H. Kelber published his groundbreaking work *The Oral and the Written Gospel*, he argued that the Gospel of Mark was written as a "counterform to, rather than extension of, oral hermeneutics."[1] "Strictly speaking, therefore, the gospel arises not from orality per se but out of the debris of deconstructed orality."[2] Although Kelber certainly recognized that the written text was recycled into orality, he appeared to imagine that it was read aloud—much as one might read aloud today—from a printed text. Since then, Kelber has done substantial further work on media differences. He has stressed, first, the great differences between a manuscript and a printed text, and second, the multiple interactions between orality and scribality in the first century, including the variability of early manuscripts.[3] He has emphasized the importance of understanding the gospel narrative *as* narrative. Furthermore, Kelber has brought cultural-memory theory to bear on Christian origins and the Gospel of Mark.[4] He understands Mark not as "cold memory," which tries to preserve faithfully the traditions of the past, but as "hot memory," which reconstructs the past in order to form and support community identity in the present. Today, Kelber is well aware of the differences between manuscript and printed cultures, of the multiple interactions of oral and scribal traditioning, and of the fluidity of both oral

1. Kelber, *Oral and the Written Gospel*, 185.
2. Ibid., 95.
3. See Kelber, "Oral-Scribal Interfaces."
4. See Kelber, "Case of the Gospels"; and Kelber, "Works of Memory."

performances and manuscript texts. Yet he still views the written Gospel of Mark as a radical departure from, and reshaping of, the oral tradition.

As I have argued elsewhere, I think that the Gospel of Mark is basically an oral narrative built on oral storytelling, employing an oral style, and plotted according to oral conventions.[5] I do not know if it was composed and performed orally and then transcribed, or whether it was composed in writing, most likely by dictation, and then performed—a writer familiar with the tradition can write in an oral style. In contrast to Kelber, then, I would argue that the Gospel of Mark as a whole does *not* represent a break with orality, but is best understood in light of oral hermeneutics of composition and reception.

Rather than developing my own position further here, I shall address and challenge Kelber's reasons for viewing Mark's gospel as a sharp break with orality. As I understand it, Kelber's overarching understanding is that early Christian oral tradition focused on Jesus as being present and alive, while the Gospel of Mark focuses on Jesus's death and absence. Kelber offers three major arguments that Mark was written as a counterform to the oral synthesis. First, Mark rejects the Christian communities that were respected as oral authorities—namely the disciples, the family of Jesus, and the prophets/Christs. Second, Mark silences the oral teachings found in the sayings material. Third, the gospel's emphasis is on death and absence rather than life and presence, which Kelber sees as a major christological shift. I shall address each of these premises in turn.[6] Basically, I will argue that Kelber has not gone far enough in considering the Gospel of Mark as narrative and in recognizing oral narrative possibilities. I look forward to continuing dialogue about these issues.

Before turning to our differences, however, I wish to affirm both how much I have learned from Kelber, and how substantial are our agreements on the significance of media issues for understanding the New Testament. I agree with Kelber that Mark's gospel is not simply a natural evolution of oral tradition (i.e., there is no inevitable linear development from Jesus to the Gospels). I agree with him also on the importance of cultural memory for the formation of the Gospels: memory continually structures and adapts tradition to support community identity and needs in the present.

---

5. See chapters 5, 6, and 10 in this volume.

6. Although I have certainly been influenced by others' responses to Kelber and by others' work on Mark, I am focusing in this article on Kelber's work. I am indebted to David Rhoads for his helpful suggestions on this essay.

I also agree that the Gospel of Mark was composed around 70 CE, in response in part to the First Roman-Jewish War and the destruction of the temple in Jerusalem. I agree that it is "hot memory" serving that present situation, not an attempt to preserve some earlier pristine past. I agree that there was some sort of *Traditionsbruch* (break in the tradition) after 70 CE, due both to the disruption caused by the war and to the passage of time and the death of the first generations.[7] Finally, I agree with Kelber that, as Tom Thatcher has summarized him, "the books of the New Testament are best understood as attempts to harness and control the forces of orality."[8] Despite these many agreements, I differ with Kelber on how the written Gospel of Mark fits into the overall media picture. Kelber sees it as the beginning of writing used to control (or at least seriously reconstruct) orality; I see it as still on the oral side of the divide. I turn now to Kelber's reasons for understanding Mark as a written counterform to orality.

Mark's Rejection of Oral Authorities

Kelber's major and continuing argument for Mark as a scribal counterform to orality is his view that the Gospel of Mark rejects all oral authorities, which are represented in the narrative by the disciples, Jesus's family, and prophets/Christs. Here I shall follow Kelber in treating each of these characters separately. Then I shall question if at the time of Mark's composition these groups were even viewed as oral authorities guaranteeing the tradition.

The Disciples

I shall begin with the disciples as the group that is perhaps the most central to Kelber's argument. For Kelber, the relationship between Jesus and the disciples in the Gospel of Mark is constructed on the oral principle of mimesis. The disciples are called to imitate the paradigm of Jesus's life and death. Yet, in Kelber's view, the narrative portrays the disciples' failures, and thus "casts a vote of censure against the guarantors of tradition."[9] I view the disciples' role rather differently. The audience is indeed called to imitate Jesus's life and death but perceives Jesus, not the disciples, as the authority.

7. See Kelber, "Case of the Gospels"; Kelber, "Works of Memory," 244.
8. Thatcher, "Beyond Texts and Traditions," 2.
9. Kelber, *Oral and the Written Gospel*, 97, 125–29.

In the narrative, the disciples provide a means to teach about discipleship and illustrate for the listening audience both successes and failures in following Jesus.[10]

Mark's gospel does not address the disciples unequivocally. Those who, like Kelber, wish to interpret the gospel as rejecting the disciples stress that the disciples deny, betray, and abandon Jesus, and thus fall under Jesus's saying, "Those who are ashamed of me and of my words in this adulterous and sinful generation, of them the Son of Humanity will also be ashamed when he comes in the glory of his Father with the holy angels" (Mark 8:38, NRSV, with author alteration). Those who view the gospel as expecting the restoration of the disciples stress that the disciples are promised a reward for following (10:29–30), that they do finally understand and accept that following Jesus and the kingdom of God entails persecution by the powers of this age (10:35–40; 14:29–31), and that the repeated pattern of prophecy and fulfillment throughout the narrative suggests the fulfillment of the prophecy that the disciples will see Jesus in Galilee (14:28; 16:7), in spite of the women's silence (16:8). I remain as convinced that the narrative expects the disciples to be restored as Kelber is convinced that their restoration is out of the question.

I suggest, then, that the portrait of the disciples in the Gospel of Mark *is* ambiguous. Certainly narrative critics today continue to interpret the disciples both positively and negatively. Here, I believe the practice of performance criticism can help us.[11] Though scholars have begun to appreciate the significance of the oral/aural first-century media world, mostly we still study the New Testament by analyzing printed texts. If we want to pay attention to the oral dimensions of the extant texts, we need to hear them, performing them ourselves in various ways—in favor of or rejecting the disciples. Performance can enhance our understandings and clarify that some interpretations do or do not work orally. Performance criticism may indeed help to show us how truly ambiguous the Markan portrait of the disciples is.

Kelber admits that, when the Gospel of Mark is performed today, there can be sympathetic responses to the disciples.[12] Yet he argues that the agonistic (that is, combative) toning and adversarial plotting of the narrative

10. J. Dewey, "Gospel of Mark."

11. See Rhoads, "Performance Criticism—Part I"; and Rhoads, "Performance Criticism—Part II."

12. Kelber, "Introduction," xxvi.

makes that unlikely in the first century. I have used the same observation of agonistic toning and adversarial plotting to argue the opposite point.[13] Because ancient audiences were accustomed to agonistic portrayals, they would simply take them less seriously than modern readers do. In fact, in antiquity, teaching was often conveyed by examples of how *not* to behave, and audiences may not have interpreted such portrayals as a rejection of the characters in question. As far as audience reception is concerned, the question must be left open, although the acceptance of Mark's gospel into the canon does suggest that it was not generally understood as rejecting the Twelve and Peter. The question of the gospel's ending is relevant here. However, even the longer endings, although they restore the disciples and present the resurrected Jesus, still leave the gospel with an ambiguous portrait of the disciples.[14]

If reception must remain open, can we say anything more certain about composition, about authorial intent in regard to the disciples? Clearly, the subplot of the disciples is used to maintain audience interest. The narrative presents three interacting levels of conflict: the cosmic conflict, the conflict between Jesus and the authorities, and the conflict between Jesus and his followers.[15] The cosmic conflict takes place between God and Satan. As Mark tells the story, the audience knows from the beginning that God is the sure victor and that Jesus is God's agent. If the audience rejects this premise, the narrative will be unconvincing. The second or middle level is Jesus's conflict with the social, political, and religious authorities, the conflict between the kingdom of God and the kingdom of Rome. These first two plotlines are established early on in the narrative: the gospel of Jesus Christ *is* good news (1:1, 15), and the authorities reject Jesus, plotting to destroy him (3:6). The narrative is not ambivalent on these conflicts: the authorities will destroy Jesus in this age, but the new age has begun with Jesus and will triumph.

The third or most embedded conflict is the conflict between Jesus and the disciples, along with the broader group of followers. These conflicts with the disciples occur in private; the conflicts between Jesus and the authorities occur in public, and in those conflicts the disciples stand

---

13. See chapter 6, above.

14. My own supposition is that the Gospel of Mark originally ended at 16:8, with the performer concluding with something such as, "Whoever has ears to hear, let them hear."

15. J. Dewey and Malbon, "Mark," 311–12. See also Rhoads et al., *Mark as Story*, 2nd ed., 73–97.

with Jesus. Thus the disciples are not grouped with the opponents within the narrative. Rather, the narrative uses the disciples to teach the hearers what following entails, to emphasize the difficulties of following, *and* to maintain plot interest as the disciples do and do not succeed in following. The disciples' misunderstandings provide Jesus with opportunities to teach the gospel's hearers the correct understandings. It is only on this third level, the followers' conflict, that the Gospel of Mark is ambiguous. While this observation does not clarify authorial intent, it does suggest that it was not a major aim of this gospel to discredit the disciples and Peter. If Mark's aim was to discredit the disciples, the narrative would be as unambiguous here as it is on the first two levels of conflict; it would not be possible for hearers or readers to expect the disciples' restoration.

The Family of Jesus

Turning now to Jesus's family as representatives of oral authority, Kelber claims that the Gospel of Mark "registers consistent hostility toward Jesus' own family."[16] First, he cites two negative instances: Mark 3:20–35, where the family is grouped with the scribes in objecting to Jesus's behavior, and Mark 6:1–6, where Jesus is rejected in Nazareth. Second, on the assumption that Mary the mother of James and Joses is understood to be the mother of Jesus in 15:40, 47 and 16:1, Kelber argues that the family of Jesus (in the person of the mother) is part of the nontransmission of the resurrection message, and thus part of Mark's rejection of the oral authorities.[17] He further asserts that there is evidence that Jesus's family was understood as oral authorities in Paul, Acts, and elsewhere.[18]

Kelber is correct that the Gospel of Mark presents a generally negative view of the family of Jesus in Mark 3:20–35 and Mark 6:1–6. Yet the narrative does not group the family of Jesus with the disciples as leaders to be rejected. Rather, to become a disciple requires one to *leave* one's family in order to join the kingdom of God. In the Markan call stories, specific disciples leave their occupations, which in antiquity were typically family businesses (Mark 1:16–20; 2:14–15). James and John explicitly leave their father as well as his business. The disciples (and other followers) who have left families are promised new families, houses, and fields in 10:29–30.

16. Kelber, *Oral and the Written Gospel*, 102.

17. Ibid., 102–4.

18. Ibid., 102.

Finally, Jesus instructs both the disciples and the crowd that "If any want to become my followers, let them deny themselves and take up their cross and follow me" (8:34). While Western readers today tend to interpret "denying oneself" in accordance with an individualistic self-understanding, in antiquity the kinship unit was central, rather than the individual. Thus the kin group is what needs to be renounced to follow Jesus.[19] The parallelism of denying kin and taking up one's cross—that is, risking persecution, even execution—suggests that these both are understood as costs of discipleship.

While other Christian literature may understand the family as leaders, and thus oral authorities, in the Gospel of Mark they are understood as a unit that must be left in order to become part of the Christian community. In regard to Mary at the empty tomb, she is no longer portrayed as family, but as part of the group of women who follow and minister to Jesus. Grouping the family together with the disciples as oral authorities to be rejected is a deductive move on the part of a modern reader; it is not part of the experience of hearing the gospel. The oral narrative of the Gospel stresses the need for the disciples to separate from their kinship group in order to be followers. The family is not so much rejected as left for a larger cause. Overall, the negative portrayal of Jesus's family in the narrative is adequately explained by the narrative itself; any historical inference that Mark is rejecting the family as oral authorities is on shaky ground.

Prophets and Christs

Turning to Kelber's final group of oral authorities, in one instance the Gospel of Mark does warn against false Christs and false prophets, rejecting them in Mark 13:21–22 precisely as leaders of the community. On the basis of 13:5–6, Kelber understands these false prophets specifically as Christian leaders.[20] He understands them as speaking in the name of Jesus, "continuing the present authority of Jesus, the living Lord. It is this oral metaphysics of presence" that Mark is objecting to, in favor of a future return of the Son of Humanity who is now absent.[21] I would argue, however, that Mark is simply separating the expectation of the return of the Son of Humanity from the events of the Roman-Jewish War. The future coming of the Son of

---

19. Malina, "Let Him Deny Himself"; J. Dewey, "Let Them Renounce Themselves."

20. That they were specifically Christian rather than Jewish proclaimers, however, is by no means certain.

21. Kelber, *Oral and the Written Gospel*, 99.

Humanity was already part of the oral tradition; it is found specifically in Q, the sayings material common to Matthew and Luke, in Luke 17:23–37 and Matt 24:26–39. One does not need to posit a rejection of oral presence to explain the warning against false Christs.

Furthermore, in Mark's narrative, the false Christs are not grouped with the disciples or with Jesus's family. In fact, it is the inner core of disciples—Kelber's core group of rejected oral authorities—who are instructed to beware of them. Kelber himself has written eloquently and often of the need to understand a narrative as narrative before making theological or historical deductions about the narrative's prehistory. It is also necessary, I would argue, to understand the narrative as narrative before making historical or theological extrapolations from it. In this particular case, an understanding of the narrative not only prohibits grouping the family of Jesus and the disciples together. In addition, while there is a clear—if isolated—warning against false prophets and Christs, an understanding of the narrative also upholds a distinction between this group and the core disciples. While disciples, family, and false Christs are each critiqued in various ways in the narrative, they are each critiqued for *different* reasons, none specifically to do with oral authority. An understanding of the narrative as narrative precludes grouping them together as oral authorities to be rejected.

Before closing this section, I wish to raise a historical question: were these three groups (disciples, family, and prophets) clearly perceived as guarantors of the Christian tradition at the time of the composition of the Gospel of Mark? In 1 Corinthians 15, Paul refers to those who have seen the risen Jesus, including Peter, the Twelve, James (family), and finally himself, as guarantors that there really was a resurrection. Does this establish these individuals as oral authorities transmitting the whole tradition? Paul certainly feels free to disagree with Peter, as seen in Galatians 1–2. Our only other pre-Markan source, the hypothetical Q, does not seem concerned with oral authorities at all. Q mentions the Twelve only to note that they are given the authority to judge the twelve tribes of Israel in the age to come (Q/Luke 22:29–30; Matt 19:28). It seems to me that it is precisely the *Traditionsbruch*, starting some forty years after Easter when the generations who knew the earthly Jesus were dying out, that led to the need to establish guarantors of the tradition. The Gospel of Mark is a bit too early.

Perhaps it is precisely because Mark was not concerned with oral authorities that he could portray Peter and the other disciples negatively in his plot to teach about discipleship. Matthew and Luke, writing later, were more concerned with establishing authority for the church, and they both softened the negative portrait of Peter. It was Matthew, writing a decade or two after Mark, who specifically established Peter as an authority for the church on earth (16:17–19). The notion of the Twelve as eyewitnesses of the earthly Jesus is first found in Acts,[22] which I would date into the second century.[23] As time goes on, there was a need to anoint authorities as guarantors of the founding narratives. However, it is only *after* the time of the composition of Mark that this need became acute. In the introduction to the second edition of *The Oral and Written Gospel*, Kelber himself notes that the notion of eyewitness guarantors of the tradition served the needs of both Christian and Jewish communities beginning in the late first century.[24] However, he does not seem to see that this may have implications for the status of Peter, the disciples, and the family of Jesus as authorities in the pre-Markan oral tradition.

The Paucity of Sayings Material in Mark

In comparison to the other canonical gospels, the Gospel of Mark contains a smaller proportion of sayings. Kelber asks why this is the case, given that Q existed prior to Mark. Here he follows Eugene Boring's argument that Mark was leery of the prophets in his community who used the sayings tradition.[25] For Kelber, this is part of Mark's rejection of material that suggests the presence of Jesus. By omission of much of the sayings tradition, Mark silences Jesus's direct speaking. Indeed, Kelber argues, even the two discourses of Jesus that the Gospel does contain, Mark 4 and 13, "function so as to disallow any oral sense of presence." The parable discourse stresses the mystery of the kingdom, and the eschatological discourse "extricates kingdom hopes from past and present . . . and projects the Son of man into the future."[26] I would argue, on the contrary, that in the very oral performance of these speeches, Jesus is made present to audiences. The hearers of the Gospel experience being directly addressed by Jesus. In the parable discourse, they are *both* being given the mystery of the kingdom *and* being

22. Acts 1:21–22; see also Luke 1:1–4.
23. See Pervo, *Dating Acts*.
24. Kelber, "Introduction," xxv–xxvi.
25. Kelber, *Oral and Written Gospel*, 101.
26. Boring, *Sayings of the Risen Jesus*; Kelber, *Oral and the Written Gospel*, 101.

admonished to try for greater understanding. Thus, Mark does not reject Jesus as a speaker; rather, he allows him to speak, and thus to be present to the listening community.

I would like to suggest that the problem of the relative lack of sayings material in Mark is a problem for modern scholars, not for ancient listeners. I am not convinced that ancient hearers would sense any dearth of sayings in Mark's gospel. As is characteristic of oral narrative in general, Mark's gospel embeds teaching in events/episodes, which makes the teaching easier to remember. As Eric Havelock notes, "information or prescription, which in a later stage of literate culture would be arranged typically and topically, is in the oral tradition preserved only as it is transmuted into an event."[27] For example, unlike Matthew 6, with its general instructions on fasting and prayer, Mark embeds fasting into the controversy over why the disciples do not fast (2:18–20), and embeds prayer into the episode of the discovery of the withered fig tree (11:20–25). The two discourses of Jesus mentioned above, Mark 4 and 13, themselves consist of narrative material: the parables are little stories, and Mark 13 is mostly narrative, albeit of future events.[28] Jesus's exhortation in Mark 13:37, "What I say to you I say to all: Watch," is easily understood in the context of oral performance, for performers often make asides to their audiences in character.[29] The gospel conforms to typical oral *narrative* techniques.

Further, I suggest that the major reason for the relative lack of sayings in the Gospel of Mark is not their content or their function in making Jesus present but rather the simple fact that too much direct discourse interrupts narrative flow. Biblical critics apparently feel that the lack of much sayings material in this Gospel is in need of explanation. Early source critics sought a textual reason for the omission: Mark did not know Q (the sayings material common to Matthew and Luke and not in Mark). Thinking in terms of the oral/scribal first-century media world, Kelber has sought a theological reason: Mark has silenced the oral teaching with its emphasis on life and presence. The paucity of sayings, however, does not necessarily mean Mark rejects sayings. I suggest that the omission is due simply to the needs of

27. Havelock, *Preface to Plato*, 174.

28. In regard to Mark 13:14, I note that "Let the reader understand" is not an address to the reader of Mark's gospel, but possibly to the public reader of Daniel's "abomination of desolation"; so also Bultmann, *Synoptic Tradition*. David Rhoads suggests the words may be an aside to the performer, and are not meant to be performed at all (personal communication).

29. Başgöz, "The Tale-Singer"; Ong, *Orality and Literacy*, 161.

narrative for oral performance. The Gospel of Mark as a whole works as oral performance in ways that the other Gospels do not. It is no accident that Alec McGowan chose Mark's gospel to perform on stage. Long sections of teaching would interrupt the flow of episodes, and the audience (and the performer) would lose track of the plot, the story as a whole.[30] The lack of teaching does not need an external justification; the requirements of effective oral narrative alone suffice.

Life and Presence, Death and Absence

Kelber's third argument for Mark as a written counterform to the oral synthesis is that the Gospel of Mark is concerned with death and absence in contrast to the typical oral emphasis on life and presence. Kelber frequently emphasizes that oral communication binds together speaker, words, and listeners into a whole while scribality separates them, creating distance.[31] He argues that the distance and separation from an audience that writing provides are necessary for dealing with death.[32] Throughout *The Oral and the Written Gospel*, Kelber stresses the connection between life and orality, "the oral equation of the earthly Jesus with the living Lord," that he sees present in Q and elsewhere.[33] Further, he stresses the association of writing with death, citing Walter Ong's dictum, "the association of writing with death is not total, but it is manifold and inescapable," as an epigraph to his discussion.[34]

In what follows, I hope to demonstrate that although orality does reinforce life, and although scribality may indeed encourage distance and facilitate a focus on death, scribality and orality *both* deal with life, and *both* deal with death. First, I shall argue that the way Mark deals with Jesus's death and subsequent absence is possible orally—that is, that the gospel's content is compatible with oral composition. Here I am countering Kelber's specific arguments for viewing the Passion Narrative as a scribal composition. Second, I shall argue that the very performance of Mark's gospel,

---

30. When biblical storyteller Dennis Dewey performs the Gospel of John, he finds it necessary to omit considerable dialogue and monologue material in order to keep the story moving.

31. E.g., Kelber, *Oral and the Written Gospel*, 19.

32. Ibid., 19, 91–92, 193.

33. Ibid., 199, 201–3.

34. Ibid., 184; see also ibid., 197–99.

whether it was composed orally or in writing, brings Jesus and the kingdom of God alive and present to listening audiences.

Death and Life

In *The Oral and the Written Gospel*, Kelber describes Mark's Passion Narrative as a story of three deaths: Jesus's death, the temple's destruction, and the disciples' failure.[35] Having discussed the disciples already, and having noted my concurrence that Mark is reshaping the tradition to deal with the Roman-Jewish War and the destruction of the temple, I turn now to a consideration of Jesus's death and absence in the Gospel of Mark. First, orality—even within the Christian tradition—can and often does deal with death, as Kelber himself seems to acknowledge. For Kelber, Q is an example of oral hermeneutics. In *The Oral and the Written Gospel*, Kelber wrote that Q does not refer to Jesus's suffering and death.[36] More recently, however, he has noted that Q "keyed Jesus' own death to the fate of prophetic personalities in Jewish history."[37] I would add that Q also intimates the death of the disciples: Jesus' followers will be brought before the synagogues and rulers, and whoever does not carry their cross cannot be Jesus's disciple, as stated in Luke 12:11–12 and 14:26–27. Persecution, even execution, is understood as part of discipleship. Finally, the theme of Jesus's absence is also present in Q: in Luke 17:22–30, the Son of Humanity will return in the future. Thus, death and absence are to be found in the oral hermeneutics of Q.

The Gospel of Mark expands the Q tradition of rejection of the prophets, applying it to John the Baptist as well as to Jesus and the disciples.[38] All three are (or will be) handed over (*paradidōmi*): John the Baptist in 1:14; Jesus in 9:31, 10:33, 14:21, 14:41, 15:1 and 15:10; and his followers in 13:9, 11. The allegory of the wicked tenants in 12:1–10 clearly portrays the son (Jesus) as the culmination of the persecution of the prophets. The view of death in Mark is not a sharp break with the view in Q; it is aligned with it.

Mark's gospel, however, goes considerably further than Q: it *narrates* the deaths of John the Baptist and Jesus. For the Baptist, Mark includes the

35. Ibid., 185–86. In his 2005 article, "Works of Memory," Kelber restated this triad but changed the last element from the failure of the disciples to "the cessation of a generation of memories and memory carriers" (244).

36. Kelber, *Oral and the Written Gospel*, 201–3.

37. Kelber, "Works of Memory," 246; see Luke 11:49–51.

38. Mark may have known Q traditions, or both Q and Mark may have been drawing on oral traditions.

story of Herod Antipas's promise to the dancing girl, resulting in John's severed head on a platter (Mark 6:14–28). For Jesus, Mark's narrative in 14:1—15:20 leads up to the crucifixion, and then includes eighteen verses (15:21–39) on the crucifixion itself. Kelber argues that the written medium, which permitted greater distance, was necessary to bring crucifixion to narration. "The stunning realism of the passion narrative is most likely the result of artistic distanciation by written words that empty events of their immediacy. Close proximity to the event and the oral metaphysics of presence are a persistent obstacle to bringing death to language."[39] I question this claim, for the following reasons.

The difference in genre between Mark and Q remains relevant. Q consists of short discourses, it does not contain much narrative, and it certainly is not a connected narrative; the Gospel of Mark is a carefully constructed (oral) narrative. I suggest that the presence of the two death narratives in Mark is not an indication that the gospel was composed in writing. It is, rather, due to the difference in genre. *Narratives* about violent death *are* part of oral literature. To take one very notable example from the ancient world, the opening of the *Iliad* tells the audience that its narrative will be about many violent deaths: "The wrath sing, goddess, of Peleus' son Achilles, the accursed wrath which brought down countless sorrows upon the Achaeans, and sent down to Hades many valiant souls of warriors, and made the men themselves to be the spoil for dogs and birds of every kind; and thus the will of Zeus was brought to fulfillment. Of this sing from the time when first there parted in strife Atreus' son, lord of men, and noble Achilles."[40] It is even possible that the narration of Jesus's crucifixion may have fit better in oral narrative than in writing, since, as Kelber himself points out, in Mark's day crucifixions tended not to be described in writing.[41]

Kelber is correct that the Passion Narrative seems less oral in character than Mark 1–13. As he notes, oral forms are not so much in evidence in the Passion Narrative.[42] Yet it might perhaps be more accurate to say that the Passion Narrative consists of the repeated use of a single oral form, the biographical apophthegm—that is, a little story about a particular event. The Passion Narrative consists of a concatenation of short biographical

---

39. Kelber, *Oral and the Written Gospel*, 198.

40. Homer, *Iliad*, 1.1–9.

41. Kelber, *Oral and the Written Gospel*, 193.

42. Ibid., 186–87.

apophthegms. The narrative remains episodic; it does not flow the way Luke's narrative does. Its episodic character is certainly possible orally.

A second argument for scribality is that Mark's Passion Narrative is filled with allusions to the Psalms. From our print perspective, the inclusion of the Psalm allusions suggests scribal activity. Yet their inclusion could also be oral. These psalms dealing with the suffering of the righteous could well have been part of the oral or little tradition, and thus available to an oral performer.[43] In the ancient media world, the gospel was likely to have been oral, written, recycled into orality, rewritten, and so on.[44] So another possibility is that scribes in the process of transmission have clarified and extended allusions to the Psalms. Neither the narrative style of Mark 14–16 nor the allusions to the Psalms require writing; the Passion Narrative is within the realm of oral composition.

Kelber argues that the Passion Narrative needs the distance of writing in order to understand Jesus's death as salvific. He sees a real shift in Christology from the oral tradition to the Gospel of Mark. In the oral tradition, "Jesus is a wholly unambiguous figure who cures diseases and conquers evil spirits. The terrifyingly ambiguous notion that the protagonist must first be crushed himself for evil to be conquered lies outside the mental horizon of this oral christology of heroism and polarization."[45] Yet I question whether the Gospel of Mark actually presents Jesus's death as the conquering of evil. In Mark 1:12–13 Jesus overcomes Satan (evil) in the wilderness, and in 2:1–12 he forgives sins. Neither act depends on Jesus's death. Mark's emphasis on Jesus's death in the narrative is simply that it is according to the will of God. In addition to Mark's placement of the crucifixion in the tradition of the persecution of prophets and the death of innocent righteous ones, the signs of darkness and the rending of the temple curtain, the phrasing of the Passion-Resurrection traditions, and the allusion to Scripture ("For the Son of Humanity goes as is written of him") all affirm Jesus's death as God's will.[46] Given first-century understandings of the role of gods in human affairs, if the death of Jesus were not according to God's will, it would be according to some other god or goddess's will, in which case the gospel would not be good news. The Gospel of Mark shows Jesus's death as consistent with God's will. The Gospel is *not* concerned to interpret *how* it is

---

43. See Horsley and Draper, *Whoever Hears You*, 98–104.

44. Parker, *Living Text*, 19, 179.

45. Kelber, *Oral and the Written Gospel*, 55.

46. See Mark 15:33, 38; 8:31; 9:31; 10:33; and 14:21.

God's will. It simply places Jesus's death in the long-standing tradition of the persecution of the prophets and the suffering of righteous ones.

In fact, the Gospel does not include much reflection on the significance of Jesus's death in particular. A full discussion of the two passages where modern critics read a saving death into Mark's gospel is beyond the scope of this article. Briefly, the combination of body and blood at the Last Supper suggests martyrdom—which fits in with the persecution of the prophets—and not sacrifice.[47] The saying in Mark 10:45, "For the Son of Humanity came not to be served but to serve, and to give his life as a ransom for many," has come to be understood as atonement in later theological interpretation. In its own narrative context, however, it is a continuation of Jesus's life of service. Jesus's entire life and death are a model of service.[48] Theological reflection on the meaning of Jesus's death might well be facilitated by the distance that writing provides, as Kelber argues. But Mark generally eschews such theological interpretation in favor of repeated assurances *that* Jesus's death is according to God's will. This seems to me well within the possibilities of oral narrative.

In order to understand Mark's Christology and his treatment of Jesus's death, it is important to hear his story through the *both-and* hermeneutic characteristic of oral narrative, rather than reading it according to print standards of linear construction. The Gospel fits oral narrative style: it is additive and aggregative, episode piled upon episode.[49] In such narrative, new information does not negate earlier information; it is added to it. As Kelber himself notes, oral plots are cumulative and additive, so that "knowledge is gathered and multiplied more than critically developed."[50] This applies well to the Gospel of Mark, composed with oral compositional methods and heard orally. But if we read Mark's narrative according to norms of modern print, then we use an either/or rather than a both-and hermeneutic. Within this framework, the emphasis on persecution and death in the second half of the Gospel appears to call into question the hermeneutic of life in the healings, sea crossings, and feedings found in the first half. Heard with oral hermeneutics, persecution—suffering and death—is *added to* the good news of the kingdom; it does not replace it. In Mark's narrative, most normal human suffering is in fact overcome, with the healings,

---

47. Mark 14:22–25; see Mack, *Myth of Innocence*, 118.
48. Dowd and Malbon, "Significance of Jesus' Death."
49. Ong, *Orality and Literacy*, 36–41, 158; see chapter 5, above.
50. Kelber, *Oral and the Written Gospel*, 80.

feedings, forgiveness, and the new community of God's kingdom. What is added, however, is that those who join the kingdom on earth not only will experience the blessings of the kingdom now but will also be persecuted by the powers of this age as long as this age continues. The oral/aural logic is thus both-and: *both* miracles, which are to be prayed for confidently, *and* persecution, which is to be expected.[51]

Because of its episodic character, oral narrative can tolerate greater inconsistency than linear, print narrative—it can sustain the logic of both-and. Thus, contra Kelber, I contend that in Mark the heroic Christology of the miracles can coexist comfortably alongside the emphases on Jesus's death and the coming persecution of the disciples. Indeed, I suggest that for early Christian community formation, cultural memory (even prior to the composition of Mark) would require both the heroic Jesus and some understanding of Jesus's execution. No matter how much Christians emphasized that Jesus is alive, they could not simply ignore his crucifixion. The portrayal of Jesus's death does not, in my opinion, require scribality, nor does it make the written gospel a counterform to the living oral tradition.

Absence and Presence

Kelber also stresses Jesus's absence at the end of Mark, in contrast to Jesus's continuing presence. In the gospel, Jesus was present in his earthly life and will be present again when the Son of Humanity returns. Jesus is a figure of the past and the future but not of the present. Logically, Kelber is correct here. While Jesus is not left dead in the tomb (the gospel clearly affirms resurrection), he is also not immediately present to the hearer.[52] But I wonder if this absence would seem more than momentary for those first-century audiences who heard the story. The expectation is that Jesus will return soon: "Truly I tell you, there are some standing here who will not taste death until they see that the kingdom of God has come with power."[53] In Mark 13, Jesus also instructs the audience to keep alert because no one knows the day or hour.[54] In both 14:28 and 16:7, the disciples, the women, *and* listening audiences are told to go to Galilee where they will see Jesus.[55]

51. Mark 11:22–25 and 13:9–11; see chapter 6, above.

52. On the affirmation of resurrection, see Kelber, "Case of the Gospels," 77.

53. Mark 9:1; see also 13:30.

54. This happens three times: in verses 32, 33, and 37.

55. It is not clear to me whether these passages are meant to refer to resurrection

They/we are told to return to the place of the in-breaking of the kingdom of God, the place of the miracles, the healings and feedings. The end is at hand; persecution and death are not the end of the story; the good news of God's kingdom, including the presence of Jesus, will continue in Galilee.

Kelber interprets the gospel's lack of resurrection stories as a deliberate stress on Jesus's absence.[56] Once again, I suggest (as have others) that there are good narrative reasons for omitting resurrection appearances.[57] The narrative is encouraging the audience throughout to be faithful followers. The abrupt ending of the gospel implicitly exhorts the audience to continue following Jesus. As the women have replaced the disciples as followers in the narrative itself, so now the listening audience replaces the women. Any resurrection appearance would dilute the appeal to the audience. This ending would be particularly effective in performance, where the performer is interacting directly with a live audience. In a written narrative, particularly one that is read silently and not heard, there is greater distance between the text and the reader, and an ending that brings closure to the narrative becomes more desirable—as the longer endings testify.[58] For listening audiences, narrative reasons seem fully adequate to explain the lack of resurrection appearances.

Kelber is correct that in the Gospel of Mark Jesus is a figure of the narrator's and audience's past and projected future, and not of their present. In the first century or two after its composition, however, the Gospel was performed orally. This would be true whether the Gospel was originally composed orally or in writing. All ancient literature was designed for oral performance, and would be composed with a listening audience in mind. The Gospel of Mark, with its oral style, is easy to remember and perform orally. In fact, I have argued that Mark's gospel survived to become part of the four-Gospel canon precisely because it was a good story and widely performed orally.[59] If early Christian communities had relied primarily on writings for transmission of the tradition, and not oral communication, then the Gospel of Matthew would likely have completely replaced the

---

appearances or to the *parousia*, or perhaps simply to a return to the place of the in-breaking of God's kingdom. It is interesting to note that no titles are used in these prophecies. "Son of Humanity," used elsewhere both in the context of resurrection and of *parousia*, is notably absent.

56. Kelber, *Oral and the Written Gospel*, 100–101; Kelber, "Case of the Gospels," 77.

57. See J. Dewey, "The Gospel of Mark."

58. See chapter 6, above.

59. See chapter 10, below.

Gospel of Mark. There would have been little reason to recopy Mark, and it likely would have been lost as Q was lost. In fact, Augustine considered the Gospel of Mark merely an abbreviation of Matthew, and his view prevailed for centuries.

In oral performance, however, the gospel and Jesus come alive. Kelber wrote, "The challenge for the storyteller is not to contemplate Jesus with theological acumen, nor to restore his historical actuality, but rather to make him live in the imagination of the audience."[60] Kelber wrote this about the exorcism stories, but his observation applies well to the Gospel of Mark as a whole. Jesus comes alive in oral performance in the immediacy of the narrative. Jesus is present in the telling to the community. A prophet speaks in the name of Jesus; a narrative provides a different way of making Jesus present, a way that makes audiences feel as if they were there at the very events. As John Miles Foley has said, "When you voice a text, wherever and whenever you do, you cause it to live and to mean by being present; when you perform within a community, you bind the community together in a shared experience that far supersedes the authority of any artifact. That is the inimitable power of voice—to give presence, literally to 'em-body.'"[61] The experience of listening to the Gospel of Mark is not an experience of Jesus's absence but of Jesus alive and present.

The Effects of Writing

Whether composed in performance, by dictation, or in writing, the Gospel of Mark was composed in an oral style and performed orally. The Gospel remains fundamentally on the oral side of the oral/written divide. It is best understood using oral hermeneutics. In performance, the Gospel is not perceived as discrediting oral authorities, as lacking sayings, or as replacing the heroic Jesus with a suffering and dying savior. Rather, it is heard and experienced as making Jesus alive and present—both the Jesus of the miracles and the Jesus who is persecuted and executed. The Gospel, however, was surely written down relatively quickly. And then retold. And then rewritten. And so forth. This was characteristic of the oral and written media mix of the first centuries. The Gospel of Mark was likely adapted to audiences in each oral performance, and modified in each rewriting. Kelber has argued

60. Kelber, *Oral and the Written Gospel*, 55.
61. J. M. Foley, "Riddle of Q," 139.

persuasively that we should not speak of original Jesus sayings;[62] I suggest that perhaps we should not speak of the original Gospel of Mark, either.

What difference, then, does the existence of manuscripts make? Over time, over decades or centuries, the written forms gradually exert control over oral versions. This can be observed in the sixteenth-century English ballad tradition: oral versions deviated more and more from the printed text, and then returned to the printed versions as broadsheets were reissued.[63] The same trend can be observed in the northern European fairy-tale tradition. The first written (printed) versions of the northern European fairy tales were a counterform to the oral stories, taming the active and often magical roles of women and girls to make them more passive, obedient figures.[64] For these materials, we can compare the first printed versions of Perrault in 1667 and the Grimm brothers in 1812 with oral versions of the stories collected from women storytellers again in the early twentieth century. These oral versions have not yet been affected by the printed texts. The women and girls remain active agents, often with magical powers. However, with the growth of mass literacy and cheap books, it is now the printed versions that mothers tell their children today. The counterform eventually has triumphed.

The manuscript and printed gospels, which made Jesus primarily a figure of the past and indefinite future, have indeed largely triumphed over the living, speaking Jesus. The New Testament writings have ultimately silenced and largely controlled the speaking of the present, living Jesus. Here I am in fundamental agreement with Kelber. But this was a process of centuries, not of the initial composition of New Testament texts, as he proposes for Mark. The Gospel of Mark was composed and performed in an oral style to bring Jesus and the kingdom of God alive for listening audiences. The gospel was *not* a radical written counterform to oral memory. It was not trying to silence and control the oral tradition. But over time, as the manuscript and then print media triumphed and the New Testament became a sacred book, Jesus has become a figure of the past, whose death was redemptive. The written texts have in due course triumphed over the living tradition.

62. Kelber, "Jesus and Tradition."
63. Finnegan, *Oral Poetry*, 162–63.
64. See Lurie, *Don't Tell the Grown-Ups*; also chapter 8, below.

PART 3

Wider Implications of the Oral Media World

8

From Storytelling to Written Text

The Loss of Early Christian Women's Voices

STORIES HAVE POWER. STORIES are important in determining how we understand ourselves and live our lives. "We know ourselves," writes literary critic Leslie Marmon Silko, "by the stories we tell about ourselves."[1] The narrator in a recent short story by Pam Houston talks "about the way we invent ourselves through our stories, and in a similar way, how the stories we tell put walls around our lives."[2] The stories of the New Testament have helped to form Christian women's lives—both to empower them and to limit and restrict them. It matters who tells the stories (and who hears); it matters what stories are told; it matters who chooses the stories that are to be told.

The ancients were well aware of the power of storytelling, and at least some literate males were aware of the dangers of women's storytelling. Two quotations will illustrate this. The first quotation is from the fourth century BCE, from Plato's vision of utopia, *The Republic*: "We must begin, then, it seems, by a censorship over our storymakers, and what they do well we must pass and what not, reject. And the stories on the accepted list we will induce nurses and mothers to tell to the children and so shape their souls by these stories far rather than their bodies by their hands. But most of the

---

1. Long, "Writing for Our Lives," 3.
2. Houston, "How to Talk to a Hunter," 20.

stories they now tell we must reject."[3] The second is a composite quotation from the early second-century Christian author of the Pastoral Epistles: "Have nothing to do with the godless tales of old women . . . They [widows] learn to be idle, gadding about from house to house; and they are not merely idle, but also gossips and busybodies, saying what they should not say . . ." (1 Tim 4:7, author's translation; 5:13, NRSV).

One of the stories Plato and the author of the Pastoral Epistles might have wished to suppress is the story of the Syrophoenician woman (Mark 7:24–34; cf. Matt 15:21–28). I begin by retelling this familiar story as I imagine some woman in antiquity might have told it. For most people then did not read stories, nor did they have stories read to them. Rather they told stories, and heard them, and retold them, and made them their own. I invite you to imagine that you are listening to this story being told.

Imagine that you are living in a small coastal fishing village, say, on the coast of Asia Minor, just outside Ephesus, some time towards the end of the first century. It's late in the day; it's a warm, balmy evening. You have finished your day's labor; you women have cooked and cared for the children. The poorer ones among you—and that is most of you— have returned from working in the houses of the wealthy in the nearby city, cooking, cleaning, and caring for other people's children. You have returned to feed the men who have come in from the fields and the fishing boats. And now, finally, your own families are fed.

It's not yet time for bed, and your homes are small and dark and stuffy, so you have gone out to gather in the village square. The men and the boys occupy most of the square, talking about whatever it is that men talk about when they are together; and the women and girls, and all the children under, say, nine or ten, are in one corner of the square, the women's corner near the path to the community baking ovens, gossiping about your day, about how hard you've worked, and about what the children have said and done. The women are oohing and aahing over Tatia's daughter, now nearly a week old, whom Tatia has brought out for the first time.

And Chloris and I walk into the square. We've walked over from our nearby village. I've come to visit my daughter, Tatia, and see my new grandchild. Pretty soon, the women and girls begin badgering me to tell them a story. There's not much to do in the evenings, no outside

3. Plato, *The Republic* IIC, I:177.

entertainment, no books. We don't know how to read; we don't need to. Only the village scribe knows how to write a bit, and even he fishes for a living. So that's why we tell stories, and good storytellers are in demand.

Now, I pride myself on my storytelling. Wherever I go, the women gather to hear me tell stories. I have a reputation throughout the whole region. People know me as Artemisia, the teller of tales. Tonight, the girls clamor, "Tell us the story of Jesus and that woman from Tyre! That Syrophoenician woman!"

Some of the men even creep over to the outskirts of our group to hear my story. Of course, men don't spend time chatting with women in public—they think it's shameful. But *I'm* a good storyteller, better than any *they* have tonight. Besides, Tatia's husband is very fond of me, and he's one of the chief men of the village; so, as he comes to listen, the other men—some of them, anyway—come over, too. Well, I begin my story.

I'm a Christian, you know, as some of you are, too. I'm a follower of the risen Jesus who's brought me freedom and joy in this life, and the promise of greater freedom to come. I love living in my new Christian community. But my story tonight isn't my story—you've probably heard that one often enough from me or Tatia. This one is an old story that women have been telling each other since the days of Jesus or from soon after. Indeed I heard the story from my friend Philé, who heard it from her aunt, who heard it from I don't know who. I don't know exactly how or even if this story really happened, but it's the story Philé told me.

It's Justa's story, the Syrophoenician woman from near Tyre. Now she had a daughter who was possessed by a demon, and she was desperate, what with wanting to help her daughter, and being worn out trying to protect her child and keep her behaving right. Hopeless! You can't control a demon! She heard that that popular Jewish healer, Jesus, was in the village. They say Jesus was trying to keep his presence hidden, he didn't want anyone to know he was there. Did he really think he could do that? All those strangers arriving in a village? News travels fast in a village, faster than my bread burns in the oven when I get to telling a story, which is fast enough. And Justa went into the house where Jesus was, and she begged Jesus to heal her daughter, to cast the demon out of her little girl.

And you know what Jesus said? He said, "Let the children first be fed, for it is not proper to take the children's bread and throw it to the dogs." Huh! Her child isn't even a child, she's just a dog, not worth feeding! *I* would have walked out then, I think—this man wasn't going to act as patron for someone he called a dog. But Justa didn't walk out. She turned to Jesus, politely called him sir, as we've all been taught to do, and told him, "Yes, we may only be dogs, but look, sir, the little dogs under the table get the children's crumbs." And Jesus—Jesus listened to her and agreed with her. He said, "For your word, for what you've said, you may go your way. The demon has left your daughter." And when Justa got home, she found her daughter whole. We, women, Christians, people who live in Asia Minor, we have a lot to thank that Syrophoenician woman for. She taught Jesus something—we are *all* people, not dogs; we *all* need food and healing. And Jesus believed her. He praised her word, what she said, her understanding. Indeed, he went on from that house in the region of Tyre to feed some four thousand Greeks, people like us, with plenty of food left over. Maybe we owe our whole, new, glorious life in Christ to Justa, to that woman who taught Jesus that even little Greek girls should be healed. And certainly she showed that women are to be listened to!

Some of the people in the crowd clamored for me to tell another story. One of the men in the back yelled for me to tell the story of the deaf man with the speech impediment, but I told him that's his story to tell, and that I'm going in with Tatia to put my new granddaughter to bed. And we go into the house, as the last of the light begins to fade outside in the square.

The story I have retold is one of the relatively few stories about women in the Gospels in comparison to the number of stories about men. It is one of even fewer in which women are portrayed in active influential roles. Most scholars today accept the foundational work of Elisabeth Schüssler Fiorenza and her claim that women played a far more prominent role in the Jesus movement and early Christianity than they do in the New Testament canon, that the stories about women are in fact the mere "tip of the iceberg," still visible in the text.[4] In this chapter, I argue that *one* major reason for the paucity of women's stories in the canon is that while early Christianity was an oral phenomenon in which women could participate relatively fully, the writing of Christian texts and their selection for inclusion in the canon was the work of the small minority of literates who were mostly men.

4. Schüssler Fiorenza, *In Memory of Her*; 41–64; Schüssler Fiorenza, "Feminist Critical Interpretation," 24.

A study of European folktales and their transformation from oral to print media shows, first, a substantial reduction in the relative quantity of stories featuring females as heroes in comparison to those featuring males; and, second, a reportrayal of the heroines who do survive from active agents in control of their lives to more passive recipients of male violence and protection.[5] There is evidence in the Gospels of a similar restriction of the role of women, which resulted in part from, and was strengthened by, the shift in media from oral transmission to manuscripts. I will begin by describing briefly the mixed oral-literate media world of the first century.

Literary and Orality in Antiquity

Plato generated manuscripts, and so did the author of the Pastoral Epistles, but the cultural world of first-century Christianity was largely an oral world. Technically speaking, the first-century media world was a manuscript culture with high residual orality.[6] But to define it that way is to define it from the perspective of the elite, those few who could read and write. Most people living during the first century lived in an oral culture that occasionally, and for specific, very limited purposes, made use of writing; and that writing, when it was done, was done by someone else. (The following description of literacy is heavily dependent on Harris.)[7]

First-century culture is thus oral beyond anything that middle-class Americans can conceive. Those using cross-cultural anthropological models of agrarian societies estimate overall literacy at about 2 to 4 percent.[8] William Harris, studying the available evidence from antiquity, suggests perhaps a high of 15 percent for males in cities.[9] Rates would be much higher in the cities than in the villages, and much higher among men than among women. The only group for which literacy was the norm was the upper class, that is, the rulers; the owners of large, landed estates; the leisured class—approximately the top 2 percent of the population.[10] There,

5. Dundes, *Little Red Riding Hood*; Lurie, *Don't Tell the Grown-Ups*; Zipes, *Trials & Tribulations*.

6. Ong, *Orality and Literacy*, 158.

7. See Harris, *Ancient Litearcy*; J. Dewey, "Textuality in Oral Culture," 39–47; Botha, "Greco-Roman Literacy."

8. Rohrbaugh, "Social Location," 115; Bar-Ilan, "Illiteracy," 56.

9. Harris, *Ancient Literacy*, 267; also see Rohrbaugh, "Pre-Industrial City," 133.

10. Harris, *Ancient Literacy*, 248–52.

literacy would have been normal for the men, and probably fairly common for the women.[11] Virtually all the extant texts from the ancient world come from members of this small, elite class, or from retainers dependent on them. Even the novels, the historical romances, were the light reading of this group, not more popular literature for a broader social class.[12] And it is precisely this group, the uppermost class, that was not represented among early Christians.[13]

For the rest of the population there was no public education. The Roman army and bureaucrats needed writing to administer the empire, and so they trained some slaves and freedmen. Those engaged in long-distance trade needed writing; Lydia, for example, if she was involved in an international luxury trade either was able herself to read and write or employed slaves and freedmen who could do so for her.[14] Letters were used to communicate over a distance—as Paul, for example, used them—but people could easily employ a scribe to write a letter or to read it to them.

Reading and/or writing were not necessary for daily life. Wills could be oral, though they often were written if enough wealth was involved. Only very large financial transactions would be put in writing. In today's terms, purchasing a house or a car would warrant going to this trouble, but not buying a refrigerator, let alone a new CD release. People did not need to acquire the skill themselves in order to cope with the occasional major purchase, will, or apprenticeship agreement. They could easily hire the local scribe to do it for them. Thus, being able to read or write was, for the huge majority, neither an economic nor a social advantage.

Furthermore, writing materials were expensive. Potsherds were most usual, or wax-covered clay tablets gathered in codices of about ten; only fifty words or so would fit on each side of such a tablet, which made them bulky, awkward, and useless for texts of any length. Papyrus and parchment were heavily used by the elite but were exorbitantly expensive for everybody else. One estimate suggests that even in Egypt, where these materials were cheapest, a single sheet would sell for thirty to thirty-five dollars in 1988 prices.[15]

11. Ibid., 252; contra Veyne, "Roman Empire," 20.

12. Harris, *Ancient Literacy*, 227–28.

13. Meeks, *First Urban Christians*, 51–53, 73.

14. Cf. Schottroff, *Let the Oppressed Go Free*, 65.

15. Harris, *Ancient Literature*, 194–95.

Basically, then, life was conducted orally. Early Christianity was a largely oral phenomenon in a mostly oral world.[16] In such a world, official information was broadcast by public criers, but even more, knowledge was transmitted by storytellers.[17] Only a little information is available about popular nonliterate storytellers, since those who wrote manuscripts tended to ignore them.[18] Basically three groups of popular storytellers are found in antiquity: street performers, who traveled about eking out a very marginal existence; a somewhat higher-status group, who told religious and secular stories outside temples and synagogues, entertaining and teaching people; and, finally, those who did not make their living at it, but who were known in their village, town, or region as good tellers of tales.[19] Some Christian teachers and preachers may have been viewed similarly to those who told stories outside religious buildings; some were certainly among those who did not make their living performing but who were known locally or regionally, telling stories in the workplace, at meals, while traveling, or to their neighbors in the evening. Much storytelling would occur in gender-segregated groups, but much also would occur in mixed settings, whether at the workplace or in the household.

I imagined Artemesia as such a local or regional storyteller. Such storytellers were often women. There are many references in antiquity to "old women's tales" or "old wives' tales."[20] There are references to nursemaids, who were servants or slaves in the houses of the elite, and who told stories to frighten the children in their charge into obedience, or to lull them to sleep.[21] Plato, in the opening quotation, speaks of mothers telling stories to their children. Popular storytelling was associated in this way with the world of women and children.

Certainly there were Christian women storytellers. Modern folklorists have found women oral performers in all cultures, though they may perform in different settings and specialize in different genres than men

---

16. Kelber, *Oral and the Written Gospel*.

17. Sjoberg, *Preindustrial City*, 289.

18. The rhapsodes who recited Homer at this time constituted a literate craft (Harris, *Ancient Literacy* 82).

19. Scobie, "Storytellers"; Ward, "Pauline Voice"; J. Dewey, "Textuality in Oral Culture," 45–47.

20. D. R. MacDonald, *Legend and the Apostle*, 13, etc.

21. Scobie, "Storytellers," 244–51.

do.[22] Furthermore, the traditions about women found in early Christian literature suggest dependence on women's storytelling traditions: the stories of the woman with the hemorrhage and the Syrophoenician woman,[23] the women connected with the resurrection narratives,[24] and the women of the Apocryphal *Acts*.[25] The world of early Christianity was a world of oral communication in which women were full participants as active proclaimers and storytellers as well as receptive listeners.

Oral vs. Manuscript Media: Access to Authority

Christianity began as a predominately oral movement: not only was it transmitted and communicated orally, but it appealed to oral authority, to what someone had said, or to what some were saying, and not to some written document. Orally based authority is inherently democratic or egalitarian, that is, the opportunity to gain oral authority is open to most people. Everyone—almost—can speak, and good speaking requires skill, practice, and experience, but not formal education. Jesus himself is perhaps our prime example. Of course, an illiterate, uneducated woman could not compete in highly technical rhetorical contests associated with the games; but she could and apparently did gain authority in local congregations through her speech (1 Corinthians; Rom 16; Acts 18). In Christian communities of either mixed but non-elite status[26] or predominately low social status,[27] the voices of women had the opportunity to be heard and to gain authority along with the voices of men. Everyone had some access to oral authority, regardless of race, class, or gender.

Manuscript-based authority, on the other hand, tends to be very elitist. In manuscript cultures only a few are literate. Access to manuscripts and their contents requires formal education and money, both of which were limited to the few upper-class males and their retainers in a patriarchal culture such as the Roman empire. To control the most advanced media of one's day is to hold power in a society. In this day of electronic

22. Mills, personal communication.

23. D. R. MacDonald, *Legend and the Apostle*.

24. Schüssler Fiorenza, *In Memory of Her*, 121–25.

25. D. R. MacDonald, *Legend and the Apostle*; Burrus, "Chastity as Autonomy"; J. Dewey, "1 Timothy," "2 Timothy," "Titus."

26. Meeks, *First Urban Christians*.

27. Schottroff, *Lydia's Impatient Sisters*.

communications media, those who control television have power over the rest of us; in a day when the most advanced medium of communication was manuscript, those who could read and write had power over those who could not. In *Tristes Tropiques*, Lévi-Strauss wrote:

> The only phenomenon with which writing has always been con-comitant is the creation of cities and empires, that is, the integra-tion of large numbers of individuals into a political system, and their grading into castes or classes . . . it seems to have favoured the exploitation of human beings rather than their enlightenment . . . My hypothesis, if correct, would oblige us to recognize the fact that the primary function of written communication is to facilitate slavery.[28]

His viewpoint may be extreme; and perhaps print, as distinct from manuscript, in times and places of near-universal literacy may be more democratic, because it is at least cheaper. Yet the Roman empire used writing, and relied on manuscripts, in its establishment of the most totalitarian rule the West had known until that time. And Christianity, on the other hand, lived its liberating message for many years without written authority.

As long as Christianity was based on oral authority, as it was in the early urban churches, and as it remained well into the second century, full participation and leadership was open to all, regardless of class and gender. Then, as the new faith increasingly appealed to the authority of manuscripts, its leadership also became increasingly restricted to those with education, that is, to a small, male elite, to free men, to heads of house-holds, to those of the same class and gender as most of the authors of the Christian manuscripts that eventually constituted the New Testament. As long as Christianity remained orally based, women both had their own oral traditions and also were important contributors to the common or "great" tradition to which both male and female community members had access. Women's oral traditions did not end as Christian authority gradually became manuscript based. Women continued to tell and hear stories, for they, and most men also, continued to live in a largely oral media world into the modern period.

Two things, however, did happen as manuscripts proliferated and gained authority. First, the role of women was minimized and distorted as oral traditions were written down by the few relatively high-status literate men. Second, the content of oral stories, of the women's stories, was

---

28. Quoted in Harris, *Ancient Literacy*, 38.

determined less and less by their own memories and traditions, and more and more by what circulated back into oral telling from the new, increasingly authoritative manuscript tradition. These processes have been observed in modern cultures in the transformation of oral traditions to the print medium.

Before I turn to the evidence from modern culture, two caveats need to be made. In the first place, while most writers were male, there were some female writers in antiquity.[29] A few have even suggested some New Testament texts were authored by women. In 1900, Adolf von Harnack suggested that Priscilla wrote Hebrews.[30] More recently, it has been suggested that Mark could have been composed by a woman,[31] and that the Apocryphal *Acts* reflect women's writing.[32] I find these claims for Christian women's authorship very doubtful, given the portrayal of women in these texts. But there were some literate women. In the second place, the shift to primary reliance on manuscripts is not the sole reason for the increasing marginalization of women during the first centuries of Christianity. But it is an important factor; it reinforced other factors such as the growing institutionalization of the church with its increasing conformity to dominant cultural norms, and the gradual move from the private sphere of the household to a more public arena. Furthermore, it is an important factor in its own right, having a fundamental impact on the canonical portrayal of women.

Evidence from European Folktales

Although we cannot compare the oral versions of early Christian stories with the ancient manuscript versions of the same stories, we can draw conclusions from what happened to more modern oral stories as they moved from oral to print media. In the case of northern European folktales, collected primarily from women and edited and printed by men, we have a chance to compare the earliest print versions of Charles Perrault and of Jacob and Wilhelm Grimm with the still-living oral traditions collected by the folklorist Paul Delarue in the early twentieth century. We see in

29. Cole, "Greek Women"; Snyder, *Woman and the Lyre*; Kraemer, "Women's Authorship"; Lefkowitz, "Did Ancient Women Write Novels?"

30. D'Angelo, "Hebrews," 364–65.

31. Achtemeier, *Mark* (2nd ed.), 125.

32. Davies, *Revolt of the Widows*.

the folktale print versions a pattern of minimalization, trivialization, and distortion of the roles of female characters; we see the disappearance of women's independent initiative. We also find the printed versions gradually supplanting and controlling the oral stories that mothers are telling their children.

The story of Little Red Riding Hood provides a good example of the fate of female characters in print. The first written version was that of Charles Perrault in 1697.[33] The story ends with Little Red Riding Hood being eaten by the wolf, and a moral in verse reminding little girls not to talk to strangers: "One sees here that young children. / Especially young girls, / Pretty well brought-up, and gentle, / Should never listen to anyone who happens by."[34] The second version, that of the Grimms in 1812, is partly dependent on Perrault.[35] However, it ends with (male) huntsmen rescuing the little girl from the belly of the wolf.[36] Oral versions are different.[37] To begin with, they lack the red hat; more important, it is the girl who saves herself:

> Oh, Grandmother, those big ears that you have!
>
> All the better to hear with, my child!
>
> Oh, Grandmother, that big mouth you have!
>
> All the better to eat you with, my child!
>
> Oh, Grandmother, I need to go outside to relieve myself.
>
> Do it in the bed, my child.
>
> No, Grandmother, I want to go outside.
>
> All right, but don't stay long.
>
> The bzou [werewolf] tied a woolen thread to her foot and let her go out, and when the little girl was outside she tied the end of the string to a big plum tree in the yard. The bzou got impatient and said:
>
> Are you making cables?
>
> When he became aware that no one answered him, he jumped out of bed and saw that the little girl had escaped. He followed her, but he arrived at her house just at the moment she was safely inside.[38]

33. Zipes, *Trials & Tribulations*, 91–93.

34. Ibid., 93.

35. Dundes, *Little Red Riding Hood*, 7.

36. Zipes, *Trials & Tribulations*, 135–38.

37. Delarue, "Story of Grandmother."

38. Ibid., 16.

In the oral versions, the girl saves herself by her own ingenuity. In written versions, the little girl gets into trouble for playing and dallying on the way and is left either dead or needing to be rescued by a male authority figure; this is her punishment for having dared to play and disobey. In the oral version, the girl also gets into trouble, but she gets herself *out* of trouble by her own initiative and lives to tell the tale. The men editing it for print blatantly altered the story.

The example of Little Red Riding Hood is not atypical. The transmission of folktales since their first move into print also shows how women get left out, and how the printed versions affect oral memory. Alison Lurie, in her book *Don't Tell the Grown-Ups*, demonstrates that the handful of folktales we know today is not typical of the genre but is the result of the skewed selection and silent revision of what she names subversive texts. For example, in the Grimms' original *Children's and Household Tales* (1812), they printed all the tales they had collected, albeit in edited versions, to fit educated men's ideals for female behavior. Most had been collected from women. In the 1813 edition, 61 women and girl characters had magic powers, compared with only 21 men and boys—and most of the male characters with magic powers were dwarfs. But, in each subsequent edition of the Grimms' tales, the women were given less to do and less to say. By the late nineteenth century, literary men had, in effect, established a canon of the folktales they liked best, whose messages they approved—including for example Sleeping Beauty, but not the parallel story of the sleeping prince rescued by an active heroine. And it is these limited, printed versions of selected and revised tales that parents now read aloud to their children. The edited print versions have supplanted the oral traditions. The control of written tradition over oral memory can also be seen in the tradition of the sixteenth-century ballads. Oral versions would deviate from and then return to the texts of the printed broadsheets.[39] What was preserved in writing drastically influences what is remembered and told orally.[40]

Evidence from the Gospels

A survey of the gospel material suggests that similar processes of reducing the active role of women occurred in the writing of the Gospels. There are many ways of writing women out. Writers could simply forget most of

39. Finnegan, *Oral Poetry*, 162–63.
40. Lurie, *Don't Tell the Grown-Ups*, 16–28.

women's history and omit most of it from the manuscripts. In the synoptic tradition, for example, there are ten accounts of miracles happening to women (counting by the sex of the parent when the healing is of a child), as against a total of thirty-three miracles happening to men. Further, the stories concerning men are, on average, two to three verses longer than the stories concerning women, so that they take up more time in the telling and listening. Furthermore, in the miracles about women, the narrative portrays the women speaking less to Jesus, and Jesus less to them than in the men's stories. There is significantly less direct speech over all in the women's stories than in the men's.[41] The few women who do appear in miracle stories tend to lose their voices. As for the Gospel of John, which does have fully voiced women in other kinds of stories, there are no miracles at all happening to women. As men wrote the gospels, they selected, modified, and created material to include or omit. They tended to select the men's stories, which they may have known better, given that much storytelling may have occurred in gender-specific groups, such as among male leather workers or among female spinners. Even those miracle stories about women that the men did put into writing received less emphasis and less narrative development than the ones about men.

Not only are women's stories minimalized and trivialized, fundamental distortion and rewriting also occur in the gospels' transition from orality to writing as it did in the case of the folktales. In the Synoptics, besides the miracle stories, there is another group of seven stories, in thirteen versions, involving minor characters—stories such as the anointing stories, the great commandment, Zacchaeus, the widow's mite (Mark 10:17–22 and par.; 12:28–34 and par.; 12:41–44 and par.; 14:3–9 and par.; Luke 7:36–50; 10:38–42; 19:1–10). In this group, *more than half* (four of the seven) involve women. This suggests that the predominance of miracle stories involving males reflects male bias rather than just a preponderance of miracle stories about males in the oral tradition. But something strange has happened to the way these stories are presented. In these narratives (but not in the three involving men), the women *act* but they do not *speak*. Rather, what happens is that men, Jesus and others, sit around and talk to each other about what the women are doing.[42] The most striking example is the narrative picture of a woman weeping over Jesus's feet and drying them with her hair, while the men continue with their dinner party, discussing

41. J. Dewey, "Women in the Synoptic Gospels."
42. Ibid.

her behavior with each other, although Luke's Jesus does eventually speak directly to the woman herself (Luke 7:36–50). The scenario is characteristic of this group of stories: what the women do becomes an example to instruct men; the women's actions have become occasions for male discourse. The manuscript tradition appears to have seriously minimized and distorted the roles of women around Jesus.

Concluding Remarks

Plato called for controlling the stories women told their children. The invention of manuscripts, and later of print, and the rise in the West of near-universal literacy has largely made this control a reality for stories in general, and for the early Christian women's stories in particular. We remember and retell the carefully selected and edited folktales of the printed collections. The limited portrayal of women in the New Testament continues to limit and deform the roles of Christian women today.

Yet we may be surprised to find as much material as we do in the Synoptics, coming from the women's traditions; it is a tribute to the importance of women at the very beginnings of the Christian churches that so much is still present. And women today are beginning to reclaim our stories—and our right to tell stories. There are an increasing number of feminist rewritings of Little Red Riding Hood (e.g., Carter, Gearhart).[43] Jack Zipes writes in concluding his study of this story's tradition, "However, the hope in the best of the more recent re-framings of the Red Riding Hood story . . . is that women do not have to reproduce the violence of men to change the rhetoric of violence."[44]

Similarly, Christian women are reclaiming our traditions and our right to interpret and develop them in our own way. We recognize not only that what we read in the New Testament is merely the tip of the iceberg, in terms of all the stories ever told by Christians, but also that what the written stories have preserved is skewed. Spaces begin to open up in which forgotten stories may be remembered, re-imagined and told again, and voices long unheard may once more exercise their authority to speak of Jesus and the life of the new community of faith.

43. See Carter, "Company of Wolves"; Gearhart, "Roja and Leopold."
44. Zipes, *Trials & Tribulations*, 381.

9

Women on the Way

A Reconstruction of Late First-Century Women's Storytelling

Introduction

For more than twenty years, I have been performing "Women on the Way" for classes, church groups, and worship services. It is a version of the Gospel of Mark as I imagine a late first-century Gentile woman might have told the story; it is Artemisia's rendition of traditions she has heard, going back to Ruth, a disciple of Jesus. Two scholarly concerns led me to develop this performance: first, the recognition of the oral media world and the importance of oral storytelling in the spread of early Christianity, and second, the need to integrate the feminist scholarship about the women around Jesus and in early Christianity into my teaching of the New Testament. So I decided to tell the plot of the Gospel of Mark concerning discipleship as a woman storyteller might have told it to Gentiles some seventy years after Easter. I use all my knowledge of oral storytelling techniques and of first-century women's lives to inform my story.

The first-century media world is described in other articles in this volume. Perhaps overall 5 percent of people were to some degree literate, higher in urban than rural areas and higher among men than among women. Except among the few elite males, nonliteracy was neither a shame nor an inconvenience. Information was conveyed orally, often shaped as stories, which are easy to remember. Women participated actively in story-telling, telling stories to children, to women, and to mixed groups of men and women.[1] So early followers of Jesus heard and told brief stories about Jesus and also heard and told lengthier narratives about his life and death. They did not read them or hear them read aloud from a manuscript. Even after the composition of the Gospel of Mark around 70 CE, the story was told and retold, often independently of any contact with a manuscript.[2] Today for us Scripture is a fixed, printed text. The way to give students a feel for story—for oral performance—as the basic medium of early Christianity is to model it, to *tell* a story. I wished to stress that this story was not in-tended as an eyewitness account but one shaped over decades of being told with variations to different audiences. Therefore, my storyteller is a woman I name Artemisia. She lives outside Ephesus on the coast of Asia Minor (modern day Turkey). She tells a story that has been passed on to her over time that goes back to Ruth, a story she calls the Gospel of Ruth.

We are not accustomed to thinking of women as disciples of Jesus or as early Christian leaders. That is because the New Testament, like most literature, is an androcentric text. Androcentrism is the mindset or attitude in which the male is understood as the human norm; the female is embed-ded in the male, which renders her secondary and generally invisible. She is considered a deviation from this human (male) norm and of inferior value. The female is only mentioned when she is a problem to the man, when she is very exceptional, or is otherwise necessary to the story.[3] Think of the story of the ten lepers: do you think of ten men or a mixed group? Or think of the two on the road to Emmaus: do you think of them as two men or, which is more probable, a husband and wife? Mark has composed an androcentric text: he only mentions the women disciples fifteen verses before the end of his narrative, because he now needs them as characters in his plot. At the arrest of Jesus, he has portrayed the male disciples all running away. So Mark now first mentions that there have been women accompanying Jesus all along in Galilee and on the way to Jerusalem. It is these women disciples who witness the crucifixion, observe the burial, and discover the empty tomb (Mark 15:40–41, 47; 16:1–8). After Peter's

---

1. See chapter 8, above.; Hearon, *The Mary Magdalene Tradition*.

2. See chapter 10, below.

3. This definition is based on the work of Elisabeth Schüssler Fiorenza. For more information about the women around Jesus and as early Christian leaders, see Schüssler Fiorenza, *In Memory of Her*, 105–241.

denial, the male disciples are not heard from again in Mark's narrative. In my performance, I attempt to remove the androcentric lens and portray the women as present throughout the story.

The New Testament provides abundant evidence of women around Jesus and of women as leaders in early Christian churches. Women are in Jesus's discipleship community throughout his ministry (Mark 15:40–41; Matt 27:55–56; Luke 8:1–3). In all four gospels, it is the women who discover the empty tomb. In Matthew and John, they are the first witnesses of the resurrection.[4] In the Gospel of John, it is Martha, not Peter, who first recognizes Jesus as the Christ (John 11:27).[5] Furthermore, women are among early Christian leaders.[6] Women are traveling missionaries and leaders of house churches. There is no title—*minister (deacon), apostle, co-worker*—that Paul applies to a man that he does not also apply to a woman.[7] Furthermore, in all of Paul's undisputed letters, of the forty leaders named, sixteen of them, or 40 percent, are women.

So Mark's first audiences and Christians through the first centuries of the Common Era would have known women as Christian leaders, and would have known stories about women and by women who followed Jesus. When they imagined the world of Jesus, they would have pictured women as well as men accompanying Jesus. So when they heard Mark's androcentric gospel, presenting only men as the inner core around Jesus until after the crucifixion, they likely would have placed Mark's story into their own picture of Jesus's world, and imagined women in the inner circles around Jesus. After centuries of only the androcentric gospels, we need to broaden our imaginations so that we can remember these women.

Of course, we have no oral stories from women that were recorded in writing in the New Testament. We can only imagine how women told stories in early Christianity. We do know, however, about storytelling and about the roles of women. What follows is how I imagine Artemisia in the late first century might have told the story about Jesus from the perspective of Jesus's disciple Ruth.

---

4. Mark has no resurrection appearances. In the longer ending added to Mark, women again are the first witnesses of the resurrection.

5. For other prominent women around Jesus, see also Mark 7:24–30; 14:3–9; Matt 26:6–13; John 4:1–42.

6. For details, see M. Y. MacDonald, "Reading Real Women," 199–220.

7. For Junia as an apostle, see Rom 16:7; also see Epp, *Junia: The First Woman Apostle*.

Script for Performance

Introduction of Artemisia to Contemporary Audience:

We welcome Artemisia here today. She is visiting us from Ephesus where she lived about seventy years after Jesus's execution in Jerusalem. She will tell us the story of Ruth. She heard the story from her aunt Philia, who heard it from her Jewish woman friend, who heard it from others, the tradition going all the way back to Ruth, a disciple of Jesus. Welcome.

Artemisia's Narrative

I invite you to imagine yourselves living in the last years of the first century. You are living in a small coastal fishing village, say, on the coast of Turkey, just outside Ephesus, sometime in the last years of the first century. It's late in the day; it's a warm, balmy evening.

You have finished your day's labor. You women have baked and cooked and cared for the children. The poorer among you—and that's most of you—have returned from working in the houses and fields of the wealthy on the nearby estates—cooking, cleaning, and caring for other people's children. You have returned to feed the men who have come in from the fishing boats, and from cleaning their nets, some from working as day laborers in nearby fields. And now, finally, you women have fed your families; the day's work is done.

It's not yet time for bed, and your homes are small and dark and stuffy, so you go out to gather in the village square. The men and the boys take up most of the square, talking about whatever it is that men talk about when they are together. And the women and girls, and all the children under say nine or ten, you are all crowded in one corner of the square, your corner, near the path to the community baking ovens, gossiping about the day, about how hard you've worked, and about what the children have done and said.

And Chloris and I walk into the square and join the women. We've walked over from the outskirts of Ephesus, where we live. I've come to visit my daughter, Tatia, and see my grandchildren.

Pretty soon, the women and girls begin badgering me to tell them a story. There's not much to do in the evenings, no outside entertainment. We don't know how to read; we don't need to. Only the village scribe knows how to read and write a bit and even he has to fish to earn enough to live. So that's why we tell stories, and good storytellers are in demand.

Now, I pride myself on my storytelling. Wherever I go, the women gather to hear me tell stories. I have a reputation throughout the whole region. People know me as Artemisia, the teller of tales. So tonight, in the village gathering, the girls clamor: tell us the gospel according to Ruth, tell us Ruth's story.

The men even creep over to the outskirts of our group to hear my story. Of course, men don't spend time chatting with women in public—they think it's shameful. But I'm a good storyteller, better than any they have tonight. Besides, Tatia's husband is very fond of me, and he's one of the chief men of the village. So, as he comes to listen, the other men—some of them anyway—come over too. Well, I began Ruth's story.

The beginning of the gospel of Jesus Christ, Son of God. Hannah and I were at our fish place in the village market on market day selling and bartering to whoever came by. And Jesus came into the village, proclaiming, "The realm of God has arrived. Turn and trust the good news"—he proclaimed God's realm, not Caesar's, not the kingdom of Rome. And we were watching, Hannah and I, as Jesus went down by the lake. Simon and Andrew were there cleaning their nets. And Jesus looked at them, and we could see he said something, and immediately Simon and Andrew got up and left their nets and followed him. They just left their nets. Some people from the neighboring boat came over and pulled their nets the rest of the way up on shore, but Simon and Andrew just left their nets and walked off with Jesus.

And immediately Jesus came past Hannah and me. And he looked at us, and he said, "Come after me and be fishers of people." So Hannah and I, we left our place and we followed after him. It was the end of the day, most of the fish were sold, but we just left our place, and accompanied him.

As soon as it was sundown, as soon as the Sabbath started, we all went to the synagogue assembly. Thaddeus, the man with the demon, he was there disrupting the worship again. I've always felt sorry for his family—they try to care for him, they try to keep him under control. But you can't control a demon. And Jesus, Jesus commanded the demon, he told it to SHUT UP. And the demon came out of him, and Thaddeus was in his right mind. We've never seen anything like this!

And immediately we went to Martha's house, and Martha's mother was sick with a fever, and Jesus went to her, and took her hand and raised her up. And you know, she started ministering to us. And we began traveling through the villages. People kept crowding around Jesus, bringing their sick, and Jesus taught them and healed them all and cast out the demons. Sometimes scribes came and challenged him about what he was doing—healing on the Sabbath, or eating with tax collectors and sinners—but he always had a good comeback. I really love how he always has a quick retort. A little scary too, it can be risky to challenge the authorities. As we went through the villages, the crowds around Jesus got bigger and bigger.

Then Jesus chose some of us to be with him. Out of the huge crowds following, he named a group of us to be with him, to preach and to heal. He named Hannah and me and some other women; he named Simon Peter and Andrew and some of the men.

And immediately Jesus began to teach us. One day when we were indoors, Jesus's mother came with his brothers to fetch him, to take him home where he belonged. He didn't go. Rather he told us that whoever does the will of God is his mother, brother, and sister. He taught us, we are truly his relatives, his kin, we are a new family together.

And crowds followed us wherever we went. So one day Jesus got in a boat on the shore of the lake so he wouldn't get crushed by the crowd, and he taught them from the boat. He told parables, these little stories, about the seed and the sower, and all these types of soil; about the farmer who planted seed and waited and waited; and about the mustard seed that grew into a great big bush. And we asked them what the stories meant.

We asked him to explain them to us, and he told us, "To you has been given the mystery of God's realm," but then he said, "Why don't you understand this story? If you can't get this story, how will you understand all the other stories?" You know, sometimes I wish Jesus had a bit more patience, that he would explain things more, I heard James and John say the same thing. Indeed the men with us don't seem to understand any better than we do—sometimes I think they don't even get it as well.

And immediately Jesus had us get into the boat with him. Now, I don't like boats. To tell you the truth, I'm terrified of the water—I don't know how to swim. But we were all getting in the boat, so I got into the boat. And it was worse than I ever could have imagined. A storm came up, waves and wind, and we were being drenched with the spray. I was sure we'd all drown. And Jesus, Jesus was just sitting on a cushion at the back of the boat, asleep. How could he sleep through this? Even the fishermen were terrified. But there he was, sleeping through it. So we woke him up.

And you know what he did? He got up and told the wind and the sea to *shut up*, just as he had told the demon, and they did. Immediately the sea was calm, and the wind died right down. Who is this that even the wind and the sea obey him?

And we continued to go about the villages. And Jairus, the synagogue leader, came and begged Jesus to come and heal his daughter. We set off, all of us, a big crowd, after Jairus. And suddenly Jesus stopped and said, "Who touched me?" And we looked at him and said, "Who touched you? You're in the middle of this jostling, pushing crowd, and you want to know who touched you?" And Jesus said, " I felt power go out of me."

And Sarah came forward. Poor woman, she has been ill—bleeding—for twelve years. She must have slipped into the crowd—she hasn't come out in crowds much during all this time. We did visit with her some, but only when the men were away, because a few of the men think she's unclean because of the bleeding and can pollute them before God. Now when the crowd saw it was Sarah, they drew back. But Jesus didn't, he didn't accuse her, as she knelt there trembling and telling her whole story. He called her "daughter" and said her trust had made her well. So Sarah again is one of us, out and about with us. We were delighted, though a few of the men seemed a bit uneasy with the way Jesus didn't care about those purity laws.

Then Jesus sent us out in pairs to preach and heal. Hannah and I went together. We went out and we proclaimed that the realm of God is here, and we healed, we cast out demons. God has given us too these powers to bring God's realm on earth.

Then there was this feeding of thousands. Jesus had been teaching this enormous group of people, and we urged him to dismiss the crowd to go buy food. And he turned and told us to feed them. And we said, "Feed them? Do you want us to go and spend thousands to buy food for all these people?" I admit I couldn't believe what Jesus said. And Jesus said to feed them, "See what food you have." So we gathered what we could find and we found a few loaves of bread and a couple of fish.

Now Hannah and I, we've stretched food. We're pretty good at it; we've had to be. But nothing like this, nothing like this. We fed thousands, and we took up baskets of food left over. Jesus was right; gracious God provided us all with plenty to eat.

And then we got into the boat again. This time Jesus had sent us ahead, and the men were rowing hard across the lake, and this figure, this apparition, came walking on the water. We were terrified; we thought it was a ghost! And it was Jesus and he got into the boat with us. Who is this, who could walk on water?

A huge crowd gathered around Jesus again. Some scribes came down from Jerusalem to check Jesus out. They got debating with Jesus about the dietary laws, about washing pots, and he silenced them all, saying we could eat anything—that wasn't what was important. I love the way Jesus gets the best of these so-called authorities. But, you know, with all these crowds following Jesus, it makes me a bit nervous too. Authorities don't like this. This could get dangerous real fast.

And then Jesus took us to Gentile territory. This time we went to a village near Tyre and entered a house. Jesus was trying to keep himself hidden. He didn't want anyone to know he was there. Now I, Artemisia, I ask you, "Do you really think he could do that? All those strangers arriving in a village? News travels fast in a village.

Now back to Ruth's story: Ruth says a pagan woman entered the house and came in the middle of them. She begged Jesus to heal her daughter, to cast the demon out of her little girl. And you know what Jesus said? He said, "Let the children first be fed because it is not right to take the children's bread and throw it to the dogs!"

Huh! Her child isn't even a child, she's just a dog, not worth feeding! I, Artemisia, I would have walked out then and there—this man wasn't going to act as patron for someone he called a dog. But according to Ruth, they weren't surprised at Jesus's way of talking. After all, in her eyes, the woman was an unclean Gentile, and Jesus and all of them were Jews, the people of God. But the Syrophoenician woman didn't walk out, she turned to Jesus, politely called him sir, as we were all taught to do, and told him, "Yeah, we may only be dogs, but look, sir, the little dogs under the table get the children's crumbs."

And Jesus—Jesus agreed with her. He said, "For your word, for what you have said, you may go your way. The demon has left your daughter." And when the woman got home, she found her daughter healed and the demon gone.

And again Jesus asked us to feed a huge crowd—Gentiles this time. The men with us murmured a bit. As for us women, maybe we were murmuring too. Anyway, we started gathering food. Jesus blessed it and broke it and we distributed it and again a huge crowd was satisfied, and there was plenty left over.

And then we got into the boat again. I don't know which is worse—just being in the boat or what happens when we're in the boat. But at least this time nothing eerie happened. Instead we just got lectured. Jesus told us that *we* didn't understand, that *our* hearts were hardened. He asked, how many loaves did we feed the five thousand with? And we told him. And he asked how many baskets of food were left over, and we told him that. He asked, how many loaves did we feed the four thousand with? And we told him. And how many baskets were left over? And we told him that. Now Hannah and I don't need a lesson in counting. We run a fish business. If we couldn't count, we would long since have lost our choice place in the market to Miriam and her daughter. They've been coveting our spot for years. But I don't understand what Jesus is trying to tell us; he just says our hearts are hardened.

Then we went on a journey way up north. At least this was a land journey, and I didn't have to get into a boat. On the way, Jesus asked us, "Who do people say that I am?"

And we told him, "Elijah, one of the prophets of old, John the Baptist."

And then he said, "Who do *you* say that I am?"

And Peter jumped in and said "You are the Messiah!"

Do you suppose maybe he is? I do know Jesus is someone special with God.

And Jesus went right on to say, "It is necessary for the son of humanity to endure many things, be rejected, killed, and on the third day rise."

And Peter jumped right in again to correct Jesus. You never can get a word in ahead of Peter. You know, they say we women talk a lot, but we can't beat Peter. And Jesus turned to Peter, and called him Satan! But, you know, Peter had a point: why should Jesus who walks on water, who feeds thousands, and who can command demons—why should he be killed?

But Jesus didn't explain. Instead he told us it was to be our fate too. He called us and the whole crowd together and said, if we wanted to follow him, we had to turn away from our families, take up our crosses (that horrible and shameful means of execution the Romans use), and follow him. If we wanted to save our lives, we needed to lose them for his sake and the good news. But if we tried to save them, we would in fact lose them. I wish I understood Jesus better.

And again a little farther along—we were journeying south now—Jesus predicted that the son of humanity would be turned over to authorities, and they would kill him, and on the third day he would rise. The men with us, they were debating among themselves, which one of *them* was the greatest among us. Really! And Jesus knew what they were saying and rebuked them and told us all, "Whoever wants to be first among you must be least of all and servant of all." And to show what he meant, he picked up a child. As you know, these days, the child is one of the weakest, with the least power, the most downtrodden; I'm glad I'm not a child anymore. So Jesus picked up a little girl of about two. He picked her up and blessed her, and he said if we wanted to enter God's realm, we needed to be least like she was least.

And then as we were traveling along, a young man came to us—you could tell he was wealthy, not one of us, by his clothes. And he asked Jesus what he had to do to inherit eternal life. And after they talked awhile, Jesus told him "Go, sell what you have, give to the poor, and come follow me." And he went away sad; he couldn't do that.

And again Peter, Peter, asked the question: Peter said, "We've left everything and followed you." I'm glad Peter asked that. I'm not sure I would have dared after the rebuke Peter got, getting called Satan. And Jesus said, "Whoever has left houses and fathers and mothers and brothers and sisters and lands and fields for my sake and for the good news will gain again in this age mothers, sisters and brothers, fields and houses—with persecutions—and in the age to come, life of the age.

You know, he's right. We are like a family. I like this new community of which we are a part. And you notice what he didn't say: he didn't say there was a new father. We didn't get a new person to order us around, whom we women are taught it is always our duty to obey. We are indeed a group together, all with Jesus.

We were approaching Jerusalem now, with this enormous crowd of people ahead and following. And a third time Jesus predicted the son of humanity was going to endure many things, be rejected, crucified, and, on the third day, rise. By now, I'm afraid he really will be crucified. You couldn't expect to go into Jerusalem with a crowd like this and not get into trouble—unless, unless of course God's about to bring about the end of the age. You know, I've heard about all the troubles and woes, wars and famines, the birth pangs bringing in the new age, but I don't know that I like it.

And James and John are at it again. After Jesus predicted his execution and his rising, they went and asked him if they could have the seats of glory and power on his right and left in the age to come! And Jesus asked them, could they endure what he would endure; could they drink the cup he would drink, undergo the baptism he was going to undergo? I don't know if I could, but then I've borne five children, and I know what birth pangs are like. James and John said they could. But they didn't get those seats—Jesus didn't give them any reward.

He said to them, "Okay! If you are able to endure persecution, you will, but don't think it's any heroic suffering that'll get you a special reward in the new age."

And we went on into Jerusalem, and Jesus caused a big to-do in the temple. I thought Jesus would be arrested then and there, but he wasn't. We got out safely, and the next days he continued teaching everyone, besting all the authorities who tried to trap him in his speech.

And pretty soon Jesus instructed us to prepare the Passover meal, and we all ate with him, and it was really very, very sad. He told us this was his last meal with us—that he would not drink wine again until he drank it anew in the realm of God.

After dinner, we went out to the Mount of Olives. Jesus was praying, and he asked us to keep watch. But we were dozing and sleeping; it had been a big meal. Suddenly soldiers came and arrested Jesus. The men, the male disciples we've been traveling with, they all took off, they just fled, leaving us alone in the middle of the night with a bunch of soldiers. And there we were, Hannah and me and the other women. Now

Hannah said, "The men are in more danger. The soldiers were more likely to arrest them than us."

But I said to her, "True, but remember, they do crucify women too. Besides, you know what soldiers do to women out alone at night. That's not a very good idea either."

But we did get back safely to where we were staying. They must have been too busy dealing with Jesus.

The Romans crucified him the next day. We went out and watched Jesus die on the cross. Hannah and I and the other women, we went and watched. We stood a ways off. I could hardly see through my tears. I think Jesus saw us, I think he knew we were there, I think he was comforted.

And then after he cried out and died, we went and watched where they buried him. And the next morning very early, we went out to the tomb to prepare his body properly for burial, which we hadn't been able to do. And there was a young person at the tomb, someone in dazzling white, maybe an angel—he or maybe she, I don't know. The angel told us not to be afraid: Jesus had gone before us to Galilee, and to go tell Peter and the other men to go to Galilee, to the place where the realm of God began. There we will see him. We were terrified, we were awestruck. Just like the men had earlier, we now fled; we now ran away. We ran as fast as we could away from there, away. We were utterly overwhelmed. We didn't tell anyone anything. We were afraid.

Ruth said, "Every one of you has ears to hear; listen, for this is the good news of Jesus Christ." And as the daylight faded, Artemisia said to those gathered around her in the village square. "Here ends the gospel of Ruth."

Notes on Performing

The script is not meant to be read silently to oneself, as we read today. Nor is it meant to be read aloud to a group. It is meant to be performed orally from memory with lots of emotion and expression. I have not memorized the script; I am thoroughly familiar with it, and I compose it anew every time as I tell it, as ancient oral performers customarily did. There are always variations in my telling. I do use a "cheat sheet," a small two-by-six card, on which I have listed the various scenes in order. Thus, in telling, I can concentrate on the scene I am narrating, imagining it in my mind, and then glance at the sheet to check what comes next.

I encourage you to make the script your own and to tell it. Feel free to elaborate it, to ham it up, to modify it. I change my voice, I speed up the tempo, and slow it way down towards the end. Tell it as it feels right to you, and pass it on.

10

The Survival of Mark's Gospel

A Good Story?

EVER SINCE I BEGAN serious New Testament studies and learned about the hypothetical document Q, I have been intrigued by these questions: Why did the Gospel of Mark survive? Why did it not go the way of Q? Given Matthew's and Luke's incorporation of Mark, and given the nature of the manuscript medium, it ought to have gone the way of Q. Scholars who address the issue believe Matthew intended his gospel to replace Mark, and so probably did Luke. Recently, Graham Stanton has argued:

> When Matthew wrote his Gospel, he did not intend to supplement Mark: his incorporation of most of Mark's Gospel is surely an indication that he intended that his Gospel should replace Mark's, and that it should become *the* Gospel for Christians of his day. Similarly Luke. Luke's Preface should not be dismissed merely as the evangelist's way of honoring literary convention. There is little doubt that Luke expects that his more complete Gospel will displace his predecessors.[1]

If Matthew and Luke had had their way and replaced Mark, today we would be debating if a hypothetical Mark ever existed, and what exactly it

1. Stanton, "Fourfold Gospel"; so also Streeter, *Four Gospels*, 10; and Bauckham, "For Whom," 13. My argument in general may support Bauckham's thesis of the Gospels being composed for all Christians, not for specific communities. However, the Markan version could easily have been formulated first for a specific community, or more likely a specific sort of audience, and then spread quickly from there.

consisted of, and how many strata of development we could discern in it. Instead we have the Gospel of Mark. Why did Mark survive?

In this chapter, I would like to suggest that the Gospel of Mark survived because it was a good story, easily learned from hearing it and easily performed, thus easily transmitted orally.[2] These characteristics gave the gospel widespread popularity. The gospel itself, I argue, was a development and refinement of an already well-known narrative or narrative framework of Jesus's ministry, death, and resurrection. Even after it was committed to writing around 70 CE, it continued to be performed and re-performed orally, with minimal dependence on or even any connection to manuscripts. In the process of being told and retold orally during the first century or two of Christianity, it became widely known orally to Christians in diverse parts of the empire. I would argue that the reason it has survived to be part of our canon today rather than going the way of Q is because of early orthodox Christians' choice around 150–175 CE to give authority neither to a single gospel nor to a harmonization of the gospels, but to the fourfold gospel.[3] Furthermore, I suggest that it was only because the Gospel of Mark was a popular story, widely known orally, that it survived at all, and that we have a fourfold instead of a threefold gospel today.

The customary explanations for the survival of the Gospel of Mark have largely been discarded today. Papias's observation that Mark was Peter's interpreter, while quite widespread in the second century, is rejected by many scholars today. The notion of a Roman provenance is also often rejected in favor of Syria or Galilee.[4] Furthermore, even if Papias were correct, that would not in itself account for the gospel's survival. In the second century some connection to an apostle, such as that provided by Papias, was probably necessary for the Gospel of Mark to be included in the fourfold gospel codex, but it would not be sufficient. Other gospels (*Peter, Thomas*) were in circulation and certainly had greater apparent claims to apostolicity. Early in the twentieth century, in part to explain the survival of Mark, B. H. Streeter developed his theory of local texts—that is, that each of the four gospels became well established in a particular geographical area before

---

2. Mark 13:14. "Let the reader understand" refers not to the reader of Mark's gospel but to the public reader of Daniel; so also Bultmann, "*anaginōskō, anagnōi.*"

3. On the fourfold gospel as a whole, see Stanton, "Fourfold Gospel," 317–46; Gamble, *New Testament Canon*, 24–35.

4. For the second-century evidence, see Black, *Apostolic Interpreter*, 77–113. For a contemporary summary of arguments against Peter and Rome as the place of origin, see Marcus, *Mark 1–8*, 21–37.

the other gospels became common there so that Mark was local to Rome. He wrote, "Again, the survival of Mark would be adequately explained if it had had time to become an established classic in one or more important churches some time before its popularity was threatened by competition with the richer Gospels produced in other centers."[5] The theory of local texts, however, has largely been abandoned by contemporary text critics as the manuscript and patristic evidence does not seem to support it.[6] A new explanation of Mark's survival and inclusion in the fourfold gospel codex is needed.

That explanation, I argue, is to be found in the oral/aural nature of the Gospel of Mark, a gospel that developed from an already-existing oral narrative or narrative framework of Jesus's ministry and passion, and that continued to circulate orally even after it was written down. The bulk of this chapter describes the types of evidence that suggest the likelihood that Mark was building on an already-existing narrative tradition. Then I make some further remarks on the gospel's continued oral life and engage in a foray into text criticism, since some aspects of the manuscript evidence seem to support the hypothesis that the ongoing oral transmission of the Gospel was important to its survival.

I shall begin with four preliminary comments: first on storytelling in antiquity, second on the interaction of oral and written media, and then two comments on Mark as oral literature. First, as we are becoming increasingly aware, literacy rates were generally very low in antiquity. Official information was broadcast by public criers who were attached to all levels of government. Even more, information and cultural traditions were transmitted by storytellers.[7] Four types of storytellers were common in antiquity: street performers of both sexes, who eked out a marginal existence; a somewhat higher-status group, who told religious and secular stories outside temples and inside and outside synagogues, entertaining and teaching; male and female storytellers who did not earn their living at it but had local or regional reputations; and finally, women—mothers or nursemaids—who told stories

---

5. Streeter, *Four Gospels*, 12.

6. Stanton, "Fourfold Gospel," 336. The Alands' handbook (Aland and Aland, *Text of the New Testament*) does not even mention the local-text theory. Metzger does include it in his handbook, along with some modifications, and notes in his 1992 appendix that the theory has been challenged and modified (Metzger, *Text of the New Testament*, 169–73; 287).

7. Sjoberg, *Preindustrial City*, 287.

to educate, amuse, or frighten children.[8] Christian storytellers would have been found among most of these groups. Stories such as Mark's would have been told both during and outside Christian worship settings. Performance of sacred stories was a major part of synagogue worship, so most likely it was also important in early Christian worship.[9] Storytelling was ubiquitous in the ancient world, so it would certainly have been part—an important part—of early Christian experience.

Second, writing was used in support of oral performance, and oral performance could and often did continue with little reliance on, or even acquaintance with, written texts. The British text critic D. C. Parker writes, "The gospels were written rather to support than to replace the oral tradition."[10] Furthermore, in such a media world, there is continual feedback between the oral and the written: Parker continues, "the written texts are only a part of the process by which the traditions about Jesus were passed on. The traditions were told and retold, written and rewritten, in oral tradition and in successive versions of texts."[11] I believe Mark was composed and transmitted primarily orally, but that does not exclude earlier and later written versions. The boundaries between the two were very fluid.

Third, the Gospel of Mark reflects a social milieu in which oral performance without any dependence on manuscripts was the norm. Richard Rohrbaugh has argued persuasively that Mark's audience consisted primarily of nonliterate peasants.[12] Richard Horsley, extending Rohrbaugh's argument and his own thesis that Mark gave voice to subjected peoples, suggests that the gospel's audiences continued to consist primarily "of ordinary Greek-speaking people in the eastern parts of the Roman empire, most likely villagers."[13] It seems quite likely that the gospel would appeal to village communities without the resources to own or read manuscripts, but this makes the Gospel's survival into the manuscript tradition even more improbable.

8. Scobie, "Storytellers," 229–59. This article remains the classic introduction to ancient storytelling. For a recent collection and analysis of the literary remains of storytelling in Greco-Roman texts, Jewish texts, and Christian texts, see Hearon, *Mary Magdalene Tradition*, 37–73, 320–36. For a new major resource on oral performance in antiquity, see Shiner, *Proclaiming the Gospel*.

9. Georgi, *Opponents of Paul*, 82, 86–101, 112–73. See also Ward, "Pauline Voice."

10. Parker, *Living Text*, 19.

11. Ibid., 179.

12. Rohrbaugh, "Social Location," 114–27.

13. Horsley, *Hearing the Whole Story*, 51.

Fourth, the Gospel of Mark works well as oral literature. It is of an appropriate length for oral performance. A storyteller could learn it from simply hearing it performed. As I and others have argued elsewhere, its composition consists of oral-composition techniques.[14] Briefly, the story consists of happenings that can be easily visualized and thus readily remembered. It consists of short episodes connected paratactically. The narrative is additive and aggregative.[15] Teaching is not gathered into discourses according to topic but rather embedded in short narratives, which is the way oral cultures remember teaching. Indeed, I would suggest that it is the lack of a more literate chronological and topical order that Papias had in mind when he said Mark's story was *ou mentoi taxei*—"not in order."[16] It followed oral ordering procedures, not proper rhetorical form.[17]

The plot as well as the style is typical of oral composition.[18] The structure does not build towards a linear climactic plot: the plot to kill Jesus is first introduced at Mark 3:6 but not picked up and developed until Mark 11, and does not really get underway until Mark 14. Rather than linear plot development, the structure consists of repetitive patterns, series of three parallel episodes, concentric structures, and chiastic structures. Such structures are characteristic of oral literature, helping the performer, the audience, and new performers and audiences remember and transmit the material. From what we know of oral literature, there is no reason why Mark's gospel could not have been composed and transmitted in oral form.

Thus it is certainly *possible*—I would say probable—that Mark was an orally composed narrative. As John Miles Foley, among others, has shown, it is possible to write in an oral register, and there is no foolproof way of deciding if a particular text was composed orally or in writing.[19] But there is no need for writing to create the Gospel of Mark.[20] Indeed, the distin-

---

14. See chapters 5 and 6, above; Botha, "Mark's Story"; and Botha, "Historical Setting."

15. For an overview of oral composition techniques, see Ong, *Orality and Literacy*, 36–49.

16. Eusebius, *Ecclesiastical History* 3.39.15.

17. This has also been suggested by Josef Kürzinger and Donald H. Juel. See Juel, *Master of Surprise*, 12–13.

18. Ong, *Orality and Literacy*, 141–43; see chapter 5, above.

19. J. M. Foley, *Immanent Art*; and J. M. Foley, *How to Read an Oral Poem*.

20. I used to believe the gospel had to be refined in writing—and it still seems probable—because of the verbal as well as structural parallels between Mark 2:1–12 and 3:1–6 at the beginning of the narrative, and the two trial scenes at the end. An oral performer can remember structures, but not necessarily verbal parallels widely separated in a

guished scholar of oral literature Albert B. Lord noted that the Synoptic Gospels seemed to him to "have the appearance of three oral traditional variants of the same narrative and non-narrative materials."[21] But whether or not Mark was composed orally, it was undoubtedly transmitted through oral re-performance.

While writing was not essential for the creation of Mark, tradition was. In order to compose orally or in writing in an oral register, the composer must be able to draw on a body of tradition. So I turn to the question of the nature of the tradition Mark had available to him. Form criticism has customarily assumed that the small episodic units to be discerned in the Synoptic Gospels were the individual units of oral tradition, and that Mark composed the Gospel from these bits and pieces of oral tradition and perhaps a short written source or two. All that we know or can infer about how tradition operates suggests that this assumption of form criticism is wrong, deriving more from the critics' own immersion in print culture than from how tradition operates. Studies from the fields of folklore, oral tradition, and oral history all suggest that traditions are likely to coalesce into a continuous narrative or narrative framework quite quickly.

Tradition generally is remembered by gathering stories around a hero (fictional or real), not by remembering disparate individual episodes. On the basis of his study of folklore, Thorleif Boman introduced to New Testament studies the thesis that traditions typically gathered into larger continuous narratives. He concluded that no narrative based on history ever emerged out of individual items that circulated for decades independently. Rather such a narrative grew gradually into a more comprehensive narrative about a person.[22] Jan Vansina, a student of African oral traditions and oral history, asserts that traditions "adhere to the 'great man,'"[23] coalescing into larger blocks of connected narratives about that person or persons. Walter Ong writes, "Most, if not all, oral cultures generate quite substantial

---

narrative. However, Whitney Shiner has suggested that the use of repeated gestures can help the performer remember particular details, even when composing in performance (Shiner, *Proclaiming the Gospel*, 139–40).

21. Lord, "Gospels as Oral Traditional Literature," 90.

22. Boman, *Jesus-Überlieferung*, 31. Both Boman and, more recently, Samuel Byrskog want to use orality to argue for greater historicity (Byrskog, *Story as History*). In my opinion, orality does not support historicity. However, both books' information on oral tradition is very helpful.

23. Vansina, *Oral Tradition*, 108.

narratives or series of narratives."[24] All agree *against* the form-critical assumption of transmission of disparate small episodes.

Thus, what we should expect from folklore, oral history, and oral literature studies is that early oral Christianity would develop a connected oral narrative about Jesus. Individuals undoubtedly would tell particular story episodes on particular occasions, but storytellers would soon combine them into longer sequences. One performance would build on another performance, in each case varying and adapting to the particular audience. And the continuous narrative would grow. This is the typical way tales are developed. Vansina writes, "Such tales develop during performance. They never are invented from scratch, but develop as various bits of older tales are combined, sequences altered or improvised . . . Unlike poetry and its sisters there is no moment at which a tale is composed. Innovation is only incremental from performance to performance."[25] Such is likely to have happened to the traditions about Jesus, much more likely than only the transmission of isolated episodes. Furthermore, not only the tellers but also the audiences need to become familiar with the new tale gradually if they are to follow it themselves: "The tale must be well known to the public if the performance is to be a success, for the audience must not be overly preoccupied with the task of trying to follow painstakingly what is being told in order to enjoy the tale."[26]

Vansina distinguishes between the traditions that audiences considered factual (accounts), and those they considered fictional (tales or epics). Once they are formed, accounts change less, but they still change according to the needs of the present. And accounts tend to coalesce and solidify fairly quickly. He writes:

> When accounts of events have been told for a generation or so the messages then current may still represent the tenor of the original message, but in most cases the resulting story has been fused out of several accounts and has acquired a stabilized form. The plot and sequence of episodes changes only gradually after this. Nevertheless, it will be impossible to discover what the inputs into such traditions have been, even soon after the events. So there is no

---

24. Ong, *Orality and Literacy*, 140.
25. Vansina, *Oral Tradition*, 12.
26. Ibid., 35.

question of reconstructing any original or even of assuming that there was but one original.[27]

Note that the plot and the general sequence of episodes become relatively stable quite quickly. Likely to have been available to Mark was precisely such an account with a plot and sequence of episodes that had developed over time.

Folklorists and students of oral literature also stress the importance of the individual performer and the influence he or she has on the performance.[28] John S. Mbiti writes about storytelling in Kenya:

> Each person will tell the same story differently, since he has to make it personal and not simply a mechanical repetition of what he has heard or narrated before. He becomes not only a 'repeater' but also a 'creative' originator of each story . . . The plot of the story and the sequence of its main parts remain the same, but the narrator has to supply meat to this skeleton. This he will do in the choice of words, the speed of reciting, the imagery he uses, the varying of his voice, the gestures . . . The narrator puts his personality into the story, thus making it uniquely his own creation.[29]

Mark (whoever he may have been) was a gifted storyteller and, using "the plot of the story and the sequence of its main parts," he made the narrative tradition or "account" of Jesus his own. His version, I suspect, fairly quickly got put into writing by his dictation or by someone else who had learned his version of the story. And it is Mark's version that became, if you will, the standard version that was told and retold to Christians—though always, of course, with variations.

Such a recounting of the emergence of the Gospel of Mark is, of course, speculative. But it accords much better with what we know about how folklore, oral literature, and oral accounts develop, and about how ancient manuscript culture functioned, than do biblical scholars' usual assumptions about form and redaction criticism. The Gospel of Mark itself, I believe, also provides evidence that it was not the first attempt to put the story of Jesus together into a coherent narrative. Once we get accustomed to the inelegant Greek, the very episodic nature of the story, and its non-linear, nonclimactic plot structure (all very typical of oral narrative or narrative written in an oral register), we discover that the gospel is a coherent,

27. Ibid.,17.

28. Finnegan, *Literacy and Orality*, 69–73.

29. Mbiti, *Akamba Stories*, 26. Quoted in Finnegan, *Literacy and Orality,* 69–70.

well-wrought narrative, and extremely well constructed. The literary work on the gospel in the last thirty years has well demonstrated this, and productive work in this area continues.[30] The Gospel of Mark continues to offer up narrative riches.

It seems to me extremely unlikely that the first attempt to put together a large variety of disparate bits and pieces of tradition would result in such an elegant story. Twenty-five years ago Leander Keck wrote, "Thus [Mark] is assumed to have achieved three things simultaneously: create a genre (pattern) without any precedent, gain acceptance for this genre among his public, and attack the belief-structure of this same public by means of the new creation. If this is true, the author of the Second Gospel must have been some first-century Merlin!"[31] It seems much more probable that Mark was building on, refining and developing an oral tradition that had already created a continuous, more-or-less coherent narrative.

So, probably around 70 CE, some version of what we know as the Gospel of Mark was put in writing. It would be possible to argue that there were no written texts of Mark until much later. We have no manuscript fragments of Mark until P[45], a papyrus codex of the four Gospels dated to the third century. However, it seems to me more probable that the text became relatively fixed around 70 CE. My argument would be based on the specific content of Mark, particularly the apparent connection to the Roman-Jewish War, and need not be detailed here. Furthermore, it is quite likely—although not absolutely necessary—that Matthew and Luke each had access to a written version of Mark. Unless somehow they used the same manuscript of Mark, their manuscripts of course would have had differences from each other.[32]

So next the question is how the Gospel of Mark was used and transmitted, now that it existed in writing as well as in oral narrative. First, I offer a comment about manuscript traditions in general: on the one hand, the existence of a text in writing helps to fix that text. Studies of ballads printed on broadsheets in the sixteenth century and in following centuries show that the ballads differed more and more from the printed version,

30. See Rhoads et al., *Mark as Story*, 2nd ed., and the authors cited there.

31. Keck, "Oral Traditional Literature," 120.

32. Helmut Koester has proposed that Matthew and Luke used an earlier version of Mark, and that what we have today is a later edition of Mark, thus explaining the minor agreements (*Ancient Christian Gospels*, 273–86). His thesis assumes a fixity of the manuscript tradition, and lack of interaction between oral and written versions, that is simply not characteristic of the manuscript culture in antiquity. See Parker, *Living Text*, 107–10.

until a new printing was made, at which point the ballad text reverted to closer to the printed version.[33] Such a process probably happened with Mark. It is unlikely we would have anything like our Gospel of Mark if it had not been preserved in manuscript form pretty early. The written version can and often does exert some control over the oral versions. On the other hand, we need to recognize that the manuscript tradition was *not yet* fixed. According to text critics, the greatest changes in texts occur in the first 100 or 150 years of manuscript transmission, after which texts tend to stabilize.[34] Furthermore, text critics indicate that "there are often as great, if not greater, variations between the manuscript copies of each Gospel" as there are between the different Synoptic Gospels.[35] There was not yet an authoritative text; no gospels were yet Scripture. The use of the papyrus codex "declared the Gospels to be neither sacred text nor high literature, but something both different and impermanent . . .We have seen that the first generations valued the oral tradition above written documents. The mean format of their Gospels makes them aids to those memories."[36]

So, then, what difference did the existence of manuscripts of Mark make to the use and transmission of the Gospel of Mark? I suspect very little. First of all, Mark was not yet Scripture. It is only when it becomes considered scripture that it gets broken up into small segments, which are then read aloud and commented upon in worship. This transition most likely did not occur before the second half of the second century at the earliest, about the same time as the development of the four-gospel codex. Until then, the gospel was likely performed and heard as a whole, and that pattern probably continued for decades or generations even after it began to be used in small sections for sermons. Furthermore it was likely to be *performed*, not read from a manuscript. Manuscript texts without spaces between words, paragraph breaks, or editing marks are very difficult to read—let alone in low-light conditions. To read a manuscript publicly, one would have to know already what it said. Professional orators performed without scripts; surely Christian storytellers did as well.

The more important reason for the continuation of oral performance of the whole of Mark is that the existence of manuscript texts does not in itself interrupt oral tradition and transmission. As Albert Lord remarked,

---

33. Finnegan, *Oral Poetry*, 161–64.

34. Koester, "Text of the Synoptic Gospels," 19; Parker, *Living Text*, 70.

35. Parker, *Living Text*, 197.

36. Ibid., 186.

oral literature is "not a phase but a genre."[37] Eusebius reports that "Mark was the first to be sent to preach in Egypt the Gospel which he had also put into writing."[38] Regardless of the historical accuracy of his reference to Mark, Eusebius's report does stress the importance of the person telling the story. A storyteller, *not* a manuscript, was sent. There is no reason for oral transmission—that is, recomposition in performance—to stop just because a written version exists. The traditional European fairy tales were written down—printed—by Charles Perrault at the end of the 1600s, and by the Grimm brothers in the early 1800s. Yet the oral tradition continued alive and largely unaffected by the printed versions until well into the twentieth century.[39] What finally did kill off the oral versions was the existence of widespread literacy and cheap books, hardly factors in antiquity.

Once again, given the way oral and written literature work in a media culture like that of antiquity, it is highly probable that Mark as a whole continued to be performed and heard orally for a long while after the gospel was first written, and even after it was first included in the fourfold gospel codices. The evidence of the early manuscript fragments and patristic citations of the Gospels also suggests that Mark was less dependent on the manuscript tradition than were the other Gospels. Text-critical data is often ambiguous, and I am no expert in it. But I would like to venture three ways the data suggest that Mark may have been more dependent on oral transmission than were the other Gospels.

First, we know that oral transmission is more variable than manuscript tradition, and that oral transmission affects the ongoing manuscript tradition, and vice versa. If Mark was more dependent on oral transmission than the other gospels were, we would expect it to have more variants than the other gospels, and this indeed is the case.[40] The quantity of variants also suggests that text critics would have more difficulty establishing what they believe is closest to the original text for Mark. This also is true. Comparing the seven modern reconstructions of the Greek New Testament texts, from Tischendorf's final 1872 edition through the twenty-fifth edition of the Nestle-Aland text (NA²⁵), Kurt and Barbara Aland found that the Gospel of Mark had the lowest percentage of variant-free verses of any New Testament text: 45.1 percent. The aggregate figure for the entire New Testament

37. Quoted in Keck, "Oral Traditional Literature," 114.
38. Eusebius, *Ecclesiastical History*, 2.16.1.
39. Lurie, *Don't Tell the Grown-Ups*; see chapter 8, above.
40. Streeter, *Four Gospels*, 307; Kilpatrick, *Principles and Practice*, 7–8.

is 62.9 percent, and every other New Testament writing has manuscripts with over 50 percent agreement, with Matthew and Luke each being closer to 60 percent. Another way of looking at it is to count the number of variants per printed page of NA[25]. Here again, Mark leads with 10.3 variants per page. John has 8.5 variants per page, and both Matthew and Luke have just under 7; the rest of the New Testament writings have fewer yet.[41] Scholars have had greater difficulty in agreeing on the Markan text. Its greater manuscript variety is most likely due to the influence of oral performances on the written tradition.

Second, there is a definite scarcity of early manuscripts of Mark in comparison to the other gospels. We have only one Markan manuscript before the turn of the fourth century—P[45], as noted earlier—whereas there are more of the other Gospels. (Incidentally, Mark is last in order in that codex. Streeter suggests that Mark was last in some codices because it was least important.[42] However, there seems to be insufficient comparative data to conclude much from the order of the Gospels in codices.) The rubbish heap at Oxyrhynchus now provides 57 percent of all early manuscripts (and represents all existing text-types). Finds at Oxyrhynchus include thirteen fragments of Matthew, ten of John, and two of Luke; but *none* of Mark have been found.[43] These finds also include two fragments of the *Gospel of Peter*, a variety of other apocryphal New Testament writings, and a portion of Irenaeus's *Against Heresies*.[44] These findings may of course be the results of random survival. However, the pattern is sufficiently consistent to suggest that there were overall fewer manuscripts made of Mark than of the other Gospels.

The third aspect of the early evidence is the incidence of patristic citations. Here we are dealing with the writings of relatively elite men, and not surprisingly they prefer the more literary gospels to Mark. But what I find interesting and suggestive here is the sharp drop-off in the number of citations of Mark from the second century to the third century.[45] In each

---

41. Aland and Aland, *Text of the New Testament*, 29–30. These figures ignore orthographic differences; verses in which only one of the seven editions is used differed by a single word are counted as agreeing completely. Additional changes have been made, of course, in the more recent Nestle-Aland editions, but no updated figures are available (Parker, *Living Text*, 197–98).

42. Streeter, *Four Gospels*, 307.

43. Epp, "Codex and Literacy." I would like to thank Eldon Epp for his assistance.

44. Ibid., 22.

45. The second-century figures include Clement of Alexandria and Tertullian. The

case, the most cited gospel is Matthew, with about 3900 citations in the second century and 3600 in the third, and the least cited is Mark. But Mark is still thoroughly present in the second-century writings, with about 1400 citations, whereas in the third century there are only about 250.[46] The status of Mark continued to decline, with Augustine finally declaring Mark to be merely an abbreviation of Matthew.

By the third century, the fourfold gospel was well accepted as canonical, and codices containing all four were becoming the norm. Certainly Mark was included in all the great majuscules of the fourth and fifth centuries. However, it was increasingly ignored.[47] Once Mark became one more written gospel included in a collection, it failed to interest the church, or at least its leaders. But in the second century, it was still alive as oral performance and referred to by church leaders. I suggest that it is the widespread oral knowledge of the Gospel of Mark among Christians of all social locations that made it salient enough to be included in the fourfold gospel. If it had not been widely known and loved on its own, and not just as incorporated in Matthew, it easily could have been omitted as nothing more than a poorer rendition of Matthew. Harry Gamble writes, "The currency of so many gospels also shows that the eventual development of a collection of only four Gospels was the result of a selective process. Nothing dictated that the church should honor precisely four Gospels, or these four in particular."[48] In his attempt to defend a plurality of gospels, Ireneaus could have as easily defended a threefold gospel as upholding the apostolic tradition or rule of faith. He might have used the triadic formulae for the divine, or anthropological analogies such as spirit, soul, and body. But he did not. We have four Gospels. I suggest that the oral viability and popular support of the story of Mark may be the reason, or at least part of the reason, that Mark indeed made it into the fourfold gospel, into the canon, and thus that we have it today.

---

third-century figures exclude Origen.

46. Brenda Deen Schildgen has calculated these numbers from the lists in *Biblia Patristica* (Schildgen, *Power and Prejudice*, 40–41).

47. Mark was ignored in the lectionaries as well (ibid., 41).

48. Gamble, *New Testament Canon*, 25.

11

Our Text of Mark

How Similar to First-Century Versions?

WE THINK OF THE text of the Gospel of Mark as fixed. We think of our Greek text of UBS[4] established with much labor by text critics, as very close to what Mark composed and to what people consistently heard throughout the first centuries of Christianity. But is this in fact tenable? Given what we now know about first- and second-century communications media, low literacy rates, and the repeated interactions or oral and written versions of a story, is this likely?

In this chapter, I am asking questions about how oral performance, memory, and manuscript interacted in the performances of the Gospel of Mark between, say, 70 and 150 CE. For audiences in the late first and early second centuries *heard* the Gospel of Mark performed, usually in its entirety.[1] They may have heard it in Christian worship services or in synagogue assemblies. They may have heard it in the context of Christian meals, during evening storytelling settings, or in workplace settings. They may have heard it in mixed-gender contexts and in single-gender contexts. They may have heard it performed by someone who traveled from community to community as teacher/preacher telling the story, or by the local community leader or patron, or by someone local whose status derived solely from his or her ability to perform the story—or indeed by all three. My question is about

---

1. See chapters 4, 5, and 10, above.

the content of these performances. I am curious to know how similar or different the content was from performance to performance and over time.

To anticipate my conclusions, I am arguing that we cannot simply assume what early audiences heard performed was close to or nearly identical with our fourth- and fifth-century manuscripts. Indeed, I suggest that we must assume that early audiences heard a variety of gospels of Mark. Although we have to rely on our United Bible Society reconstructed text, we cannot blindly assume it was a close approximation of what early audiences heard. This chapter explores some reasons for both constraint and freedom in the performances of the gospel. First, I shall present some preliminaries and a general discussion of issues involved in performing the gospel, and then I shall present several models of possible interaction of between manuscript and oral performance.

First, a few preliminaries. *The time frame of 70 to 150 CE.* Seventy CE seems an appropriate starting point since most scholars believe it was about the time the gospel of Mark was composed and probably put in writing. The year 150 CE seems a suitable endpoint, not because oral performance ended at that time (it did not), but rather because it is about that time when patristic quotations from the gospels tend to be more exact and less free-form, and when the codex of the fourfold gospel emerged.[2] Both developments suggest that the gospels were becoming thought of as Scripture, that is, as authoritative writings whose wording mattered. In the period I am discussing, the Jesus traditions and the gospels were not yet considered Scripture.

I distinguish two different uses of the term "memory." The first use concerns memory arts: composition in memory *or* memory technique. Ancient literate composers typically composed in memory and then dictated to a scribe.[3] Nonliterate performers also worked with tradition in memory and composed during performance. It is memory, memory arts, and memory cues that enable a story to be remembered and retold. Composition in memory and performance also allow for improvisation and adaptation to changed circumstances.

Composition in memory makes use of memory cues. Memory cues include repetitions of all sorts: verbal parallelism, syntactic and thematic parallels and echoes. Memory cues are superabundant in the gospel of

2. See chapter 10, above, and the references there.

3. Lee and Scott, *Sound Mapping the New Testament,* 11–57; and Small, *Wax Tablets of the Mind,* 177–201.

Mark.[4] Their presence implies that the gospel was composed *for* and used *in* oral performance—whether it was initially composed orally or in writing. Memory cues are clearly important for maintaining the stability of a story, to keep it being told in the same way since they help the performer to recall the material. It also suggests that the gospel may have been honed through repeated performance. At times the memory cues are so frequent and so elegant that it seems probable that they were expanded and perfected in the course of repeated performances. We cannot assume that all the memory clues in our present Greek text were all present in the early performances.

The second use of memory is "social memory," the social or cultural memory of a culture, group, or subgroup. Social memory deals with the content of tradition, not the *how* of remembering. Social-memory theorists and oral historians alike argue that accounts or traditions tend to solidify in about forty years after the events.[5] The oral historian Jan Vansina writes: "When accounts of events have been told for a generation or so . . . the resulting story . . . has acquired a stabilized form. The plot and sequence of episodes changes only gradually after this."[6] Most scholars agree that Mark was composed about forty years after Jesus's life and death, right about the time the tradition is stabilizing. I suggest that Mark was working with a somewhat stabilized tradition of Jesus's ministry and death, of plot and sequences. I imagine him to have been a particularly gifted storyteller, who put his stamp on the narrative. The social memory has by then acquired some fixity but is still open to development, new interpretations, and adaptations to current situations. Social memory does not produce a final unchanging product, but it does put some constraints on a story, giving it some stability.

My basic argument consists of four interacting points. First, the Gospel of Mark was generally performed in its entirety. Second, oral performances vary from one another. Third, the manuscript tradition was also quite fluid in this early period. Finally, the oral and the written traditions did not develop in opposition to each other but in repeated interaction with each other. So the tradition consists of ongoing oral performances, manuscript versions that would be recycled into the oral traditions, followed by new manuscript editions and continuing oral performances. There was an evolving tradition involving both oral and written media.

4. See chapters 3, 4, and 5, above.

5. Kirk, "Social and Cultural Memory," 1–24, and the literature cited there.

6. Vansina, *Oral Traditions*, 108.

First, then, the Gospel of Mark was usually performed orally in its entirety. It is a suitable length for oral performance in antiquity. Pieter J. J. Botha suggests the gospel would take about an hour and fifteen minutes to perform.[7] Given the extremely low literacy rates, if people knew the gospel at all, they would know it through having heard it. (I will return to the question of the relation of performance to manuscript below. My point here is that the gospel would have been performed orally as a whole.) The existence of a manuscript does not stop oral transmission. As Albert Lord posited, oral literature is "not a phase but a genre."[8] Further as late as the fourth century, Eusebius reports, "They say Mark was the first to be sent to preach in Egypt the Gospel which he had also put into writing."[9] Regardless of the historical accuracy of the report, it shows that the storyteller/performer was needed, not the manuscript. Knowledge of the gospel spread not through sending manuscripts but through traveling storytellers. Indeed, if the gospel had not become widely known and appreciated through oral performance, it most likely would have disappeared, going the way of Q, as by all rules of ancient manuscript copying and transmission it should have. The gospel had an ongoing oral existence over an extended period of time.

Next, *oral performances vary from one another.* No two oral performances are identical. The telling may be more or less formal depending on the setting—a worship service, evening storytelling, a Christian meal. Performing before a live audience inevitably affects the telling. The performer will adapt the telling to the audience: Jews, Gentiles, men, women, peasants, wealthy landowners, and so forth. Are the community's patrons present or not? Are Roman officials present? Furthermore, the storyteller will shorten or expand the story depending on audience interest. Walter Ong writes: "A real audience controls the narrator's behavior immediately . . . a given story may take a skilled . . . storyteller anywhere from ten minutes to an hour and a half, depending on how . . . the audience relates."[10] The performer will adapt the story to the interests of whatever particular audience he or she is addressing. So even hearing the gospel performed by the same storyteller at different times , a listener likely heard a somewhat different story that varied in length and in details. And different storytellers would likely tell

7. Botha, "Writing in the First Century," 81.

8. Quoted in Keck, "Oral Traditional Literature," 114.

9. Eusebius, *Ecclesiastical History* 2.16.1.

10. Ong, *Interfaces of the Word*, 69.

it differently. We have to suppose that early audiences heard the Gospel of Mark performed with considerable variations.

Further, over time a story is likely to develop and change. Social-memory theorists debate among themselves how much faithfulness there is to older content and how much is totally revised to reflect any given present.[11] We may expect both some retention of older material that is no longer relevant and also incorporation of new material. So there is both some stabilization of plot and sequence of episodes solidifying about the time Mark was first composed, and also changes and adaptations over time to accommodate new situations

Third, *even the manuscript tradition of Mark was not fixed in the early period.* We tend to import our notions of textual fixity based on our experience of print. Yet, no two manuscripts are identical. We know that scribes edited or corrected texts as they copied.[12] Manuscripts are clearly more stable than oral performances, but they are far from fixed. We have no access to any written texts of Mark until the great Bibles of the fourth and fifth centuries. (The only fragment of Mark prior to 300 CE is P[45] (dated to the mid-third century), which contains a few portions of Mark 4–9 and 11–12.) Furthermore the early years of manuscript transmission tend to be the most fluid. In what follows I am presenting in particular the views of D. C. Parker and Eldon Epp.[13] They argue that there is *no* concern evident to maintain verbal accuracy in New Testament manuscripts prior to Constantine. Copiers were concerned for the true text, not the historically accurate text. Indeed, the greatest changes in any manuscript traditions generally occur in the first 100 or 150 years of transmission (that is, before we have *any* texts of Mark), after which manuscripts tend to stabilize.[14] Parker concludes about all the Gospels, "The possibility [is] that whatever forms of text were like in the year 100, they were very different from the late second-century forms still available to us."[15] Manuscripts are a great deal more stable than oral tradition; however, the manuscript tradition was not stable or fixed in the beginning.

11. Kirk, "Social and Cultural Memory."

12. Ehrman, *Orthodox Corruption*; Ehrman, *Lost Christianities*, 215–27.

13. See Parker, *Living Text*; Epp, "Multivalence." See also Schröter, "Jesus and the Canon."

14. Parker, *Living Text*, 70; Koester, "Text of the Synoptic Gospels," 19.

15. Parker, *New Testament Manuscripts*, 346.

Last, *the oral and the written traditions did not develop in isolation from each other but in repeated interaction with each other.* There is no great divide. Rather the manuscript tradition and the oral traditions interacted and impacted each other. Whichever began first, oral or written Mark, it would influence the other, which in turn would influence the first, and so on. Parker writes, "The written texts are only a part of the process by which the traditions about Jesus were passed on. The traditions were told and re-told, written and rewritten, in oral tradition and in successive versions of texts."[16] Furthermore, the written versions may well have been in service of the oral performances. Parker concludes, "We have seen that the first generations valued the oral tradition above written documents[, which] makes them aids to those memories."[17] So, in conclusion, I suggest that our reconstructed text of Mark does *not* represent the original text (the gospel as composed around 70 CE) but the gospel as it was recomposed at a considerably later date.

So far I have argued that we cannot assume that the Gospel of Mark performed in the first and early second centuries closely resembles the Gospel of Mark of our latest United Bible Society Greek edition. Oral performances are always adapted to their particular contexts, social memory adapts to new situations, and the manuscript tradition itself is developing. We cannot simply assume what early audiences heard performed was close to or nearly identical with our fourth- and fifth-century manuscripts. In fact, we should assume that considerable change has occurred.

I turn now to somewhat different questions: How did manuscripts interact with individual oral performances? Were they typically used in performing, and if so, in what ways? These questions are relevant, for if performances were dependent on or closely tied to manuscripts, then the manuscript tradition would have exerted greater control over oral performances from the beginning, limiting variations. And if there was greater manuscript control of the tradition, then there was greater control by the small group of more educated, more literate, and most likely male elements of the Christian population. Given the realities of oral performance and scribal practices, early control by the manuscripts seems unlikely. I shall lay out a spectrum of models of the possible relationships of manuscripts to performance, moving from what seems to me least likely—total dependence on a manuscript—to reliance on memory with or without contact

16. Parker, *Living Text,* 179.

17. Ibid., 186.

with a manuscript, which I consider most probable. Certainly more than one model may have had currency, and perhaps all of them occurred occasionally in some form or other.

1. *Reading a manuscript individually.* For most of the centuries of critical biblical scholarship this has been our default mode. Extrapolating from our own experience with print, we assumed people read the Gospel of Mark individually, in silence. Now more aware of the low literacy rates, the ubiquity of reading aloud, and the substantial differences between the oral/aural/manuscript media of antiquity and the print medium, we know this view is anachronistic.

2. *Public readings to audiences.* Today a common way to imagine the publication and transmission of the gospel is to imagine someone reading the manuscript aloud to audiences or congregations, much as we read portions on Scripture in church and synagogue services today. But is this likely? Unless a reader already knows what a manuscript says (has it in his or her memory), reading a manuscript lacking punctuation and spaces between words while managing to unroll and roll a scroll is no easy feat. William Graham writes, "At the most basic level, the oral text was the 'base text,' if only because reading a manuscript text virtually demanded prior knowledge of the text."[18] The sheer difficulty of reading a manuscript and the difficulty of maintaining audience interest during a long reading suggest to me that reading aloud to groups was not a common mode of presentation and transmission of Mark. Reading aloud a small portion of a manuscript and then preaching on it came in later in the second or even in the third or fourth century, once the gospels had become considered Scripture to be commented on during worship.

   However, public readings were certainly part of elite culture, and often enjoyed by more than the elite. How was this done? The public reader (the author?) would already be familiar with the manuscript and would have prepared to read it. He or she (most likely he) would have practiced reading aloud or performing the manuscript. Moreover, the ancient notion of accuracy was not our notion of accuracy but rather of gist: Jocelyn Small writes, "Once we understand that the ancient standard of 'accuracy' is 'gist,' we can also understand why

18. Graham, *Beyond the Written Word*, 36.

they would so willingly rely on their memories for retrieval."[19] For literates in antiquity the term *to memorize* covers two distinct practices: first, verbatim, that is word-for-word (or better, syllable-by-syllable) memorization of a text—what we generally mean by memorization today; and second, having the general gist in memory, the order and essence of their speeches but not the precise wording.[20] When ancients wrote of memorization, we often assume they meant word-for-word or verbatim memorization when they actually meant having the gist in memory. For public readings by good readers, the gist was probably pretty close to the text. Even in public readings, I would wonder if the reader was free to include digressions or make serious abridgements of a text if audience interest appeared to flag.

3. *Memorizing the manuscript word for word, performing it as memorized.* Were performances then like public readings, largely from memory but sticking closely to the written text, the performer perhaps holding a scroll in one hand, as seen in art on vases? I am restricting the term *memorization* to our usage today: verbatim memorization. In this instance a performer would memorize the text—if literate, by reading it aloud, or more likely by hearing it read aloud repeatedly, probably by a slave. Verbatim memorization suggests enough wealth to own a manuscript; they were expensive. And verbatim memorization requires literacy, or at least the possession of a literate slave.

We know that verbatim memorization did occur in some instances in antiquity. It was used for short poems; it was Quintilian's preferred process for elite orators to prepare a speech. However, Quintilian's views on this were not typical. Spontaneity and improvisation were also highly valued. For the few who did attend school, the education system among Jews and Greeks seems to have begun with memorization and recitation Was the purpose of this memorization to inculcate verbatim memorization, or was the purpose more to get the approximate texts into people's memories so they could work with them in their heads, in memory, as was the general practice of literate composers? I suspect the latter.

Unlike reading a text, performance based on verbatim memory would permit a lively telling. The performer would not be hindered by having to manipulate a scroll and to somehow keep his or her place.

19. Small, *Wax Tablets,* 189–93; the quotation is from 192.
20. Shriner, *Proclaiming the Gospel,* 103–21.

Performance from verbatim memorization is possible—barely. If it occurred with any frequency, it would suggest the content of performances mirrored the content of early manuscripts. However, it would also suggest that performers valued precise verbal accuracy above the values of spontaneity and keeping their audiences' attention. Early concern for precise wording does not appear to have existed in the Jesus traditions. Rather the oral/rhetorical culture of antiquity centered on persuasion of audiences. I question that there was much if any verbatim memorization of Mark from 70 to 150 CE. The freedom of the manuscript tradition and the free wording of early patristic citations suggest that close accuracy was not even desired. It is only after Mark's gospel becomes considered authoritative as Scripture that precise wording becomes a value. For first-century audiences to have heard Mark's gospel very close in wording in various performances, they would have had to hear verbatim performances. While some probably did occur, I suspect the great preponderance of performances were much freer.

4. *Having the Story in Memory, Composing in Performance.* Most likely, this was the predominate practice for both literate and nonliterate performers.[21] Given what we know about how few were literate in antiquity and about the social makeup of early Christianity, which did not yet include the elite (the only group for whom literacy was normal), nonliterate performers probably well outnumbered literate performers. And it is quite possible that many of the nonliterate performers never had contact with a manuscript or heard a verbatim performance. A good storyteller, already familiar with the tradition, could hear a story like Mark once, and be able to retell basically the same story. For nonliterate performers, composing in performance would be the norm, basically the only option. The oral literature scholar Albert Lord wrote, the storyteller "does not memorize a text, no matter how stable, from someone else. One is not concerned with transmission of text, but with transmission a) of the art of composition and b) of the story itself."[22] I suggest that the same was true for literate performers as well. Given the cost of ancient manuscripts,

---

21. This is how I perform "Women on the Way" (chapter 9, above). I do have a script that I use for refreshing my memory, but I do not have it memorized, and I never tell it exactly the same way twice.

22. Lord, "Gospels as Oral Traditional Literature," 37.

it is unlikely that many possessed their own copies of Mark. There are very few early manuscript remains of any gospel, and fewer still of Mark. More important, the centrality of composition in memory seems characteristic of what we know of the compositional practices of ancient writers.[23] So I would argue that composition in performance from memory—the reliance on memory arts—was the typical and nearly universal means of performing the Gospel of Mark, carried out by literate and often by nonliterate performers.

So then the question becomes how close or how free were these renditions of the Gospel of Mark, assuming it was composed in performance by both nonliterate and literate storytellers? What evidence or analogies can we bring to bear on this question? I shall briefly consider Matthew's and Luke's use of Mark, and then two later examples of interfaces of oral and written transmission.

Matthew's and Luke's use of Mark might seem to imply early stability. However, it is not clear in scholarly discussion that our text of Mark is needed to account for Matthew and Luke. On the one hand, oral knowledge of Mark may be sufficient to explain the parallels. Albert Lord argued that the three Synoptic Gospels seemed to him to be typical oral variants of a tradition, varying in ways oral narratives often vary.[24] Or, using manuscript copying as the basis, Helmut Koester argues there was a proto-Mark, then Matthew's and Luke's Gospels, then Secret Mark, then finally our canonical Mark.[25] My point is, our present text of Mark is not necessary to explain Mark's overlaps with Matthew and Luke.

Two later examples of the interaction of written texts and oral performances may provide some evidence about the process of change. Neither is a direct analogy. They both are about oral performance in a time of craft literacy, that is, a 20–35 percent literacy rate, with most nonagricultural males literate and most women and peasants not literate. This is a much higher literacy rate than that found in antiquity. Both also were recorded in print, a much easier medium to read than manuscripts. Further, neither deals with a community's social memory. Yet both provide evidence on the nature of change. The examples involve ballads and fairy tales.

---

23. Small, *Wax Tablets of the Mind,* 177–201; Lee and Scott *Sound Mapping the New Testament,* 11–57.

24. Lord, "The Gospels as Oral Traditional Literature," 33–91.

25. Koester, *Ancient Christian Gospels,* 273–303.

Studies of English ballads printed on broadsheets in the sixteenth century and in following centuries show that the sung versions of ballads differed more and more extensively from the printed version, until a new printing was made, at which point the sung ballad reverted to closer to the printed version.[26] Applying this sequence to the Markan tradition suggests, first, that there were indeed oral variations; and, second, that the manuscript tradition did exert some control over the oral tradition, at various points bringing some performers back to a closer rendition of whatever the manuscript tradition was at that point. This seems quite likely. The reissue of the ballads, however, was the same print version that was earlier circulated. In the case of the Gospel of Mark, the reissue (so to speak) might well have been rather different, incorporating some material from oral performances and dropping other material.

The second example suggests that written versions may have selectively edited the oral performances, not maintaining the full breadth of the oral tradition. They may have substantially reduced and modified the roles of women found in oral versions. We can compare the northern European fairy tales collected from women, first printed by Charles Perrault in 1697, and again by the Grimm brothers in 1812, with versions collected by the folklorist Paul Delarue in the twentieth century. Perrault and the Grimms severely edited the tales for their printed versions, reducing female natural and supernatural characters from major protagonists to what they considered more appropriate docile and subordinate roles. Little Red Riding Hood provides a good example: in the printed versions of the tale, she was either eaten by the wolf or rescued by male hunters. In the oral women's versions, the girl very cleverly extricates herself from the wolf and lives to tell the tale. She rescues herself.

The fate of the fairy-tale tradition also illustrates the power of writing (in this case print) to control the oral tradition. These women's stories remained almost entirely untouched by the printed versions until well into the twentieth century. What finally did them in was the presence of mass literacy and cheap books, hardly conditions that existed in antiquity. And it is the stories from the edited, printed editions, with their restricted roles for women, that people know today.[27]

In the fairy tales, we can document the drastic restriction of the roles of women as the tales moved from women's oral storytelling to printed

26. Finnegan, *Oral Poetry*, 161–64.

27. For more on the fairy tales, see chapter 8, above, and the references cited there.

texts edited by educated males. So I ask if something similar happed to the Gospel traditions as the moved from oral storytelling to manuscripts. I suggest that it is likely that some groups and subgroups may have performed versions of Mark with substantial differences, particularly in the portrayal of women. There is sufficient evidence in the gospel tradition that women were important followers of Jesus. There is also sufficient evidence that women and women's stories were written out of the manuscript traditions.[28] As Elisabeth Schüssler Fiorenza insists, what is left in the gospels about women is just the tip of the iceberg. So, were there early oral versions of Mark (or the gospel story) in which women were far more prominent that they are in our New Testament gospels? Did men and women tell versions to mixed audiences that were noticeably less androcentric than our present gospels? Did women storytellers tell different versions to women, still with the same general plot and sequence but with an abundance of women's stories?[29] Did these versions continue to exist over a period of time? While proof is not possible, it seems to me quite likely that there were versions of Mark persisting over decades or even centuries in which women were far more prominent, central in their own right, not as they are portrayed now in the Gospel of Mark, a mere remnant used primarily as examples to teach men.[30] And if the manuscript tradition seriously distorts and minimizes the role of women around Jesus, are there also other systematic distortions as the tradition moved into manuscripts involving lower classes, peasants, slaves? How closely do our surviving texts reflect the breadth of early Christianity?

In summary, I have suggested that in the last decades of the first century and the early decades of the second century, Mark was performed not verbatim but from memory by composition in performance by both literate and more commonly by nonliterate performers. I expect that there was considerable variety, including renditions that differ substantially from what we would recognize today as Mark. Some oral performances may have been greatly influenced by the manuscript tradition; others may have been entirely independent of manuscripts as a continuation of the ongoing oral tradition. Mine is a preliminary exploration of these issues. More research is needed to confirm or modify my description.

---

28. See chapter 8, above; Schüssler Fiorenza, *In Memory of Her*, 41–95.
29. See chapter 9, above, where I have imagined such a story.
30. J. Dewey, "The Gospel of Mark," 508.

My conclusion, I hope, will stand: that we cannot assume what early audiences heard was close to or nearly identical with our fourth-century manuscripts of the Gospel of Mark. Indeed, I suggest that early audiences heard a variety of Marks. We should not assume that our reconstructed Greek text is a close approximation of what Mark composed or early audiences heard. This has implications for our understanding of Mark and our reconstructions of early Christianity. Recognition of the realities of the first- and second-century oral media world impacts our whole understanding of Christian development.

Bibliography

Achtemeier, Paul J. *Mark*. 1st ed. Proclamation Commentaries. Philadelphia: Fortress, 1975.

———. *Mark*. 2nd ed. Proclamation Commentaries. Philadelphia: Fortress, 1986.

Aland, Kurt, and Barbara Aland. *The Text of the New Testament: An Introduction to the Critical Editions and to the Theory and Practice of Modern Textual Criticism*. 2nd rev. ed. Translated by Erroll F. Rhodes. Grand Rapids: Eerdmans, 1995.

Albertz, Martin. *Die synoptischen Streitgespräche: Ein Beitrag zur Formengeschichte des Urchristentums*. Berlin: Trowitzsch & Sohn, 1921.

Anderson, Janice Capel, and Stephen D. Moore, editors. *Mark & Method: New Approaches in Biblical Studies*. Minneapolis: Fortress, 1992.

Aune, David E. *The New Testament in Its Literary Environment*. Library of Early Christianity 8. Philadelphia: Westminster, 1987.

———. "Worship, Early Christian." In *ABD* 6:973–89.

Babcock, William S., editor. *Paul and the Legacies of Paul*. Dallas: Southern Methodist University Press, 1990.

Bacon, Benjamin W. *The Beginnings of the Gospel Story*. New Haven: Yale University Press, 1909.

Bar-Ilan, Meir. "Illiteracy in the Land of Israel in the First Centuries CE." In *Essays in the Social Scientific Study of Judaism and Jewish Society*, edited by Simcha Fishbane and Stuart Schoenfeld with Alain Goldshläger, 2:46–61. 2 vols. Hoboken, NJ: KTAV, 1992.

Barr, David. "The Apocalypse as a Symbolic Transformation of the World: A Literary Analysis." *Int* 38 (1984) 39–50.

Barth, John. "How to Make a Universe." In *The Friday Book: Essays and Other Nonfiction*, 13–25. New York: Putnam, 1984.

Başgöz, İlhan. "The Tale-Singer and His Audience." In *Folklore: Performance and Communication*, edited by Dan Ben-Amos and Kenneth S. Goldstein, 143–203. Approaches to Semiotics 40. The Hague: Mouton, 1975.

Bauckham, Richard. "For Whom Were Gospels Written?" In *The Gospels for All Christians: Rethinking Gospel Audiences*, edited by Richard Bauckham, 9–48. Grand Rapids: Eerdmans, 1998.

Black, C. Clifton. *Mark: Images of an Apostolic Interpreter*. Studies on Personalities of the New Testament. Columbia: University of South Carolina Press, 1994.

Boer, Martinus C. de "Which Paul?" In *Paul and the Legacies of Paul*, edited by William S. Babcock, 45–54. Dallas: Southern Methodist University Press, 1990.

Boman, Thorleif. *Die Jesus-Überlieferung im Lichte der neueren Volkskunde*. Göttingen: Vandenhoeck & Ruprecht, 1967.

Boomershine, Thomas E. "Biblical Megatrends: Towards a Paradigm for the Interpretation of the Bible in Electronic Media." *SBLSP* 26 (1987) 144–57.

———. "Jesus of Nazareth and the Watershed of Ancient Orality and Literacy." *Semeia* 65 (1994) 7–36.

Boring, M. Eugene. *Sayings of the Risen Jesus: Christian Prophecy in the Synoptic Tradition.* SNTSMS 46. Cambridge: Cambridge University Press, 1982.

Botha, Pieter J. J. "Greco-Roman Literacy as Setting for New Testament Writings." *NovT* 26 (1992) 195–215.

———. "The Historical Setting of Mark's Gospel: Problems and Possibilities." *JSNT* 51 (1993) 27–55.

———. "Letter Writing and Oral Communication in Antiquity: Suggested Implications for the Interpretation of Paul's Letter to the Galatians." *Scriptura* 42 (1992) 17–34.

———. "Mark's Story as Oral Traditional Literature: Rethinking the Transmission of Some Traditions about Jesus." *HvTSt* 47 (1991) 304–31.

———. "Writing in the First Century." In *Orality and Literacy in Early Christianity,* 62–88. Biblical Performance Criticism 5. Eugene, OR: Cascade Books, 2012.

Boyarin, Jonathan, editor. *The Ethnography of Reading.* Berkeley: University of California Press, 1993.

Bultmann, Rudolf. "*anaginōskō, anagnōi.*" In *TDNT* 1:343–44.

———. *The History of the Synoptic Tradition.* Translated by John Marsh. New York: Harper & Row, 1963.

Burrus, Virginia. "Chastity as Autonomy: Women in the Stories of the Apocryphal Acts." *Semeia* 38 (1986) 101–17.

Byrskog, Samuel. *Story as History—History as Story: The Gospel Tradition in the Context of Ancient Oral History.* Boston: Brill, 2002.

Carter, Angela. "The Company of Wolves." In *The Trials & Tribulations of Little Red Riding Hood,* edited by Jack Zipes, 282–91. 2nd ed. New York: Routledge, 1993.

Cartlidge, David R. "Combien d'unités avez-vous de trois à quatre?: What Do We Mean by Intertextuality in Early Church Studies?" *SBLSP* 29 (1990) 400–11.

Cassel, Jay. "Strategy and Irony in the Resurrection Stories of Mark and Matthew." Paper for the Literary Aspects of the Gospels and Acts Group, Society of Biblical Literature, 1986.

Clanchy, Michael T. "Remembering the Past and the Good Old Law." *History* 55 (1970) 165–76.

Cohen, Abner. "The Social Organization of Credit in a West African Cattle Market." *Africa* 35 (1965) 8–9.

Cole, Susan Guettel. "Could Greek Women Read and Write?" In *Reflections of Women in Antiquity,* compiled by Helene P. Foley, 219–45. New York: Gordon and Breach Science Publishers, 1981.

Couch, Carl J. "Oral Technologies: A Cornerstone of Ancient Civilizations?" *Sociological Quarterly* 30 (1989) 587–602.

Crossan, John Dominic. *The Birth of Christianity: Discovering What Happened in the Years Immediately after the Execution of Jesus.* San Francisco: Harper San Francisco, 1998.

———. *The Historical Jesus: The Life of a Mediterranean Jewish Peasant.* San Francisco: HarperSanFrancisco, 1991.

D'Angelo, Mary Rose. *Hebrews.* In *The Women's Bible Commentary,* edited by Carol Newsom and Sharon H. Ringe, 364–67. Louisville: Westminster John Knox, 1992.

Daube, David. *The New Testament and Rabbinic Judaism*. Jordan Lectures in Comparative Religion 2. London: Athlone, 1956.

Davies, Stevan L. *The Revolt of the Widows: The Social World of the Apocryphal Acts*. Cabondale: Southern Illinois University Press, 1980.

Delarue, Paul. "The Story of Grandmother." In *Little Red Riding Hood: A Casebook*, edited by Alan Dundes, 13–20. Madison: University of Wisconsin Press, 1989.

Dewey, Arthur J. *Spirit and Letter in Paul*. Studies in the Bible and Early Christianity 33. Lewiston, NY: Mellen, 1996.

Dewey, Joanna. "1 Timothy," "2 Timothy," "Titus." In *The Women's Bible Commentary*, edited by Carol A. Newsom and Sharon H. Ringe, 353–61. Louisville: Westminster John Knox, 1992.

———. "1 Timothy," "2 Timothy," "Titus." In *The Women's Bible Commentary*, edited by Carol A. Newsom and Sharon H. Ringe, 444–52. Rev. ed. Louisville: Westminster John Knox, 1998.

———. "The Gospel of Mark." In *Searching the Scriptures: A Feminist-Ecumenical Commentary*, edited by Elisabeth Schüssler Fiorenza, 2:470–509. 2 vols. New York: Crossroad, 1994.

———. "Images of Women." In *The Liberating Word: A Guide to Nonsexist Interpretation of the Bible*, edited by Letty Russell, 62–81. Philadelphia: Westminster, 1976.

———. "Jesus' Healings of Women: Conformity and Non-Conformity to Dominant Cultural Values as Clues for Historical Reconstruction." *BTB* 24 (1994) 122–31.

———. "'Let Them Renounce Themselves and Take up Their Cross': A Feminist Reading of Mark 8:34 in Mark's Social and Narrative World." In *A Feminist Companion to Mark*, edited by Amy-Jill Levine, 23–36. Feminist Companions to the New Testament and Early Christian Writings 2. Sheffield: Sheffield Academic, 2001. Reprinted, *BTB* 34 (2004) 98–104.

———. "Mark as Aural Narrative: Structures as Clues to Understanding." *STRev* 36 (1992) 45–56.

———. *Markan Public Debate: Literary Technique, Concentric Structure, and Theology in Mark 2:1–3:6*. SBLDS 48. Chico, CA: Scholars, 1980.

———, editor. *Orality and Textuality in Early Christian Literature*. Semeia 65. Atlanta: Scholars, 1995.

———. "Point of View and the Disciples in Mark." SBLSP 118 (1982) 97–106.

———. "Women in the Synoptic Gospels: Seen but Not Heard?" *BTB* 27 (1997) 53–60.

Dewey, Joanna, and Elizabeth Struthers Malbon. "Mark." In *Theological Bible Commentary*, edited by Gail R. O'Day and David L. Petersen, 311–24. Louisville: Westminster John Knox, 2009.

Dibelius, Martin. *From Tradition to Gospel*. Translated by Bertram Lee Woolf. New York: Scribner, 1934.

Donahue, John R. *Are You the Christ?: The Trial Narrative in the Gospel of Mark*. SBLDS 10. Missoula, MT: Society of Biblical Literature, 1973.

———. "A Neglected Factor in the Theology of Mark." *JBL* 101 (1982) 563–94.

Doty, William G. *Letters in Primitive Christianity*. Guides to Biblical Scholarship: New Testament Series. Philadelphia: Fortress, 1973.

Dowd, Sharyn Echols. *Prayer, Power, and the Problem of Suffering: Mark 11:22–25 in the Context of Markan Theology*. SBLDS 105. Atlanta: Scholars, 1988.

Dowd, Sharyn and Elizabeth Struthers Malbon. "The Significance of Jesus' Death in Mark: Narrative Context and Authorial Audience." *JBL* 125 (2006) 271–297.

Duling, Dennis C., and Norman Perrin. *The New Testament: Proclamation and Parenesis, Myth and History.* 3rd ed. Fort Worth: Harcourt Brace, 1994.

Dundes, Alan, editor. *Little Red Riding Hood A Casebook.* Madison: University of Wisconsin Press, 1989.

Elliott, John H. "Man and the Son of Man in the Gospel according to Mark." In *Humane Gesellschaft: Beiträge zu ihrer sozialen Gestaltung,* edited by Trutz Rendtorff and Arthur Rich, 47–59. Zurich: Zwingli, 1970.

Epp, Eldon Jay. "Appended Note 2 on Additional Newly-Published Oxyrhynchus Papyri of the New Testament." In *Perspectives on New Testament Textual Criticism: Collected Essays, 1962–2004,* 548–50. NovTSup 116. Leiden: Brill, 2005.

———. "The Codex and Literacy in Early Christianity and at Oxyrhynchus: Issues Raised by Harry Y. Gamble's *Books and Readers in the Early Church." CRBR* 10 (1997) 15–37.

———. *Junia: The First Woman Apostle.* Minneapolis: Fortress, 2005.

———. "The Multivalence of the Term 'Original Text' in Textual Criticism." *HTR* 92 (1999) 245–81.

Ehrman, Bart D. *Lost Scriptures: Books that Did Not Make It into the New Testament.* Oxford: Oxford University Press, 2003.

———. *The Orthodox Corruption of Scripture: The Effect of Early Christological Controversies on the Text of the New Testament.* Oxford: Oxford University Press, 1993.

Eusebius. *The Ecclesiastical History.* 2 vols. LCL. Cambridge: Harvard University Press, 1965.

Finnegan, Ruth H. *Literacy and Orality: Studies in the Technology of Communication.* Oxford: Blackwell, 1988.

———. *Oral Poetry: Its Nature, Significance, and Social Context.* Cambridge: Cambridge University Press, 1977.

———. "What Is Orality, If Anything?" *Byzantine and Modern Greek Studies* 14 (1990) 139–49.

Foley, John Miles. *How to Read an Oral Poem.* Urbana: University of Illinois Press, 2002.

——— *Immanent Art: From Structure to Meaning in Traditional Oral Epic.* Bloomington: Indiana University Press, 1991.

———. "The Riddle of Q: Oral Ancestor, Textual Precedent, or Ideological Creation?" In *Oral Performance, Popular Tradition, and Hidden Transcript in Q,* edited by Richard Horsley, 123–140. SemeiaSt 60. Atlanta: Society of Biblical L, 2006.

———. *The Singer of Tales in Performance.* Voices in Performance and Text. Bloomington: Indiana University Press, 1995.

Fowler, Robert M. *Let the Reader Understand: Reader Response Criticism and the Gospel of Mark.* Minneapolis: Fortress, 1991.

———. *Loaves and Fishes: The Function of the Feeding Stories in the Gospel of Mark.* SBLDS 54. Chico, CA: Scholars, 1981.

———. "Reader-Response Criticism: Figuring Mark's Reader." In *Mark & Method: New Approaches in Biblical Studies,* edited by Janice Capel Anderson and Stephen D. Moore, 50–83. Minneapolis: Fortress, 1992.

———. "Reading Matthew Reading Mark: Observing the First Steps toward Meaning-as-Reference in the Synoptic Gospels," *SBLSP* 25 (1986) 1–16.

Funk, Robert W. *Parables and Presence: Forms of the New Testament Tradition.* Philadelphia: Fortress, 1982.

Furnish, Victor Paul. "On Putting Paul in His Place." *JBL* 113 (1994) 3–17.

Gamble, Harry Y. *Books and Readers in the Early Church: A History of Early Christian Texts*. New Haven: Yale University Press, 1995.

————. *The New Testament Canon: Its Making and Meaning*. Guides to Biblical Scholarship: New Testament Series. Philadelphia: Fortress, 1985.

Gearhart, Sally Miller. "Roja and Leopold." In *The Trials & Tribulations of Little Red Riding Hood*, edited by Jack Zipes, 331–42. New York: Routledge, 1993.

Georgi, Dieter. *The Opponents of Paul in 2 Corinthians: A Study of Religious Propaganda in Late Antiquity*. Philadelphia: Fortress, 1986.

Goody, Jack, and Ian Watt. "The Consequences of Literacy." In *Literacy in Traditional Societies*, edited by Jack Goody, 27–68. Cambridge: Cambridge University Press, 1968.

Graham, William A. *Beyond the Written Word: Oral Aspects of Scripture in the History of Religion*. Cambridge: Cambridge University Press, 1987.

Grimm, Jacob, and Wilhelm Grimm. "Little Red Cap (Rotkappchen)." In *Little Red Riding Hood: A Casebook*, edited by Alan Dundes, 7–12. Madison: University of Wisconsin Press, 1989.

Grob, Rudolf. *Einführung in das Markus-Evangelium*. Zurich: Zwingli, 1965.

Haenchen, Ernest. "Die Komposition von Mk VIII 27—IX 1 und Par." *NovT* 6 (1963) 81–109.

Harbsmeier, Michael. "Writing and the Other: Travellers' Literacy, or Towards an Archaeology of Orality." In *Literacy and Society*, edited by Karen Schousboe and Mogens Trolle Larsen, 197–228. Copenhagen: Akademisk, 1989.

Harris, William V. *Ancient Literacy*. Cambridge: Harvard University Press, 1989.

Havelock, Eric A. *The Muse Learns to Write: Reflections on Orality and Literacy from Antiquity to the Present*. New Haven: Yale University Press, 1986.

————. "The Oral and the Written Word: A Reappraisal." In *The Literate Revolution in Greece and Its Cultural Consequences*, 3–38. Princeton Series of Collected Essays. Princeton: Princeton University Press, 1982.

————. "Oral Composition in the *Oedipus Tyrannus* of Sophocles." *New Literary History* (1984) 175–97.

————. *Preface to Plato*. A History of the Greek Mind 1. Cambridge: Belknap, 1963.

Hay, Lewis S. "The Son of Man in Mark 2:10 and 2:28." *JBL* 89 (1970) 69–75.

Hays, Richard B. *Echoes of Scripture in the Letters of Paul*. New Haven: Yale University Press, 1989.

Hearon, Holly E. *The Mary Magdalene Tradition: Witness and Counter-Witness in Early Christian Communities*. A Michael Glazier Book. Collegeville, MN: Liturgical, 2004.

Hedrick, Charles W. "What Is a Gospel?: Geography, Time and Narrative Structure." *PRSt* 10 (1983) 255–68.

Hezser, Catherine. *Jewish Literacy in Roman Palestine*. Texts and Studies in Ancient Judaism 81. Tübingen: Mohr/Siebeck, 2001.

Homer. *The Iliad*. With an English translation by A. T. Murray. Revised by William F. Wyatt. 2 vols. 2nd ed. LCL 170–71. Cambridge: Harvard University Press, 1999.

Horsley, Richard A. *Hearing the Whole Story: The Politics of Plot in Mark's Gospel*. Louisville: Westminster John Knox, 2001.

————. *Jesus and the Spiral of Violence: Popular Jewish Resistance in Roman Palestine*. San Francisco: Harper & Row, 1987.

Horsley, Richard A., with Jonathan A. Draper. *Whoever Hears You Hears Me: Prophets, Performance and Tradition in Q*. Harrisburg, PA: Trinity, 1999.

Houston, Pam. "How to Talk to a Hunter." In *Cowboys Are My Weakness: Stories*. New York: Norton, 1992. Quoted in Gail Pool, "Hunting the Hunter." *The Women's Review of Books* 9 (1992) 20.

Howe, Nicholas. "The Cultural Construction of Reading in Anglo-Saxon England." In *The Ethnography of Reading*, edited by Jonathan Boyarin, 58–79. Berkeley: University of California Press, 1993.

Hultgren, Arland J. "The Formation of the Sabbath Pericope in Mark 2:23–28." *JBL* 91 (1972) 38–43.

Humphrey, J. H., editor. *Literacy in the Roman World*. Journal of Roman Archaeology Supplementary Series 3. Ann Arbor: Journal of Roman Archaeology, 1991.

Iersel, B. M. F. van. "Locality, Structure, and Meaning in Mark." *LB* 53 (1983) 45–54.

Jauss, Hans Robert et al. "Levels of Identification of Hero and Audience." *New Literary History* 5 (1974) 283–317.

Johnson, Sherman E. *The Gospel according to St. Mark*. Black's New Testament Commentaries. London: A. & C. Black, 1960.

Juel, Donald H. *A Master of Surprise: Mark Interpreted*. Minneapolis: Fortress, 1994.

Keck, Leander E. "The Introduction to Mark's Gospel." *NTS* 12 (1966) 352–70.

———. "Oral Traditional Literature and the Gospels: The Seminar." In *The Relationships among the Gospels: An Interdisciplinary Dialogue*, edited by William O. Walker Jr., 108–13. Trinity University Monograph Series in Religion 5. San Antonio: Trinity University Press, 1978.

Kee, Howard C. *Community of the New Age: Studies in Mark's Gospel*. Philadelphia: Westminster, 1977.

Keenan, J. G. "Ancient Literacy." *Ancient History Bulletin* 5 (1991) 101–7.

Kelber, Werner H. "The Case of the Gospels: Memory's Desire and the Limits of Historical Criticism." *Oral Tradition* 17 (2002) 55–86.

———. "Introduction." In *The Oral and the Written Gospel: The Hermeneutics of Speaking and Writing in the Synoptic Tradition, Mark, Paul, and Q*. Voices in Performance and Text. Bloomington: Indiana University Press, 1997.

———. "Jesus and Tradition: Words in Time, Words in Space." *Semeia* 65 (1994) 139–67.

———. "Language, Memory, and Sense Perception in the Religious and Technological Culture of Antiquity and the Middle Ages." *Oral Tradition* 10 (1995) 409–450.

———. "Modalities of Communication, Cognition, and Physiology of Perception: Orality, Rhetoric, Scribality." *Semeia* 65 (1994) 193–216.

———. *The Oral and the Written Gospel: The Hermeneutics of Speaking and Writing in the Synoptic Tradition, Mark, Paul, and Q*. Philadelphia: Fortress, 1983.

———. "Orality, Scribality, and Oral-Scribal Interfaces." Paper presented at Society for New Testament Studies, Halle, Germany, 2005.

———. "The Works of Memory: Christian Origins as Mnemohistory—A Response." In *Memory, Tradition, and Text: Uses of the Past in Early Christianity*, edited by Alan Kirk and Tom Thatcher, 221–48. SemeiaSt 52. Atlanta: SBL, 2005.

Kelber, Werner H., and Tom Thatcher. "'It's Not Easy to Take a Fresh Approach': Reflections on *The Oral and the Written Gospel* (An Interview with Werner Kelber)." In *Jesus, the Voice, and the Text: Beyond "The Oral and the Written Gospel,"* edited by Tom Thatcher, 27–43. Waco: Baylor University Press, 2008.

Kermode, Frank. *The Genesis of Secrecy: On the Interpretation of Narrative*. The Charles Eliot Norton Lectures, 1977–1978. Cambridge: Harvard University Press, 1979.

Kilpatrick, G. D. *The Principles and Practice of New Testament Textual Criticism: Collected Essays*. Edited by J. K. Elliott. BETL 96. Leuven: Leuven University Press, 1990.

Kirk, Alan. "Social and Cultural Memory." In *Memory, Tradition, and Text: Uses of the Past in Early Christianity*, edited by Alan Kirk and Tom Thatcher, 1–24. SemeiaSt 52. Atlanta: SBL, 2005.

Knox, Bernard M. W. "Silent Reading in Antiquity." *GRBS* 9 (1968) 421–35.

Koester, Helmut. *Ancient Christian Gospels: Their History and Development*. London: SCM, 1990.

———. *Synoptische Überlieferung bei den Apostolischen Vätern*. Texte und Untersuchungen zur Geschichte der altchristlichen Literatur 65. Berlin: Akademie, 1957.

———. "The Text of the Synoptic Gospels in the Second Century." In *Gospel Traditions in the Second Century: Origins, Recensions, Text, and Transmission*, edited by William L. Petersen, 19–37. Notre Dame: University of Notre Dame Press, 1989.

———. "Writings and the Spirit: Authority and Politics in Ancient Christianity." *HTR* 84 (1991) 353–72.

Kolenkow, Anitra Bingham. "Beyond Miracles, Suffering and Eschatology." *SBLSP* 2 (1973) 155–202.

Kraemer, Ross S. "Women's Authorship of Jewish and Christian Literature in the Greco-Roman Period." In *"Women Like This": New Perspectives on Jewish Women in the Greco-Roman World*, edited by Amy-Jill Levine, 221–42. Early Judaism and Its Literature 1. Atlanta: Scholars, 1991.

Kuhn, Heinz-Wolfgang. *Ältere Sammlungen im Markusevangelium*. Göttingen: Vandenhoeck & Ruprecht, 1971.

Kümmel, Werner G. *Introduction to the New Testament*. 14th rev. ed. Translated by A. J. Mattill Jr. New Testament Library. Nashville: Abingdon, 1966.

Lafontaine, René, and Pierre Mourlon Beernaert. "Essai sur la Structure de Marc, 8,27–9,13." *RSR* 57 (1969) 543–61.

Lambrecht, Jan. "La structure de Mc, XIII." In *De Jésus aux évangiles: tradition et rédaction dans les Évangeles synoptiques*, edited by Ignace de la Potterie, 141–64. BETL 25. Gembloux: Duculet, 1967.

Lane, William L. *The Gospel according to Mark*. NICNT. Grand Rapids: Eerdmans., 1974.

Lang, Friedrich G. "Kompositionsanalyse des Markusevangeliums." *ZTK* 74 (1977) 1–24.

Lanser, Susan Sniader. *The Narrative Act: Point of View in Prose Fiction*. Princeton: Princeton University Press, 1981.

La Potterie, Ignace de. "De compositione evangelii Marci." *VD* 44 (1966) 135–41.

Lee, Margaret Ellen, and Bernard Brandon Scott. *Sound Mapping the New Testament*. Salem, OR: Polebridge, 2009.

Lefkowitz, Mary R. "Did Ancient Women Write Novels?" In *"Women Like This": New Perspectives on Jewish Women in the Greco-Roman World*, edited by Amy-Jill Levine, 199–219. Early Judaism and Its Literature 1. Atlanta: Scholars, 1991.

Lenski, Gerhard E. *Power and Privilege: A Theory of Social Stratification*. McGraw-Hill Series in Sociology. New York: McGraw-Hill, 1966.

Lenski, Gerhard E., and Jean Lenski. *Human Societies: An Introduction to Macrosociology*. 2nd ed. New York: McGraw-Hill Press, 1974.

Lévi-Strauss, Claude. *Tristes Tropiques*. Translated by John and Doreen Weightman. New York: Atheneum, 1974.

Lewis, Thomas et al. *A General Theory of Love*. New York: Random House, 2000.

Lindemann, Andreas. "Paul in the Writings of the Apostolic Fathers." In *Paul and the Legacies of Paul*, edited by William S. Babcock, 25–45. Dallas: Southern Methodist University Press, 1990.

Lohmeyer, Ernst. *Das Evangelium des Markus*. 16th ed. Göttingen: Vandenhoeck & Ruprecht, 1963.

Lohr, Charles H. "Oral Techniques in the Gospel of Matthew," *CBQ* 23 (1961) 403–35.

Long, Priscilla. "Writing for Our Lives." *The Women's Review of Books* 9/5 (1992) 3.

Lord, Albert B. "The Gospels as Oral Traditional Literature." In *The Relationships among the Gospels: An Interdisciplinary Dialogue*, edited by William O. Walker Jr., 33–91. Trinity University Monograph Series in Religion 5. San Antonio: Trinity University Press, 1978.

———. *The Singer of Tales*. Harvard Studies in Comparative Literature 24. Cambridge: Harvard University Press, 1960.

Lund, Nils. *Chiasmus in the New Testament*. Chapel Hill: University of North Carolina Press, 1942.

Lurie, Alison. *Don't Tell the Grown-Ups: Subversive Children's Literature*. Boston: Little, Brown, 1990.

MacDonald, Dennis R. "Apocryphal and Canonical Narratives about Paul." In *Paul and the Legacies of Paul*, edited by William S. Babcock, 55–70. Dallas: Southern Methodist University Press, 1990.

———. "From Audita to Legenda: Oral and Written Miracle Stories." *Forum* 2 (1986) 15–26.

———. *The Legend and the Apostle: The Battle for Paul in Story and Canon*. Philadelphia: Westminster, 1983.

MacDonald, Margaret Y. "Reading Real Women through the Undisputed Letters of Paul." In *Women and Christian Origins*, edited by Ross Shepard Kraemer and Mary Rose D'Angelo, 199–220. New York: Oxford University Press, 1999.

Mack, Burton L. *A Myth of Innocence: Mark and Christian Origins*. Philadelphia: Fortress, 1988.

Malbon, Elizabeth Struthers. "Echoes and Foreshadowing in Mark 4–8: Reading and Rereading." *JBL* 112 (1993) 211–30.

———. "Mark: Myth and Parable." *BTB* 16 (1986) 8–17.

———. "Narrative Criticism: How Does the Story Mean?" In *Mark & Method: New Approaches in Biblical Studies*, edited by Janice Capel Anderson and Stephen D. Moore, 23–49. Minneapolis: Fortress, 1992.

———. *Narrative Space and Mythic Meaning in Mark*. New Voices in Biblical Studies. San Francisco: Harper & Row, 1986.

Malina, Bruce J. "'Let Him Deny Himself' (Mark 8:34 & Par): A Social Psychological Model of Self-Denial." *BTB* 24 (1994) 106–19.

Malina, Bruce J., and Richard L. Rohrbaugh. *Social Science Commentary on the Synoptic Gospels*. Minneapolis: Fortress, 1992.

Marcus, Joel. *Mark: A New Translation with Introduction and Commentary*. Vol. 1, *Mark 1–8*. AB 27. New York: Doubleday, 2000.

Mbiti, John S. *Akamba Stories*. Oxford Library of African Literature. Oxford: Clarendon, 1966.

Meeks, Wayne. *The First Urban Christians: The Social World of the Apostle Paul*. New Haven: Yale University Press, 1983.

Metzger, Bruce M. *The Text of the New Testament: Its Transmission, Corruption, and Restoration.* 3rd ed. New York: Oxford University Press, 1992.

Mills, Margaret A. Personal Communication. 1995.

Mitchell, Margaret M. "New Testament Envoys in the Context of Greco-Roman Diplomatic and Epistolary Conventions: The Example of Timothy and Titus." *JBL* 111 (1992) 641–62.

Moore, Stephen D. "Deconstructive Criticism: The Gospel of the Mark." In *Mark & Method: New Approaches in Biblical Studies,* edited by Janice Capel Anderson and Stephen D. Moore, 84–102. Minneapolis: Fortress, 1992.

———. *Mark and Luke in Poststructuralist Perspective: Jesus Begins to Write.* New Haven: Yale University Press, 1992.

Neisser, Ulric, and Nicole Harsch. "Phantom Flashbulbs: False Recollections of Hearing the News about *Challenger.*" In *Affect and Accuracy in Recall: Studies of "Flashbulb" Memories,* edited by Eugene Winograd and Ulric Neisser, 9–31. Emory Symposia in Cognition 4. New York: Cambridge University Press, 1992.

Oakman, Douglas E. "The Countryside in Luke-Acts." In *The Social World of Luke-Acts: Models for Interpretation,* edited by Jerome H. Neyrey, 151–79. Peabody, MA: Hendrickson, 1991.

Ong, Walter J. *Interfaces of the Word: Studies in the Evolution of Consciousness and Culture.* Ithaca, NY: Cornell University Press, 1977.

———. *Orality and Literacy: The Technologizing of the Word.* New Accents. London: Methuen, 1982.

———. *The Presence of the Word: Some Prolegomena for Cultural and Religious History.* The Terry Lectures. New Haven: Yale University Press, 1967.

———. "The Writer's Audience Is Always a Fiction." *PMLA* 90 (1975) 9–21.

Parker, D. C. *An Introduction to the New Testament Manuscripts and Their Texts.* Cambridge: Cambridge University Press, 2008.

———. *Living Text of the Gospels.* Cambridge: Cambridge University Press, 1997.

Perrin, Norman. "The Creative Use of the Son of Man Traditions by Mark," *USQR* 23 (1968) 357–65.

———. *The New Testament: An Introduction.* New York: Harcourt Brace Jovanovich, 1974.

———. "Towards an Interpretation of the Gospel of Mark." In *Christology and a Modern Pilgrimage: A Discussion with Norman Perrin,* edited by Hans Dieter Betz and Norman Perrin, 1–78. Claremont: New Testament Colloquium, 1971.

———. *What Is Redaction Criticism?* Guides to Biblical Scholarship: New Testament Series. Philadelphia: Fortress, 1969.

Pervo, Richard I. *Dating Acts: Between the Evangelists and the Apologists.* Santa Rosa, CA: Polebridge, 2006.

Pesch, Rudolf. *Das Markusevangelium.* 2 vols. Herders Theologischer Kommentar zum Neuen Testament 2. Freiburg: Herder, 1976.

———. *Naherwartungen: Tradition und Redaktion in Mark 13.* Kommentare und Beiträge zum Alten und Neuen Testament. Düsseldorf: Patmos, 1968.

Petersen, Norman R. *Literary Criticism for New Testament Critics.* Guides to Biblical Scholarship. 1978. Reprinted, Eugene, OR: Wipf & Stock, 2008.

———. "'Point of View' in Mark's Narrative." *Semeia* 12 (1978) 97–121

———. "'When Is the End Not the End?': Literary Reflections on the Ending of Mark's Narrative." *Int* 34 (1980) 151–66.

Plato. *The Republic*. 2 vols. LCL. Cambridge: Harvard University Press, 1953.

Pomeroy, Sarah B. "*Technikai kai Mousikai*: The Education of Women in the Fourth Century and in the Hellenistic Period." *American Journal of Ancient History* 2 (1977) 51–68.

————."Women in Roman Egypt: A Preliminary Study Based on Papyri." In *Reflections of Women in Antiquity*, edited by Helene P. Foley, 303–22. New York: Gordon & Breach, 1981.

Radloff, Wilhelm. "Samples of Folk Literature from the North Turkic Tribes." Translated by Gudrun Böttcher Sherman and Adam Brooke Davis. *Oral Tradition* 5 (1990) 73–90.

Rhoads, David. *Dramatic Performance of the Gospel of Mark*. VHS videotape. Columbus, OH: Select, 1985.

————. "Jesus and the Syrophoenician Woman." In *Reading Mark, Engaging the Gospel*, 63–94. Minneapolis: Fortress, 2004.

————. "Performance Criticism: An Emerging Methodology in Second Testament Studies—Part I." *BTB* 36 (2006) 118–33.

————. "Performance Criticism: An Emerging Methodology in Second Testament Studies—Part II." *BTB* 36 (2006) 164–84.

————. "Performing the Gospel of Mark." In *Body and Bible: Interpreting and Experiencing Biblical Narratives*, edited by Björn Krondorfer, 102–19. Philadelphia: Trinity, 1992.

Rhoads, David, and Donald Michie. *Mark as Story: An Introduction to the Narrative of a Gospel*. Philadelphia: Fortress, 1982.

Rhoads, David et al. *Mark as Story: An Introduction to the Narrative of a Gospel*. 2nd edition. Minneapolis: Fortress, 1999.

Robbins, Vernon K. "The Healing of Blind Bartimaeus (10:46–52) in the Marcan Theology." *JBL* 92 (1973) 224–43.

————. *Jesus the Teacher: A Socio-Rhetorical Interpretation of Mark*. Philadelphia: Fortress, 1984.

————. "Oral, Rhetorical, and Literary Cultures: A Response." *Semeia* 65 (1994) 75–91.

————. "Summons and Outline in Mark: The Three-Step Progression." *NovT* 23 (1981) 97–114.

Robinson, James M. "Mark's Understanding of History." *SJT* 9 (1956) 393–409.

Rohrbaugh, Richard L. "The Pre-Industrial City in Luke-Acts: Urban Social Relations." In *The Social World of Luke-Acts: Models for Interpretation*, edited by Jerome H. Neyrey, 125–49. Peabody, MA: Hendrickson, 1991.

————. "The Social Location of the Marcan Audience." *BTB* 23 (1993) 114–27.

Russell, Letty, editor. *The Liberating Word: A Guide to Nonsexist Interpretation of the Bible*. Philadelphia: Westminster, 1976.

Saldarini, Anthony J. *Pharisees, Scribes, and Sadducees in Palestinian Society*. Wilmington, DE: Glazier, 1988.

Schildgen, Brenda Deen. *Power and Prejudice: The Reception of the Gospel of Mark*. Detroit: Wayne State University Press, 1999.

Schmidt, Karl L. *Der Rahmen der Geschichte Jesu: literarkritische Untersuchungen zur ältesten Jesusüberlieferung*. Berlin: Trowitzsch & Sohn, 1919.

Schottroff, Luise. *Let the Oppressed Go Free: Feminist Perspectives on the New Testament*. Translated by Annemarie S. Kidder. Gender and the Biblical Tradition. Louisville: Westminster John Knox, 1993.

————. *Lydia's Impatient Sisters: A Feminist Social History of Early Christianity.* Translated by Barbara and Martin Rumscheidt. Louisville: Westminster John Knox, 1995.

Schröter, Jens. "Jesus and the Canon: The Early Jesus Traditions in the Context of the Origins of the New Testament Canon." In *Performing the Gospel: Orality, Memory, and Mark,* edited by Richard A. Horsley et al, 104–22. Minneapolis: Fortress, 2006.

Schüssler Fiorenza, Elisabeth. "A Feminist Critical Interpretation for Liberation: Martha and Mary: Luke 10:38–42." *Religion & Intellectual Life* 3 (1986) 21–36.

————. *In Memory of Her: A Feminist Theological Reconstruction of Christian Origins.* New York: Crossroad, 1983.

————. *Jesus: Miriam's Child, Sophia's Prophet: Critical Issues in Feminist Christology.* New York: Continuum, 1994

Schweizer, Eduard. *The Good News according to Mark: A Commentary on the Gospel.* Translated by Donald H. Madvig. Richmond: John Knox, 1970.

Scobie, Alex. "Storytellers, Storytelling, and the Novel in Graeco-Roman Antiquity." *Rheinisches Museum für Philologie* 122 (1979), 229–59.

Scott, James C. *Domination and the Arts of Resistance: Hidden Transcripts.* New Haven: Yale University Press, 1990.

Scott, James M. "Paul's Use of Deuteronomic Tradition." *JBL* 112 (1993) 645–65.

Scott, M. P. "Chiastic Structure: A Key to the Interpretation of Mark's Gospel." *BTB* 15 (1985) 17–26.

Shiner, Whitney. *Proclaiming the Gospel: First-Century Performance of Mark.* Harrisburg: Trinity, 2003.

Silberman, Lou H., editor. *Orality, Aurality and Biblical Narrative. Semeia* 39. Decatur, GA: Scholars, 1987.

Sjoberg, Gideon. *The Preindustrial City: Past and Present.* Free Press Paperback. New York: Free Press, 1960.

Slusser, Michael. "Reading Silently in Antiquity." *JBL* 111 (1992) 499.

Small, Jocelyn Penny. *Wax Tablets of the Mind: Cognitive Studies of Memory and Literacy in Classical Antiquity.* London: Routledge, 1997.

Snyder, Jane McIntosh. *The Woman and the Lyre: Women Writers in Classical Greece and Rome.* Bristol: Bristol Classical Press, 1989.

Standaert, Benoît. *L'Évangile selon Marc: Commentaire.* Lire la Bible 61. Paris: Cerf, 1983.

————. *L'Évangile selon Marc: Composition et genre littéraire.* Zevenkerken: Brugge 1978.

Stanton, G. N. "The Fourfold Gospel." *NTS* 43 (1997) 317–46.

Stock, Brian. *Listening for the Text: On the Uses of the Past.* Parallax : Re-visions of Culture and Society. Baltimore: Johns Hopkins University Press, 1990.

Streeter, Burnett Hillman. *The Four Gospels: A Study of Origins, Treating of the Manuscript Tradition, Sources, Authorship, & Dates.* London: Macmillan, 1924.

Sundwall, Johannes. *Die Zusammensetzung des Markusevangeliums.* Acta Academiae aboensis: Humaniora IX:2. Abo: Abo Akademi, 1934.

Tannehill, Robert C. "The Disciples in Mark: The Function of a Narrative Role." *JR* 57 (1977) 386–405.

————. "The Gospel of Mark as Narrative Christology." *Semeia* 16 (1979) 57–95.

Taylor, Vincent. *The Gospel according to St. Mark.* 2nd ed. London: Macmillan, 1966.

Thatcher, Tom. "Beyond Texts and Traditions: Werner Kelber's Media History of Christian Origins." In *Jesus, the Voice, and the Text: Beyond the Oral and the Written Gospel,* edited by Tom Thatcher, 1–26. Waco, TX: Baylor University Press, 2008.

Tolbert, Mary Ann. "1978 Markan Seminar: Response to Robert Tannehill." Presented to the Seminar on Mark at the Society of Biblical Literature Annual Meeting, New Orleans, 1978.

———. *Sowing the Gospel: Mark's World in Literary-Historical Perspective*. Minneapolis: Fortress, 1989.

Townsend, John T. "Ancient Education in the Time of the Early Roman Empire." In *The Catacombs and the Colosseum: The Roman Empire as the Setting of Primitive Christianity*, edited by Stephen Benko and John J. O'Rourke, 139–63. Valley Forge: Judson, 1971.

Trocmé Étienne. *The Formation of the Gospel according to Mark*. Translated by R. A. Wilson. Philadelphia: Westminster, 1975.

Turner, Cuthbert H. "Marcan Usage: Notes, Critical and Exegetical, on the Second Gospel." *JTS* 25 (1924) 377–86.

Vanhoye, Albert. *Structure and Theology of the Accounts of the Passion in the Synoptic Gospels*. Collegeville, MN: Liturgical, 1967.

Vansina, Jan. *Oral Tradition as History*. Madison: University of Wisconsin Press, 1985.

Veyne, Paul. "The Roman Empire." In *A History of Private Life*. Vol. 1, *From Pagan Rome to Byzantium*, edited by Paul Veyne, 5–233. Cambridge: Belknap, 1987.

Ward, Richard F. "Pauline Voice and Presence as Strategic Communication." *Semeia* 65 (1994) 95–107.

Weeden, Theodore J. *Mark: Traditions in Conflict*. Philadelphia: Fortress, 1971.

Williamson, Lamar Jr. *Mark*. Interpretation. Atlanta: John Knox, 1983.

Wire, Antoinette Clark. *The Corinthian Women Prophets: A Reconstruction through Paul's Rhetoric*. Minneapolis: Fortress, 1990.

Yaghjian, Lucretia B. "Ancient Reading." In *The Social Sciences and New Testament Interpretation*, edited by Richard L. Rohrbaugh, 206–30. Peabody, MA: Hendrickson, 1996.

Zipes, Jack, editor. *The Trials & Tribulations of Little Red Riding Hood*. 2nd ed. New York: Routledge, 1993.

Index of Ancient Documents

Author Index

Made in the USA
Columbia, SC
19 July 2021